THE FUTURE
OF
LEADERSHIP

RISE OF AUTOMATION, ROBOTICS AND ARTIFICIAL INTELLIGENCE

By
Brigette Tasha Hyacinth

ALSO BY BRIGETTE TASHA HYACINTH

PURPOSE DRIVEN LEADERSHIP:
BUILDING AND FOSTERING
EFFECTIVE TEAMS

THE ULTIMATE LEADER:
LEARNING, LEADING AND
LEAVING A LEGACY OF HOPE

THE EDGE OF LEADERSHIP:
A LEADER'S HANDBOOK
FOR SUCCESS

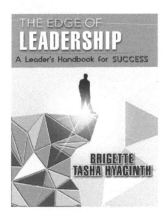

Dedication

First and foremost, I have to thank God for His mercies, grace, and loving kindness towards me, and for blessing me with wisdom to complete this book.

This book is dedicated to my family. I love you all so much.

My heartfelt thanks goes to my dear mother, Marguerite Joseph, who has made huge sacrifices for me to be where I am today. She is the best mother ever. She is a beautiful, loving, diligent, intelligent, and godly woman, and I am so glad to have her as my mom.

A big thank you to Frank Hyacinth, my father, and to my brothers and sisters—Troy Hyacinth, Onica Hyacinth, Gavery Enrico Hyacinth—and to Alicia Hyacinth (my sister-in-law), Che Nigel Hyacinth (deceased), Cheron Hyacinth, Ezra (Tricia) Ramlall, and Brent John for the huge support they provided.

Thank you to my nieces and nephew Nicholas Hyacinth, Celeste Hyacinth, Jessie Ramlall, Tinique Hyacinth and Sarah Davis. I am so proud of you all. May you continue to grow in the grace and knowledge of our Lord and Saviour, Jesus Christ. The world is yours for the taking. Once you put God first, nothing shall be impossible unto you. Think big, always look up, and never give up. May God richly bless you now and forevermore.

PREFACE

|||||||||||||||||||||||||||||||||||||||||||||||||||||||||||||||||||||||||||||||||||||||||||||||||||||||||||||||||||

We are now on the brink of a technological revolution that will alter the way we live, work, and relate to each other. The pace of technological innovation is faster today than ever before. Artificial Intelligence (AI) is in the early stages of development and the possibilities are vast. Should you fear or embrace AI? This question revolves around the assumption that we may have a choice to control its implementation. Opposition to automation, robotics and AI is about as futile as it would have been in the 20th century to oppose electricity.

AI and Robotics will become a new reality whether we decide to embrace it or not. Everything that can be automated, will be automated. There will be a massive disturbance. Incorporating these new technologies is similar to a change process. Most people resist change. They prefer the familiar until they get acquainted with the benefits. As leaders, we need to be change agents. Our responsibility should be to make sure everyone is informed and prepared for the upcoming changes. I invite you to take a glimpse into the future of leadership.

Table of Contents

SECTION THREE:
THE FUTURE OF LEADERSHIP

SECTION ONE

RISE OF AUTOMATION, ROBOTICS AND ARTIFICIAL INTELLIGENCE

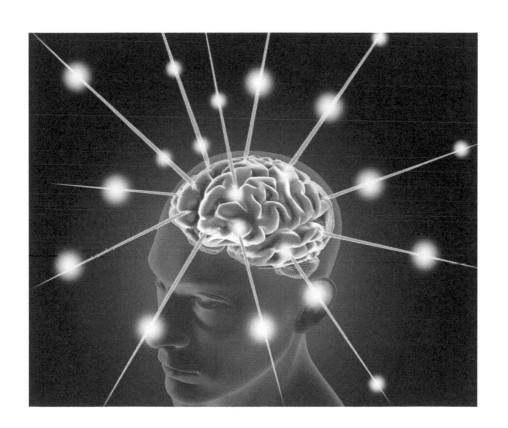

CHAPTER ONE

THE GREAT ARTIFICIAL INTELLIGENCE AWAKENING

Artificial Intelligence (AI) has been pushing the boundaries of human imagination and has transformed from a futuristic concept to a powerful force. If you haven't been living under a rock, you've definitely come across the terms AI, Machine Learning, and Natural Language Processing, etc. There is an overall fear that surrounds AI. For many, it is human nature to be fearful of the unknown and, hence, the future. The Wright brothers' first powered flight would not have been achieved if it was not for conquering fear. The Luddites feared that textile machines would replace them and yet we all benefit from affordable clothing. AI is a key feature of today's automation, if not the defining feature. As we look back in history, at the beginning of the Industrial Revolution, we can see that each technological innovation was heralded as the dawn of a golden age or would bring about the destruction of humanity. Examples throughout history have been the automobile, the airplane, software, and now even AI. When you look back at the adoption rate of electricity, personal computers, cell phones, you can see that these were not just isolated to a single country. These took the world by storm. We are now on the brink of a technological revolution that will alter the way we live, work, and relate to each other. One of the main differences between this and the other revolutions will be the speed of change. Previous industrial revolutions may have happened over many decades, and a few are still ongoing today in developing countries, but with software and AI we could see this condensed into a much shorter timeframe. Regardless of our sentiments, the only choice is to adapt to this new technology.

Robotics and AI are here to stay and they are coming to a neighborhood near you. "We are moving … to an AI first world" (Google), "In five years AI will impact every decision we make" (IBM). Citizens, businesses, and governments alike cannot escape the disruption of AI. If you are a Star Trek fan, you already know that a lot of gadgets from the show are real today as motion sensors, sliding doors, and communicators—today's mobile phones. Robots like R2-D2 and C-P30 in movies like *Star Wars* or even Rosie the robot maid in *The Jetsons* made us laugh, but the reality is that we are using robots and AI in our everyday lives, now. They've been in development for decades. You just haven't recognized them as Robots or AI. Drones, autopilot on airplanes, `machines' in factories, and Siri on your iPhone. Today, AI technology has made its way into a host of products, from search engines like Google, voice assistants like Amazon's Alexa, autonomous vehicles, to a range of "smart" consumer devices and home appliances. The machines today are capable of doing a lot of things that we could not imagine doing 20 years ago. These rapid advances will disrupt the very fabric of our business frameworks and lives.

The term "artificial intelligence" was coined by John McCarthy in his 1955 proposal for the 1956 Dartmouth Conference. The workshop, which took place a year later, during the summer of 1956, is generally considered as the official birthdate of the field. So what is AI? Artificial Intelligence is a branch of computer science that emphasizes the creation of intelligent machines or programs that think, learn, and react like human beings. It is defined as the intelligence exhibited by machines by which it mimics cognitive functions that humans use, while interacting with other humans. In one line, AI is human intelligence exhibited by a machine. It refers to "a broad set of methods, algorithms, and technologies that make software 'smart' in a way that may seem human-like to an outside observer," said Lynne Parker, director of the division of Information and Intelligent Systems for the National Science Foundation.

AI is made up of both software and hardware technologies which rely on intelligence to reason, predict, communicate, and act faster than humans ever could. Back in 1997, a computer that had been built by IBM, known as Deep Blue, beat Garry Kasparov, the then world champion of chess. A paradoxical turning point had been reached: AI was able to beat man at a game as complicated as chess. I've been following IBM's AI developments for a quite a while now and it is safe to say they helped jump-start the current cycle of AI with the introduction of Watson back in the 2000s. Fast forward to August 2017, OpenAI's Dota 2 bot beat the world's most celebrated professional players in one-on-one battles in competitive eSports, which is more complex than traditional board games such as Chess and Go.

Over the past few years, AI has exploded—especially since 2015. The application of these concepts has now become more mainstream. Given that the field of AI has been around for over 60 years, one might wonder what has changed. This can be attributed to the vast increases in inexpensive computational power, exponential growth in the capability of technology, burgeoning use of the Internet of Things (IoT), and the volume of cheap and accessible data. IoT also provides the data AI needs in order to make smart decisions. As more consumers around the globe purchase smartphones and other gadgets which link them to the web, the expanse of IoT will only grow ever greater. Add to this, the storage and compute capacity of the cloud.

The more data we produce, the more of it we can feed into AI systems. These models can therefore be trained with large datasets—producing great performance in real-world applications. Successful systems often use a training set of data with thousands or even millions of examples. A combination of these events has helped AI gain the critical-mass necessary for it to become the center of attention for technology investment. The recent increased investment in AI has also led to a rapid expansion of the AI industry.

The other part of the answer is powerful algorithms and data science. We have seen dramatic improvements in specific areas over the last years such as Machine Learning, Deep Learning, Natural Language Processing, and Robotics. These have all brought AI out of the research lab and into the real world.

1 Machine Learning (ML) - The term was *coined* by computer scientist Arthur Samuel in 1959. ML is often used as a synonym for AI, but it's actually a different, albeit related discipline. While AI refers to a computer program able to "think" for itself without programmed instructions, ML is one process by which a computer can learn its trade. ML is about providing AI with lots of data. It refers to a wide variety of algorithms and methodologies that enable software to improve its performance over time as it obtains more data. The essential task is to create a predictor of future outputs from the set of inputs. Amazon's ML makes product recommendations based on

the customer's purchasing behavior and browsing history almost instantly. Thus, for ML to work reliably, the technology requires continual access to massive volumes and a broad variety of data—referred to as big data. It also requires the right learning algorithm and accurate data sets. We use ML to solve real-world problems. ML is increasingly being used to help companies collect billions of data points, boil them down to what is actually meaningful, and predict what is likely to happen in the future.

➢ **Deep Learning**

In 1951, Marvin Minsky and Dean Edmunds build SNARC (Stochastic Neural Analog Reinforcement Calculator), the first artificial neural network, using 3000 vacuum tubes to simulate a network of 40 neurons. By 1969, Arthur Bryson and Yu-Chi Ho describe backpropagation as a multi-stage dynamic system optimization method. This learning algorithm for multi-layer artificial neural networks, has contributed significantly to the success of deep learning in the 2000s and 2010s.

Some of the most impressive recent advancements in ML have been in the subfield of Deep Learning (DL). DL is a subset of ML. DL is an algorithm that is inspired by how the human brain works and solves problems typically in the way humans solve. DL uses a structure called an artificial neural network where a neural network is arranged into multiple "layers" between an input, such as the pixels in a digital image, and an output, such as the identification of a person's face in that image. It focuses on algorithms that are built on the model that the human brain is built. The power of DL lies in its ability to determine the features of a model from the data, rather than having features defined upfront by an expert. It uses artificial neural networks to discern complex statistical correlations. Once the neural network is supplied with a large enough labeled data, it can then establish a suitable mathematical relation between the different factors (or variables) by comparing it with the desired output. DL enables computers to "see" or distinguish objects and text in images and videos much better than before.

DL has enabled many practical applications in the field of AI. Image recognition by machines trained via DL in some scenarios is better than humans, which can range from identifying cats to tumors in MRI scans. Today's deep learning will seem basic to humans in 5–10 years.

2 Natural Language Processing (NLP) is an application domain for ML techniques. The program STUDENT, written in 1964 by Daniel Bobrow for his PhD dissertation at MIT is one of the earliest known attempts at natural language understanding by a computer. A year later in 1965, Joseph Weizenbaum developed ELIZA, an interactive program that carries on a dialogue in English language on any topic. Natural Language Processing (NLP) is about making a machine "understand" the structure and the meaning of natural language as used by humans. It allows machines to interact with us. The goal of NLP algorithms is to get relevant linguistic structure and use that information to understand the user's question or instruction. The Google Assistant on your smartphone also uses NLP. When you ask a question, it interprets human language and

then performs actions to give you a reply. It allows machines to understand human language. NLP can use ML based models to help it interpret language.

3 **Robotics** is a field of engineering which incorporates multiple disciplines to design and manufacture robotic machines. The term robot was first introduced by Czech novelist Karel Čapek in his hit play, R.U.R. or Rossum's Universal Robots, which opened in Prague in January 1921. In 1929, Makoto Nishimura designs Gakutensoku, Japanese for "learning from the laws of nature," the first robot built in Japan. It could change its facial expression and move its head and hands via an air pressure mechanism. Robots are programmable machines which are able to carry out a series of actions autonomously, or semi-autonomously. They interact with the physical world via sensors. They are more flexible than single-function machines. The word "robotics" was first used by the famous science fiction author Isaac Asimov in his 1941 story "Liar!" An incredible visionary, Asimov started the world thinking about the potential challenges technology might have on the world of humanity. He also proposed the three laws of robotics. Is robotic process automation the same thing as robotics? Robotic Process Automation (RPA)—in spite of its name—has nothing to do with physical robots. It refers to "software robots" which are configured to execute steps identically as a human operator would. These robots are used to automate physical tasks, such as in manufacturing. Also, many branches of robotics have nothing to do with automation. Industrial automation involves using physical machines and control systems to automate tasks within an industrial process. A fully autonomous factory is an example. In 1961, the first industrial robot, Unimate, started working on an assembly line in a General Motors plant in New Jersey.

Is robotics a part of AI? Many people assume robotics is a subset of AI, or the same thing. Despite being related in some ways, they are different fields of study. The two fields can intersect, but neither is dependent or contingent on the other. For example, a factory robot is programmed to do the same tasks over and over again until someone switches it off. This is not AI. Artificial intelligence is software that learns and self-improves, whereas robotics is useful to allow AI to interact with the world. AI is emulation of the mind. It is an algorithm, to embed machines with decision making ability. Robotics, on the other hand, is about interacting with or manipulating real physical things. I like to think of robotics as the hardware and AI as the software when they are combined—brain and body. The combination of *robots* and AI is a significant area of research. In 1966, Shakey, the world's first robot to embody artificial intelligence was developed at the Stanford Research Institute. Robots combined with AI are potentially a powerful force, due to their physical nature and ability to change and rapidly improve without human direction or control. One of the earliest attempts at creating an AI through human interaction was made by Rollo Carpenter in 1988. He developed the chatbot Jabberwacky to "simulate natural human chat in an interesting, entertaining and humorous manner."

The marriage of robotics and AI will offer powerful competitive advantage, which will accelerate development. Bank of America Merrill Lynch estimates that combining AI with robotics will increase productivity by 30% in many industries within a decade. It can also reduce manufacturing labor costs by as much as 33% over the same time period.

Japan has spent decades developing robots. They've made humanoid robots to make people curious about their capabilities. Honda's Asimo robot can act on its own without human intervention. It has a sophisticated sense of touch and can walk and run well. Asimo even kicked a ball to President Barack Obama during his 2014 visit to Japan.

Hanson Robotics, in the USA, has developed robots that are extremely humanlike. Sophia is Hanson Robotics' latest and most advanced robot. She has also become a media sensation having given numerous interviews to multiple media outlets. One of her interviews has generated billions of views. She is capable of natural facial expressions and can also remember faces and the interaction.

Predictions for State of AI & Robotics in 2025 by Pew Research Center Lists:

- ❖ Domestic: Cleaners, homecare, nannies, and companions
- ❖ Commercial: Packing, drawing, printing, media (robots are writing news articles now), pharmacy, retail, and hospitality
- ❖ Transport: Cab/truck drivers and waste removal truck drivers
- ❖ Medical: In hospitals and surgeries, diagnostics, and scans for disease and cancer cells which require precision and 100% accuracy
- ❖ Industrial: Repetitive work in factories and farms or in hazardous situations like nuclear disasters, and recovery and containment
- ❖ Sea: Salvage and recovery operations
- ❖ Law and Enforcement: Police and traffic cops
- ❖ Military: Soldiers, drones, tank drivers, and disarming bombs
- ❖ Space: Construction/digging/maintenance work on Mars and space stations, and explorations such as the ESA's Philae, which landed on a comet 12 Nov 2014

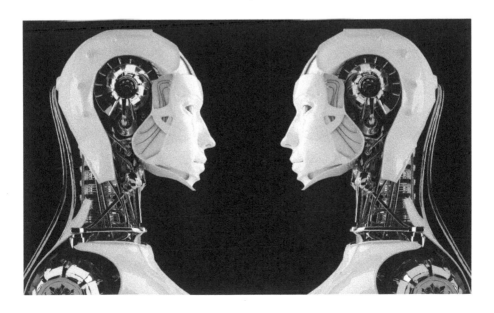

Robots are being loaded with more sensors and capabilities. In many cases they used to perform tasks that are difficult for humans to perform or perform consistently. *NASA's* Valkyrie humanoid, officially known as R5, is one such example. There are only a handful of these in the world, and one of them is owned by NASA. They are a platform for establishing human-robot interaction, and were built in 2013 by a Johnson Space Center (JSC) Engineering directorate. This humanoid robot is designed to be able to work in damaged and degraded environments. According to a white paper by Bell-Hawk systems, real-time AI techniques originally developed for the USAF and NASA are being applied to manufacturing organizations. *Research and Markets* expects that $226 billion will be spent on robotics by 2021. It also believes that 2016 was the crossover point after which the majority of robots will be used in nonindustrial applications. Forrester estimates that by 2021, there will be over 4 million robots doing office, administrative, sales, and other related tasks. Softbank's Masayoshi Son will invest $100 billion in AI and robotics. In terms of specific areas, SoftBank said its areas of focus include IoT, AI, robotics, infrastructure, telecoms, bio tech, fintech, mobile apps, and more.

"A number of economic and technical barriers to wider adoption are beginning to fall," says the Boston Consulting Group's 2015 report. "As a result, a dramatic take off in advanced robotics is imminent." Since AI systems can recognize optical patterns and identify objects, machines can leave the virtual and join the real world. Very soon, robots will be operating and moving about in society and not only limited to commercial buildings. We will have to learn to coexist with them.

AI can be categorized in any number of ways, but here are two examples:

Artificial intelligence today is rightly known as narrow AI (or weak AI), in that it is designed to perform a particular task (e.g. only internet searches or only driving a car). Virtual personal assistants, such as Apple's Siri, are a form of weak AI. They are highly specialized and are often better than humans at the same task. However, they need large sets of data and weeks/months/years of training by humans. One of the biggest drawback is that these narrow AI cannot transfer knowledge. However, the long-term goal of many researchers is to create artificial general intelligence (AGI or strong AI). In 1950, Alan Turing published "Computing Machinery and Intelligence" in which he proposes "the imitation game" which later become known as the Turing Test. The Turing Test is a method used to determine if a computer can actually think like a human. While narrow AI may outperform humans at whatsoever its specific task is, such as solving equations, AGI would outperform us at nearly every cognitive task.

Alan Turing said in his famous 1950 paper: "Most of the programmes which we can put into the machine will result in its doing something that we cannot make sense (if at all, or which we regard as completely random behaviour. Intelligent behaviour presumably consists in a departure from the completely disciplined behaviour involved in computation."

The proliferation of intelligent technology is resulting in advanced machines than can act and do more than humans ever thought possible. And innovation seems likely to get faster, since tech giants and venture capitalists are pouring investment into new AI applications. Last year, according to research conducted by McKinsey, tech companies spent somewhere between $20bn and $30bn on AI, mostly in research and development. Another study, performed by Forrester Research, predicted an increase of 300% in investment in AI this year (2017), compared to last year. IDC estimated that the AI market will grow from $8 billion in 2016 to more than $47 billion in 2020.

Intel invests $1 billion in the AI Ecosystem to Fuel Adoption and Product Innovation. In a statement published on their website, their CEO Brian Krzanich states: "AI will make the impossible possible: advancing research on cancer, Parkinson's disease and brain disorders; helping to find missing children; and furthering scientific efforts in climate change, space exploration and oceanic research."

THE RACE FOR AI:

Approaching the end of 2017, there continues to be a record number of Mergers and Acquisitions of AI companies, with giants like Apple, Amazon, Facebook, Microsoft, and Alphabet Inc. leading the transactions. Consolidation in any market is expected, but AI is consolidating at such an early stage, by so few companies, that there are strong reasons to be concerned. Alphabet's Google led the race to acquire AI and ML startups in the past 5 years, followed by Apple. It's no surprise that Google is leading the pack. In 2013, Google picked up deep learning and neural network startup DNNresearch, an acquisition that reportedly helped Google make major upgrades to its image search feature. Consolidation in AI will create the worst monopoly in US history. When five companies have dominant control over an emerging and transformational field such as AI, it hurts everyone and limits access to smaller companies who don't have the financial backing. Keep in mind, all these companies are building platforms for both immediate need, and strategic expansion of future businesses.

China aims at becoming the world leader in AI by 2030

China has laid out a development plan to become the world leader in AI by 2030, aiming to surpass its rivals and build an AI industry worth almost US$150 billion. The National Development and Reform Commission, China's top economic planner, has already given the green light to the creation of 19 national engineering labs this year, 3 of which are dedicated to AI research and application, including DL, brain-like intelligence, virtual reality (VR), and augmented reality (AR) technologies.

The European AI Landscape

According to research on "The European AI Landscape" conducted by Asgard, The main findings are as follows:

- Europe has a growing and thriving AI industry
- The UK has by far the strongest AI ecosystem, followed by Germany, France, and Spain
- London is Europe's number one hub for AI companies, followed by Berlin, Paris, Madrid, Stockholm, and Amsterdam
- Switzerland has the most AI companies per citizen
- Most AI companies are in the data analytics market
- There are some mature and well-funded AI companies in Europe
- Only 60% of companies claiming to be AI firms actually are

The European General Data Protection Regulation (GDPR)

The demand for uniform privacy regulations has led to the creation of the European General Data Protection Regulation (GDPR), which will take effect in May 2018. The GDPR imposes strict rules on how to handle personal data and may create a challenge for AI companies. It forces companies offering a product or service to a European citizen (it doesn't matter where in the world they are headquartered) to follow Privacy by Design principles. It basically states that whoever collects data about citizens of the 28 European countries needs to follow the General Data Protection Regulation (GDPR) by May 25, 2018. Fines for noncompliance are 4% of global revenue, including USA revenue. This could amount to billions of dollars for large corporations. This is why many US companies made this their top legal priority in 2017. The regulation states that the data subject can ask for their personal data to be transferred directly to a new provider, without hindrance, and in a machine readable format. It also states European residents have a "right to explanation" when an automated decision was made about them. The reason behind it is to avoid discrimination and unseen bias by enabling people to go to court if they feel unfairly treated. But, this could also prohibit the use of Deep Learning. Laws similar to GDPR will spread worldwide— it's only a matter of time.

THREE INDUSTRIES THAT AI WILL DISRUPT IN THE NEXT 10 YEARS

➢ **Healthcare**

Robots are also making healthcare services available 24/7, even when a patient is between doctor visits. AI nurses and caretakers can help monitor a patient's at-home condition and prompt them to take their medication. Through data-driven algorithms, machines will be able to respond to health concerns and even make diagnoses. Boldest Digital Health Influencer nominee Dr. Emmanuel Fombu says, "Artificial intelligence is arguably the single biggest disruptor for the healthcare industry. It'll free up physicians' time by taking care of menial tasks, it'll aid in the discovery of new drugs and treatments and it'll help to provide personalized healthcare to every single patient in the system. The possibilities are mind-blowing." AI could dramatically cut down on the thousands of annual deaths that occur due to adverse reactions to medication.

➢ **Finance**

Four in five bankers believe AI will "revolutionize" the way in which banks gather information, as well as how they interact with their clients, said the Accenture Banking Technology Vision 2017 report, which surveyed more than 600 top bankers. The report forecasts that AI will become the primary way banks interact with their customers within the next 3 years.

Even today, financial advice is becoming automated, with a growing trend towards Robo Advisors. Robots can use a variety of algorithms to provide personalized recommendations that best meet clients' saving and investment habits. According to a survey conducted by Narrative Science in conjunction with the National Business Research Institute, 32% of financial services executives surveyed confirmed using AI technologies such as predictive analytics, recommendation engines, voice recognition, and response. However, the adoption of AI in the banking sector has been slowed by fear and a rigid structure within the industry that keeps data secure.

➢ **Transportation**

AI is also used to power autonomous driving systems, and self-driving vehicles will become a reality within the next 5 years. Self-driving cars are very safe compared to human drivers. Google's self-driving car drove 1.8 million miles and was involved in only 13 accidents—all of which were caused by the other car. This may also lead to making human driving illegal. This is great news, since 1.3 million people die in road traffic accidents every year.

LIMITATIONS OF AI

The effectiveness AI systems is limited by the machine's current inability to explain their decisions and actions to human users. Machines help solve the "how," not the "what" nor the "why." We are not at the level yet where we can completely rely on AI, we will still need the human factor. Another factor is if you present a machine with data that varies even slightly from the training data with which they were taught, it may not be able to compute a result. AI is still being developed and is in its somewhat infancy stages in terms of true commercial viability in many industries. There is lots of development still to come.

The majority of the data in the world is not well defined or structured (incorrect, missing, not timely, irrelevant) and secondly—we humans do not understand well enough how our own brains work so our models are also limited in that respect.

A DL limit is one that considers truth simply as what it spots more frequently in the data, and false as what's statistically more infrequent. If a DL model is trained over 100 books on hate and love, with 60 telling how hate is good, the DL will end up supporting hate. Have a look at what happened to Microsoft's chatbot "Tay" on Twitter. AI can't be left unattended.

Image recognition has improved dramatically and is even replacing ID cards at corporate headquarters. However, vision systems such as those used in self-driving cars, formerly made a mistake when identifying a pedestrian. Mistakes like these can have serious implications resulting in loss of life. Additionally, image recognition isn't always successful in environments where lighting conditions, angles, image resolution, and context may be very different. Even "deep learning," which uses artificial neural networks to discern complex statistical correlations in huge amounts of data, often comes up short. Some of the best image-recognition systems can make major errors, such as mistaking a simple pattern of yellow and black stripes for a school bus.

Learning is about crunching lots of data using statistics. The difficult part is to collect enough data, cleaning, selection of proper features, and choice of ML algorithm. These high-profile examples of AI we read about daily, rely on clever programming and extensive training datasets to accomplish intelligent tasks. Unless the algorithms or training sets specifically account for a particular element, situation, or circumstance, ML systems are thwarted, unable to determine what to do. If there is not enough up-to-date data, statistics cannot deliver the best fit for your problem. Statistics rely on information from the past. It can only extrapolate the past to the future, which is about driving a car while looking at the rear mirror. Statistics has particular problems when it comes to predicting the future, particularly if there is going to be a change in the trend. While the trend is maintained, it can predict accurately.

In his Pulitzer Prize-winning book, *Gödel, Escher, Bach: an Eternal Golden Braid*, Douglas Hofstadter explores the themes of intelligence. He believes that intelligence is an emergent property built on self-referential layers of logic and abstractions. In an interview with the Atlantic Magazine he states, "I don't want to be involved in passing off some fancy program's behaviour for intelligence when I know that it has nothing to do with intelligence. And I don't know why more people aren't that way."

AI can reach a very logical conclusion but it is not "creative." It delivers an output that is perfectly logical, given the internal modeling of the neuron network and the function coefficients for each neuron that resulted of applying ML. It might be true that AI is first of all inspired from our intelligence, but it has to have the same subjective tendencies as humans. AI systems will never be able to predict something that hasn't already happened, adds Anne Moxie, a senior analyst at Boston-based research and advisory firm Nucleus Research. "They're learning from past events but won't be able to predict something that's unexpected," she says, "They can't think the way humans can and speculate on something they don't have any data for."

Machine Learning pioneer Geoffrey Hinton, said at an AI conference that he was "deeply suspicious" of back-propagation and stated, "My view is throw it all away and start again." A neural network learns through training using an algorithm called backpropagation, which is an abbreviation for the backward propagation of errors. He has a valid point. The brain assumes that the world is deterministic, not probabilistic. As Judea Pearl said, "humans are not probability thinkers but cause-effect thinkers." Other scientists at the conference said backpropagation still has a main role in AI's future. But Hinton said that, to push materially ahead, entirely new methods will probably have to be invented.

The truth is our intelligence is very complex and part of this is because we are directly connected to the physical world.

In an interview, Mark Riedl, associate professor at the Georgia Tech School of interactive computing, stated, "If we want computers to understand how the real world works and what we want, we have to figure out ways of slamming lots of common sense, everyday knowledge into them." He went on to say that robots will always be capable of making mistakes. "We'll always want an operator in the loop who can push this big red button and say: 'Stop. Someone is about to get hurt. Let's shut things down.'"

Bringing artificial intelligence more in line with our own mental powers.

Google has started adding Imagination to its DeepMind AI. Researchers have started developing AI with imagination. "When placing a glass on the edge of a table, for example, we will likely pause to consider how stable it is and whether it might fall," explain the researchers. "On the basis of that imagined consequence we might readjust the glass to prevent it from falling and breaking." The team working at Google-owned lab DeepMind says this ability is going to be crucial in developing AI algorithms for the future, allowing systems to better adapt to changing conditions that they haven't been specifically programmed for.

Computer scientists are even finding ways to code curiosity into intelligent machines. Additionally, a new program funded by the federal government's intelligence arm, Intelligence Advanced Research Projects Activity (IARPA), aims to bring AI more in line with our own mental powers. Three teams composed of computer scientists and neuroscientists will attempt to figure out how the brain performs visual identification, and then make machines that can do the same. No one has yet attempted to reconstruct a piece of brain at this scale. Researchers are focusing on a part of the cortex that processes vision—a sensory system that computer scientists have long striven to emulate. "Today's machine learning fails where humans excel," said Jacob Vogelstein, who heads the program at the Intelligence Advanced Research Projects Activity (IARPA).

The race is definitely on to bring AI more in line with the brain. Engineering researchers at the California NanoSystems Institute at the University of California, Los Angeles (UCLA) are building a device that is "inspired by the brain to generate the properties that enable the brain to do what it does," according to Adam Stieg, an associate director of the institute, who leads the project with Jim Gimzewski, a professor of chemistry at UCLA. This device, a 2-millimeter-by-2-millimeter mesh of silver nanowires connected by artificial synapses may look chaotic and random, but its structure and behavior resemble those of neurons in the brain. It can recall its experiences and can solve simple problems. Its inventors hope it points the way to devices that match the brain's energy-efficient computing prowess.

It seems that this structure enables memory and processing ability to be combined as it does not have the separation that exists in our Turing machines. Personally, I want to learn more about the fabrication and how you communicate—send signals to this silver mesh. There is a soon to be published paper cited on this research and it's what I'm really interested in. I would like to learn how they execute logic operations against this device.

CONCLUSION

"By far the greatest danger of Artificial Intelligence is that people conclude too early that they understand it."—Eliezer Yudkowsky

Machines are learning to do more, and they are learning fast. It is expected that they will learn even faster from their user's behavior and predict a person's needs to the point where they are basically making decisions for them. It is estimated that AI will add nearly $16 trillion to the global economy by 2030. Most companies are rethinking their strategy about business models, services, and architecture in a hyper connected world of intelligent machines and big data. According to a Narrative Science report, just 38% percent of the companies surveyed used AI in 2016—but by 2018, this percentage will increase to 62%. The effects of AI will be magnified in the coming decade and most industries will transform their core processes and business models to take advantage of the new developments. The bottleneck now is in management, and implementation.

A joint report by The Boston Consulting Group and MIT Sloan Management Review revealed three-quarters of executives believe AI will enable their companies to move into new businesses. Almost 85% believe AI will allow their companies to obtain or sustain a competitive advantage. At the same time, the survey of 3,000 business executives in 112 countries and 21 industries revealed that the current level of AI adoption at most companies is alarmingly low. The gap between ambition and execution is large at most companies. Only 5% of executives said that their companies were already extensively leveraging AI. In other words, 95% are playing catch up. Consequently, chasing the hype of AI— or any advanced technology—is not at all uncommon. I am close to a company (that shall remain unnamed) that is now falsely selling themselves as an AI enabled platform. I am also seeing many companies adding this. Investors need to be cautious because adding AI is a label, and executing it successfully are two very different things that require specific skill sets and management competence. Saying you are AI enabled because you have a job posting for a ML expert is not being AI enabled. Solitary successful execution of a backpropagation algorithm does not make one AI enabled.

Should you fear or embrace AI? This question revolves around the assumption that we have a choice to control its implementation. AI will eventually become a new reality, whether we decide to embrace it or not. While there might be a temptation and tendency to "wait and see" this could be very risky. The change when it happens will accelerate quickly, leaving unprepared businesses, governments, and societies paralyzed. It is far better to anticipate imminent shocks and act now, to be better able to cope with the upcoming technological upheaval.

Most industries that don't want to be left behind are looking to employ AI in some form, "The convergence of emerging technologies including the Internet of Things, robotics, and AI is creating new market value and displacing existing products and services. These technologies are driving profound changes impacting industries and business models as well as life, society, and the environment," said Tim Zany, Global and US Technology Sector Leader at KPMG. The combination of these factors means we are at the start of a new age of developments, one that will have a profound effect on every person's life. Artificial Intelligence is the future. AI will propel a transformation of unprecedented progress that governments, businesses, and individuals will need to prepare for an era of continuous adaptation and life-long learning.

At the same time, this also affords humans the opportunities to learn to work together with robots and machines. The future of robotics is going to be interesting with passing time. Claims that AI will be superior to existing approaches ignores the fact that AI needs data—data that's often not captured. AI does not mysteriously create data. AI success stories so far are based on very well defined sets of data when algorithms can do a discovery based on relatively simple models. AI is as smart as the combination of the underlying data and humans that design the underlying models. AI still requires a lot of human intelligence to frame the relevant use cases and train the platform. Years of research in this field has helped to come up with algorithms that help machines to identify the problems and to come up with novel approaches to solve them. But still, a great deal of code is written by researchers; hence years of research is still required to reach a level where machines can learn by themselves and come up with solutions without human help. The smartest AI systems can't stack up against adaptive biological intelligence. AI cannot replace cognitive human reasoning and thinking. A robot will not be able to plan, negotiate a business proposal, and decide if it is in need of care now or later. A machine will never replace humans, for they are not independent rational beings. They are devoid of compassion, feelings, empathy, and life.

According to John Launchbury, the Director of DARPA's Information Innovation Office, there are "Three waves of AI technology". We are currently witnessing the "The 2nd Wave of AI", which are essentially systems that are very good at 'learning' but not so good at 'reasoning'. By definition, "Reason is the capacity for consciously making sense of things, applying logic, establishing and verifying facts, and changing or justifying practices, institutions, and beliefs based on new or existing information."

In September 2017, Harry Shum *Executive Vice President, Microsoft AI and Research Group,* told an audience at the recent opening of the GIX U.S. China tech institution, "While this is very exciting, I think people might get confused that most AI problems are solved. That's definitely not true. I want to caution everyone — we're still very early in this AI thing. Computers today can perform specific tasks very well, but when it comes to general tasks, AI cannot compete with a human child."

We must never lose sight of the fact that systems only imitate what we do in real life; systems do not think objectively, as there is always subjectivity. If we keep in perspective the meaning of "life," this is the critical difference as a machine doesn't experience "life." It doesn't feel emotions, doesn't appreciate mortality, so it is unable to be compassionate, loving, or understanding. A machine is capable of ingesting, analyzing, and objectively providing solutions and/ or recommendations based on what humans have programmed or taught it; but will never make decisions based on the emotional and unknown—that is what makes us human.

Intelligent machines and applications can learn a few tricks on their own, but they cannot decipher or predict human emotions. Even if you are married, your spouse cannot know what you want if you do not say it. How do you expect AI researchers to know how to do that? Could your partner guess what you want by spying data on your past activities? Communication between people is impossible without understanding. Understanding is an intuitive attribute of human beings. Machines cannot read your mind to figure out your intentions, desires, and goals and your understanding about how to satisfy them. They don't take the route that goes by the river because there's an absolutely beautiful sunset this evening which will ease your stress.

AI's most important attribute isn't processing scores of data or executing programs, but rather learning to fulfill tasks we humans cannot so we can reach further. It's a partnership: we humans guide AI. To invest in ML and see results, you can't just invest in the technology. You also need to make sure you have the right people in place to guide the systems and allow them to create the most impact. Man and machine partnerships will become more important than ever in the next decade. We will need to have ethical committees in place to oversee the advancement of

DL to determine if developments will cause more harm than good to human civilization on a case-by-case basis. Where jobs are lost, others will be created, but we must be open-minded and agile in order to adapt. That means reconsidering our current economic and political systems to complement our evolving technological advancements for the greater good of society.

History is abounding with the wreckage of technological innovation that failed to provide a consequent advantage to human endeavors. Scientific, technological, and industrial developments have frequently involved side-effects, and trade-offs that have had global scale impacts on our environment and society—plastics, power stations, and the internal combustion engine have had the side effects of global pollution, and climate change. The sources of many of today's issues can be found in the amoral nature of scientific and technological developments. It's never easy to accurately predict the future, and the true capabilities of AI may not yet be realized. By 2030, advances in technology and innovations will mean that robots and AI will be in our lives in a big way. It's unavoidable. Robots and AI are capable of much more than vacuuming or packing our groceries. Depending on code and software written for them, they may be able to think independently, like Asimo. It's important that we stay up-to-date with technology, but learning or implementing something before we understand how the technology will help us is a bad idea. AI when used correctly, is extremely powerful and beneficial.

CHAPTER TWO

WILL ROBOTS TAKE YOUR JOB?

The recent anxieties about technological change are hardly new. Writing in the 1930s, the economist Maynard Keynes counseled patience, promising that any jobs lost to technology marked only a "temporary phase of maladjustment."

The relationship between new technologies and jobs is complex. New technologies enable better-quality products and services at more affordable prices, but they also increase efficiency, which can lead to a reduction in jobs. New technologies are arguably good for society overall because they can improve healthcare and broadly raise living standards; however, when they lead to job loss, they can threaten not only livelihood but individual sense of identity.

Steam power drove industrialization for most of the nineteenth century, until the adoption of electric power in the twentieth century, leading to tremendous advances in industrialization. We are in the early stages of a technology-driven industrial revolution which is both eliminating and creating jobs. Just like blacksmiths and weavers were replaced in the First Industrial Revolution, many of the jobs we see today will be replaced now that we are moving from an Industrial Revolution to a Digital Revolution. The Fourth Industrial Revolution will cause widespread disruption, not only to business models but also to labor markets over the next 5 years, with enormous change predicted in the skill sets needed to thrive in the new landscape. *The Future of Jobs* report, published by the World Economic Forum stated, 5 years from now, over one-third of skills (35%) that are considered important in today's workforce will have changed. Microsoft's *FutureProof Yourself* report suggested that 65% of today's school students will be doing jobs that don't exist yet. This means that many of today's students may be spending time and money on a degree or qualification for jobs which may become obsolete in the near future.

By 2025, the Fourth Industrial Revolution will have brought us AI, autonomous transport, and advanced robotics. These developments will transform the way we live, and the way we work. Some jobs will disappear and there will be new ones. Rapid advancement in AI will enable smart machines the ability to learn more and process data faster than any human can, while making much fewer mistakes. Smart machines don't have human limitations. Smart machines will not require sleep nor suffer from bias decision making or emotional influence.

According to statistics published by the International Federation of Robotics, nearly 1.3 million new robots will be working across the globe by 2018. Already, the average robot density in the manufacturing industry of developed countries is as high as 20 to 50 robots per 1,000 human workers. A joint research by MIT and Boston University studied the effects of increased use of industrial robots between 1990 and 2007. Results estimate an extra robot per 1,000 workers could potentially cut 5.6 human jobs. In that period, industrial robots alone have eliminated up to 670,000 American jobs. China is also building fully automated factories. In some cases, 1 robot can do the work of 140 human workers. "They don't get sick, they don't complain about bad working conditions." Foxconn replaced 60,000 factory workers with robots in May 2016. They cut their human workforce from 110,000 to 50,000. Their unhappy workers tended to commit suicide by jumping off the roof. Foxconn put nets on the ground level to catch them. That didn't work, so instead of fixing conditions, they replaced them with robots. Profits come first. How long can the other 50,000 human workers keep their jobs?

Economists generally emphasize the benefits of automation: Machines reduce costs, and they free up workers to do other jobs. For example, 41% of Americans were farmers a century ago, due to mechanical harvesters and tractors but only 2% work in agriculture today. A factory in Dongguan, China, replaced most of its workers with robots and it saw a rise in productivity. Despite this reduction in staff, not only is the factory producing more equipment (a 250% increase), but it's also ensuring better quality (defects dropped by 80%). According to Monetary Watch, the Changying Precision Technology Company focuses on the production of mobile phones and uses automated production lines. The factory used to be run by 650 employees, but now just 60 people with the robots gets the job done. Luo Weiqiang, the general manager, says the number of required employees will drop to 20 at some point. Adidas is another company which has already announced a shift towards robot-only factories.

According to the researchers, there's a 50% chance that AI will outperform humans in all tasks in just 45 years. In a new study, researchers from Oxford University's Future of Humanity Institute, Yale University, surveyed 352 machine learning experts to forecast the progress of AI in the next few decades. Within the next 10 years alone, the researchers found AI will outperform humans in truck driving, language translation, and writing high-school essays. By 2049, they'll be able to write a bestseller and by 2053, they'll be working as surgeons, the report said.

Historically, technology has generated jobs to the point of break even, maybe. In a recent report, the World Economic Forum predicted that robotic automation will yield a net loss of more than 5 million jobs across 15 developed nations by 2020. The International Labour Organization estimates that as many as 137 million jobs across Indonesia, the Philippines, Thailand, Cambodia, and Vietnam are at risk of replacement by robots. This represents approximately 56% of the total workforce of these countries.

Some of the changes are suddenly coming at such a rapid pace that "traditional" industries and jobs can't keep up. A recent article contained a forecast that by 2020, more than 3 million truck drivers in the US will be displaced by autonomous vehicles. The US Robotics Industries Association (RIA) estimates that more than 265,000 robotics installations are currently deployed at factories across the US. China and Japan have considerably more robotics deployments. Studies at The Center for Business and Economic Research at Ball State University suggested that between 2000 and 2010, 5.6 million manufacturing jobs were lost, where 85% of these losses were due to technology developments. Currently, robots have replaced approximately 10% of manufacturing jobs, and this could rise to 25% by 2025.

The writing is already on the wall. The issue I see with AI is the speed which the technology is coming upon us. People are not able or willing to adapt and learn so they can move on to new jobs while their current positions are being taken away by this technology. This could eventually cause a problem with displaced workers. There is not one area of business that this is not going to be affected. Self-driving vehicles will usher in the elimination of millions upon millions of jobs; fast food restaurants are beginning to introduce automated kiosks and prep systems—millions of jobs lost; drone delivery and automated warehouses; AI-driven robotic factories that can also handle repair and maintenance; increasingly sophisticated AI systems entering into law, medicine, science, business, news/media, you name it. Technology enhancements will continue to increase exponentially; new jobs for humans will not. Japan also has the world's first "Autonomous Corporation," that is, it operates with no operational personnel. To be clear, these are deliberate human replacing initiatives.

Who is Most at Risk?

Almost every human job requires us to perform some combination of the following four basic types of tasks:

- ➤ Manual repetitive (predictable)
- ➤ Manual nonrepetitive (not predictable)
- ➤ Cognitive repetitive (predictable)
- ➤ Cognitive nonrepetitive (not predictable)

Robotic process automation is rapidly advancing from handling traditional applications for repetitive tasks to handling continuously changing tasks. Martin Ford, futurist, explains the jobs that are most at risk are those which "are on some level routine, repetitive, and predictable." Some of the jobs include, accountants, air control traffic controllers, babysitters, car dealers, customer service representatives, pharmacists, secretaries, teachers, telemarketers, wealth managers, retail workers, postal workers, military jobs, pilots, and paralegals.

Forrester Research recently predicted that robots alone would replace 16% of US jobs by 2025, but create the equivalent of 9% of jobs for a net loss of 7% by 2025. The research found that office and administrative support staff would be the most rapidly disrupted. Forrester states that the cognitive era will create new jobs that require higher skills such as robot monitoring professionals, data scientists, automation specialists, and content curators. Forrester forecasts 8.9 million new such jobs in the US by 2025.

According to the Future of Employment, these are some of the least safe and safest jobs:

- ➤ **The least safe jobs**
  - ❖ Telemarketer   Chance of automation 99%
  - ❖ Loan office   Chance of automation 98%
  - ❖ Cashier   Chance of automation 97%

- ❖ Taxi driver   Chance of automation 89%
- ❖ Fast food cook   Chance of automation 81%
- ❖ Paralegal and legal assistant   Chance of automation 94%

> **The safest jobs**

- ❖ Occupational therapist   Chance of automation 0.35%
- ❖ Dietitian and nutritionist   Chance of automation 0.39%
- ❖ Physician and surgeon   Chance of automation 0.42%
- ❖ Clergy   Chance of automation 0.81%
- ❖ Mental health and substance   Chance of automation 0.3%
  abuse social worker

An important 2015 study by YouGov showed that fear of technology rises with primarily those with lower incomes who feel threatened by the "rise of AI," whereas mistrust drops with higher incomes. As estimated by Deloitte, around 39% jobs would be replaced in legal services and around 6% jobs are supposed to be replaced in the next 5 years. Similarly accountant jobs have 95% chance of being replaced. Jobs like insurance underwriters and claims representatives, bank tellers and representatives, financial analysts and construction workers, inventory managers and stock listing, taxi drivers, and manufacturing workers jobs are coming into extinction. All of these fields employ a huge headcount. These implementations will lead to better customer experience, lower costs, but great job losses.

Blue collar manufacturing jobs are being replaced at an increasing rate by the hundreds of thousands as robots are being deployed into many factories and workplaces across the world. For example, an assembly line worker performs mostly manual repetitive tasks which, depending on complexity and a cost/benefit analysis, can be automated. On the other hand, a CEO performs mostly cognitive nonrepetitive tasks which are much harder to automate. While repetitive jobs are always thought to be first on the chopping block, automation will impact many tasks of white collar jobs as well. As technology becomes more sophisticated, some activities previously completed by employees can be handled by computer programs. A Zdnet article focusing on this research emphasizes that if the AI boom continues, it will soon expand into sectors so far considered immune to automation. From the financial industry to journalism and education, new jobs are going to be created which, without AI, would simply be impossible. HR professionals have already found that AI can perform candidate searches and determine best matches for jobs. Using technology can help make candidate reviews more manageable. Some companies already offer some AI-related assistance to track candidates or monitor workers. It is possible to receive alerts if employees have poor performance or if they are not where they should be at work. In early 2017, a Japanese insurance company, Fukoku Mutual Life Insurance, replaced 34 claims workers (30%) with a $1.7m IBM Watson based AI investment. According to Raja Subramanian, group enterprise architect at tech services company Xchanging, robots processing insurance-related tasks can clear more than 30,000 cases a month, reducing processing time from 5 minutes to less than 10 seconds. Other Japanese insurance companies and US companies have also started using AI to replace staff. Will there be a net creation rather than destruction of jobs? The potential impacts are becoming more serious. This not only represents loss of jobs but leads to mass unemployment and depression.

This is just the beginning. The AI-driven robot "Flippy," by Miso Robotics, is marketed as a kitchen assistant, Flippy features a number of different sensors and cameras to identify food objects on the grill. Flippy is capable of deep frying, chopping vegetables, and even plating dishes. As part of its "Experience of the Future" initiative, McDonald's announced plans to roll out digital ordering kiosks that will replace cashiers in 2,500 of its locations. The company will also extend its customer self-service efforts, deploying mobile ordering at 14,000 locations. Meet SAM (Semi-Automated Mason), a bricklaying robot designed and engineered by Construction Robotics out of New York. While SAM can do the work of 6 masons each day, he never requires a break, benefits, or a pay check.

Robots and Chatbots at the Frontier of Human Replacement

A recent report by *The Economist* confirmed that most consumers expect a business to be available 24/7. They demand a continuous and quick service. Chatbots offers the solution here. Call centers, and many types of human-driven customer services, are quickly becoming obsolete. Chatbots are like apps but they are in a conversational format. Many companies have begun to implement similar interfaces to service customers. One example is Reserve, which allows you to book a table at a restaurant through an SMS simulated platform. The entire booking process happens inside an in-app chatbot that feels like a text message conversation. Some of the responses in the conversation are automated, while others are managed by members of the reserve support team. This combination of man and machine creates a uniquely personal and magical experience.

At the Chatbot Summit in Tel Aviv. Leaders from the chatbot community came from all over the world to discuss the challenges and the potential. In his opening speech, Yoav Barel, who founded the conference said, "We are at the threshold of a revolution that would affect the daily lives of billions of people during the next decade... Chatbots are essentially a new user interface which provides consumers the ability to communicate with brands the same way they communicate with friends and family—via a natural conversation. In the not so distant future, we will be able to communicate with our bank, get recommendations on movies and order a cup of coffee from a friendly chatbot." Research from the acclaimed Nomura Research Institute asserts that by 2035, almost 50% of all jobs in Japan will be taken by robots, chatbots, or other AI applications.

As business bots become more intelligent, their ability to perform complex operational tasks will move beyond simple chat applications like customer service and scheduling support, to impact business in more profound ways. For example, the Operations bot will manage production schedules and the Sales and Marketing bot will optimize e-commerce channels…etc.

Research from KPMG suggests that Robotic Process Automation (RPA) offers a 40% to 75% reduction in costs. RPA-based processes run nonstop, 24 hours a day, 365 days a year and they're fast. Automation is no longer an option in the 21st-century enterprise. The speed of technological evolution is exponential. Across industries, it is already driving efficiency, productivity, and optimization. Companies are going through the intelligent automation journey (or digital operations journey) by digitalizing their process activities using robots. AI can improve business efficiency, reduce costs, enhance customer experience (internal and external clients), and reach a higher level of process excellence (e.g., improve quality, accuracy).

While automation is good, someone needs to manage the transition to such a domain or job loss will become unmanageable and societal problems will balloon. The problem society faces is that the pace of technological change is much faster (and getting faster by the minute) than the ability to change careers or invest in our own education to quickly learn today the skills needed in the "new" world. Basically the rate of human labor displacement is faster than the rate of job creation necessary to absorb the labor displaced. How are people who lose their jobs today supposed to pay their monthly bills, save for the future, and ensure their kids are receiving the education they need for these future jobs that don't exist yet?

The US Bureau of Labor Statistics (BLS) reports over the past 7 years that companies added 136,748 robots to factory floors. The BLS also determined that while robots were being added to factories, 894,000 new manufacturing jobs were also created as a result of automation. The more we rely on automation, the more we will need individuals with the relevant skills to deal with the complex code and systems. These jobs being created require specialist skills. This creates a raft of new careers, disciplines, and areas of expertise not existing today.

Some economists claim automation will create many jobs. Boston University economist James Bessen stated that "in the 45 years since the introduction of the automated teller machine, the number of human bank tellers employed in the United States has roughly doubled." What Bessen doesn't take into account is that the US population increased by roughly 120 million people since the introduction of the ATM into the US, so population (as well as increased services) helped to contribute to an increase in bank tellers.

For business futurist Morris Miselowski, job shortages will be a reality in the future. "I'm not absolutely convinced we will have enough work for everybody on this planet within 30 years anyway. I'm not convinced that work as we understand it, this nine-to-five, Monday to Friday, is sustainable for many of us for the next couple of decades."

I have no doubt that technology will create new job roles, but will displace many more jobs than it creates and at a much faster pace than in previous revolutions. Jobs will be lost at a greater pace than ever before, a rate that might pass the threshold of our ability as a nation to provide a reasonable level of employment for all persons. This isn't like the earlier Industrial Revolutions, this is not replacing some jobs by machinery, it is replacing people with intelligent machinery. There's a fundamental difference in eliminating some jobs from the labor market (to be replaced by other jobs), and eliminating humans in general from the labor market (to be replaced by machines). The previous industrial revolution involved human augmentation. This coming revolution involves human replacement. The entire point of automation is to reduce overhead. How do you do that? You remove salaries, benefits, and human error. What happens to the humans? Robots and AI will take jobs and not everyone can be re-trained.

When we look at previous economic transitions, for example agriculture to manufacturing there was an increase in employment, and new jobs were created. The transition to a manufacturing economy developed a need for management, design, planning, forecasting, and a variety of other skills. That is, latent human capabilities were engaged in an economically productive way. However, this time, Industry 4.0 technologies (AI, Robotics, IoT, etc.) are increasingly assuming these advanced economically productive human capabilities. The range of human capabilities that only humans can perform is rapidly shrinking. Previous economic transitions involved the economic deployment of unused but economically productive human capability. This may still be the case, however, the human capabilities not yet subsumed under AI or Robotics includes: creative, advanced analytical, or a few highly specialized skills. That is only a very small percentage of the population will fill jobs that require these skills; everyone else is at risk of jobs displacement. There are structural issues in our global society that will accelerate the adverse effects of AI and Robotics on global employment.

Automation and AI will affect multiple, horizontal marketplaces at the same time. For example, think of the tractor taking farm jobs. Now think of the tractor not only taking the farm jobs but all the jobs leading up to the arrival of the tractor on the farm. The potential for a "compounding" impact as change takes place within an "industry sector" and also across a number of "sectors".

The comparison between "then" and "now" that many use, is stark and invalid. The reason is that "then," people made the machines that improved productivity; today, machines make machines. In the tractor example above, when one man can plough in a day what formerly required, say, 20 workers, that's a productivity increase. And, by the way, the tractor could dig deeper so quality was improved as well. So what happened to those other 19 farmers then out of a job? Most simply moved to the cities and became assembly line workers—more tractors and other machines, like automobiles, were being built. They had to learn new skills, but that bar was fairly low.

Contrast that with "now" where an industrial robot is assembled by machine-made components and is installed into an application where one person can now manage the work previously performed by four. Where do the other three people go? It doesn't take three people to program that robot; on the contrary, one programmer can support dozens of robots. Or let's look at the looming self-driving vehicle. One of the largest employee bases in the US is truck driver. Once driverless trucks are on the road, where do all the truck drivers find work? They won't build the trucks—that's done by machine; they won't program the trucks—that's done by some IT specialist. The dilemma is not just one of manual skills. Jobs like accounting, electrical, and mechanical troubleshooters, clerical and service functions, even creative activities, are all being replaced by software. The fact is, culture adapts to it. Eventually I won't need some clerk trying to sell me an outfit off the rack when I can make my choice online from the comfort of my home and have custom-tailoring delivered within 2 days. The examples are endless. If machines can do the work of more people, then fewer people are required. It's the same intellectual blind spot that led to the notion that more unhealthy people can be insured at lower cost. And millions of otherwise intelligent individuals buy into these impractical conclusions.

You could train farmers to use a tractor, far less likely you can train unskilled workers today to adapt to AI. Also, the speed of technological evolution is exponential. I am not sure the mass populace can rise to the educational demands required to keep up with technology replacing their jobs. The trend of technology is to always replace the lowest strata of workers. Many of these are unwilling or incapable of improving their intellectual capacity to get ahead of the curve. It's easier to go from using a hoe to driving a tractor, than a forklift operator to robot programmer. Even if they did, I don't think the market will have enough opportunities for all, regardless of whether they transform themselves or not into more relevant professionals. So even if new training programs are developed, a big part of today's workforce will still become redundant. Secondly, the ageing population of Western mature countries reinforces the point above.

The question then is: What happens to those people who, for whatever reason, are unable to adapt to the disruption or do not have sufficient opportunities to learn the new skills? Ultimately, we need to ask ourselves whether the disruption can be handled in a more humane manner and not just treat all human beings as replaceable. Simply put, machines may replace human beings, but we need a new world order where human beings are not treated as disposable objects but as people with families, emotions, and who need to live a life of dignity, and be given the chance to be productive and earn their living.

Andrew Ng, the cofounder of Coursera and former chief scientist at Chinese technology powerhouse Baidu, called for more educational opportunity, especially as people are pushed out of the jobs they used to hold. "I think we're reaching a point where we need to maybe rebuild our educational system, or at least add some new components to our educational system, so that someone whose job is displaced has a good shot at getting themselves the training they need in order to find meaningful work," he said.

Pervasive job disruption can lead to global social unrest and exacerbate the challenges of companies and governments to retrain their aging workforce. We need to do a better job of helping these people to transition to other occupations and managing the process by which technology is upending society. So, the real question is how do we deal with people that will lose their jobs and do not have the skill sets to take on higher level, more technical challenges? Coal miners are one example; most coal miners simply do not have the skill sets/education to work in "clean energy tech," so what are they to do? There has to be a sharp focus on the re-skilling of people. The new jobs created by AI will require different and higher-level skills than the ones they replaced. Many people with degrees can't find good jobs now, so what will the situation be when they are displaced by machines.

Bill Gates has suggested robots be taxed and many experts are recommending a Universal Basic Income (UBI) to compensate for the huge job displacements. I will discuss UBI in more details in Chapter 4—The Two Edged Sword of Artificial Intelligence.

I believe that employers who lay off workers should be required to contribute to a fund that will help finance further education or retraining for the displaced. These workers cannot go back, so they must learn new trades or obtain more education in another field. Educational institutions are also part of the mix. They must be prepared to stay out in front and prepare a younger and aging workforce for new job categories.

Educating our labor force for the jobs of tomorrow will be of paramount importance, although technology will be changing the face of education itself in the years to come. Our education systems usually generate great test takers but do not teach the necessary developmental work to that focus on high levels of social and emotional intelligence. Young people have no formal training on how to apply critical thinking, how to effectively collaborate, how to become emotionally engaged, or how to listen effectively. Change won't wait for us: business leaders, educators, and governments all need to be proactive in up-skilling and retraining people so everyone can benefit from the Fourth Industrial Revolution.

This pace of change is only going to get faster thanks to rapid advances in the fields of robotics, driverless transport, AI, biotechnology, advanced materials, and genomics, according to the World Economic Forum's latest annual Human Capital Index.

We are moving from a commodity based capital to intellectual capital. These changes may seem marginal today. But the level of job disruption will be unprecedented and accelerate without much warning and cause crises for companies that aren't prepared. Businesses will benefit the most. They will no longer be forced to pay human workers the billions of dollars that they have. Add to that the billions of dollars spent on employee insurance, workplace safety renovations, overtime compensation, and workers compensation claims and anyone could see the benefits of replacing manpower with machine power. With its one time purchasing cost and the minimal cost of upkeep, it's no wonder that businesses nationwide fought against raising the minimum wage to a mere $15 an hour.

WHAT CAN YOU DO?

All of us have some tendency to become comfortable and complacent with things simply because they are familiar to us. When a new way of doing something is thrust upon us, our natural instinct is often to resist for no other reason than because it is "different." By accepting change, you put yourself on more solid footing in dealing with the unexpected.

We need to be aware that the future of management will not always be the management of humans by humans. Business leaders will remain but lower and middle management may be replaced. You need to accept in the not so distant future your boss may be a robot.

We must adapt, simply adapt. Think of adaptability as a habit, something to practice. In the future, we will be competing against mechanically-enhanced workers who can work longer and harder than us—a new breed of elite super-workers emerges.

Robots will be in almost every sector. The idealized company for owners is one without employees. Robots can't get unionized or strike. They are a cost effective and compliant workforce. They are able to work incessantly, don't require breaks or vacations, sick leave, maternity leave, don't ask for raises, don't gossip or get disgruntled over missing a promotion, don't need weekends off, never leave the premises, don't lie, cheat, steal, antagonize, or complain. But coupled with AI, robots will be enabled and trusted to do much more.

According to PwC, these forces will result in four potential futures: one where humans come first, one where innovation rules, one where companies care, and one where corporate is king. Imagine what it will be like when you are no longer just competing for a job with another human. What will you think when your competition for a job is a smart machine with a serial number?

Despite the massive potential of AI systems, they are still far from replacing many kinds of tasks that people are good at or tasks that require creativity, innovation, or empathy.

I saw this funny poster *"Humans need not apply"* which was felt as an exacerbated factor of robotics and AI. Automation, like every other form of industrial rivalry is designed to transfer wealth from those less equipped and slower to adapt to those who are ahead of the curve. Don't resist the progress of technology but rather work to make it fruitful and complementary. We should embrace AI as soon as possible so as not to fall too far behind. Society will feel a tremendous impact—so it's better to be ahead of the curve, to be proactive in learning new skills.

Individuals will have to make a conscious effort to grow in their lives and careers. If service jobs are going to become obsolete, then it's up to each and every individual to manage and find a way to transform themselves. Become a better brand and a better version of yourself. While we have had robots which have replaced minor jobs, we are still quite some time away from robots being so advanced that they can replace complex tasks such as persuading or negotiating. Communication, emotional and social intelligence, creativity, innovative thinking, empathy, critical thinking, collaboration, and cognitive flexibility will become the most sought-after abilities.

I believe we could see a world where data and technology replace entire classes of employment. We need to be paying close attention and invest in the job skills and education sectors that are anticipated to grow.

Regardless if you think AI is coming for your job or not, it's in your best interest to become a perpetual learner:

1 Start by getting a high-level understanding of the changes coming from the Fourth Industrial Revolution, beyond AI, robots, and automation. Keep abreast of new developments and changes. This will help you to not only understand where risks to your career may come from but also identify opportunities for your future.

2 Take a SWOT analysis. SWOT is the acronym for strengths, weakness, opportunities, and threats. Be sure to include not only your learned technical skills but also soft skills interests and passions as well.

3 Pay attention to tangential areas related to your career, not just to what is directly in front of you.

4 Think of other areas where your skills can be applicable. You will need to create every advantage to stay ahead. Consider alternative career paths and work on bridging the gap, think beyond your role.

5 Be a continuous learner, take classes online, volunteer, participate in discussions, and network. Keep learning. Keep growing.

New technologies will create new opportunities in many fields. There's an unprecedented shortage of programmers, data scientists, cybersecurity experts and IT specialists, among others. For example, there's currently a 1 million shortage of skilled workers in the cybersecurity sector. According to ISC2, that number will rise to 1.5 million by 2020. Additionally, a study of job ads from April found more than 10,000 vacancies in the US for people with AI or machine-learning skills.

Moreover, here's a selection of 10 occupations that weren't around in 2006: App developer, iOS developer, Android developer, Driverless car engineer, Cloud computing specialist, Big data analyst/data scientist, Sustainability manager, Drone operators. Digital marketing specialist, UI/UX designer.

Upwork, the largest freelancing website, released the 20 fastest-growing skills for freelancers in Q2 2017.

The 20 fastest-growing freelance skills in Q2 2017 all experienced more than 150% year-over-year growth, while the top ten grew more than 300% compared to the same time period last year (Q2 2016). 1) Virtual reality, 2) Natural language processing, 3)Econometrics, 4) Learning Management System (LMS), 5) Neural networks, 6) Penetration testing, 7) SEO auditing, 8) Image processing, 9) Asana work tracking, 10) Facebook API development, 11) Swift development, 12) Marketing analytics, 13) Geographic Information System (GIS), 14) Docker development, 15) Adobe Photoshop Lightroom, 16) Machine learning, 17) AngularJS development, 18) Video advertising, 19) Shopify development, and 20) Pardot marketing.

CONCLUSION

We're entering a new age of automation and technology, where we don't have to work repetitive, unchallenging jobs and can instead focus on other things. The problem is...there might not be other things. Every single technological advance in human history has brought new economic opportunities and increased the living standards of everyone. That is because every single technological advance in human history has leveraged the productivity of everyone. AI will enormously leverage the productivity of those very few who can use creative and analytical thought to solve the problems of the rich. The remainder will be surplus to requirements. It will destroy minimum wage jobs, but will create more specialty jobs.

Both the Canadian Government and the US Department of Commerce have authored reports suggesting that up to 40% of the jobs currently performed in our economies are in danger of automation within 10 years. This is a very fast, very large change that is simply going to leave some people behind. Not everybody is cut out to do technology work...and what about older workers? Some are saying that age discrimination is now taking place as young as 45, particularly in technology and knowledge driven fields.

While every technological advancement in the past made multiple professions obsolete but created a greater number of new jobs, this "knowledge revolution" is different. Just look at the size of the most valuable companies in the world less than a generation ago. They employed millions or hundreds of thousands of workers. Look at the most valuable companies today: Google is worth around $500B and has 72K employees. Facebook with a value of around $350B has 17K employees, and Waze was sold for $1.3B when it had 115 employees. This is a growing trend where more and more value is attributed to less and less people. Most US college graduates have a meaningless degree that will not land them a job, while the average student in the US has an outstanding debt of $35K ($1.2T total). This current knowledge revolution will necessitate fewer people with higher skills. This brave new world will demand initiative and entrepreneurship from everyone, while only a small portion of the population have the required spirit.

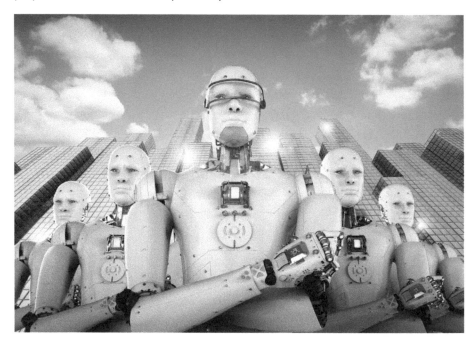

The fundamental mathematics of investment and finance require every company to pursue one basic objective: Spend as little as you can in order to produce the most and the best output (products and services) that you can. This forces every company to use capital equipment rather than employees in every situation where the capital equipment does more and/or better for less cost. This has always been true, but now robotics and AI are vastly increasing the proportion of work activities to which this imperative applies. Of course, this means that every company is forced to reduce its workforce as much as possible, while relying on other companies to keep employing workers so that someone can buy the products of the job cutter. Meanwhile, those other companies are doing the same thing. This will not end well. Thus far, the only people that are optimistic are those selling the technology, and the company owners who may benefit in the short term from reductions in labor costs. They soon won't be so full of bliss when they finally realize that the mass technological unemployment they create will result in very few people being able to afford to buy their goods and services.

We've entered an era when computers can understand speech, respond to customer support questions, develop music, create novel art, and even generate new summaries and reports from data. Increasingly, we will struggle to distinguish between machine-generated and human-generated. **Companies will have to eventually disclose if a product is made by a human or machine—natural or artificial.** Products made by humans will be more expensive. Companies will need to view future competitive advantage, processes, and organization from a man-and-machine angle. Economic theory suggests that AI will substantially raise the value of human judgment.

It was once believed that the purpose of enterprise is to provide employment. This is no longer the case as boosting shareholder value has taken precedence. Businesses are looking for every method to reduce cost and/or human error so they can maintain a competitive edge in the global market place. It's about competition and they will reasonably do what they have to, to survive. Outsource or automate—whatever will reduce costs. So take active steps to keep yourself relevant in the job market.

CHAPTER THREE

TECHNOLOGIES AND FUTURE TRENDS

AI promises to be the biggest technological shift in our lifetime. For the foreseeable future, AI is there augmenting our capabilities, allowing us to do more, with better accuracy, in less time. However, every industry will have to fundamentally reassess how it operates in order to incorporate AI and coexist with machines that will become invaluable partners in solving real problems. One thing is certainly clear: technology is changing and the ramifications of this evolution will be felt in every aspect of business. Seeing the shifts and some of the early-stage technology out there being tested, will give you an early indication of trends that are about to go mainstream.

THE NEW DIGITAL NATION

At the end of 1991, following the breakup of the Soviet Union, a small group of government officials got together to discuss the challenges they faced with the biggest one being this: how can a tiny player of a country, with only around 1 million people, survive and compete in a world dominated by "big players"? The country was Estonia, and the people suddenly had the opportunity to build a government and a country from the start. The then Ambassador to the United States, Toomas Hendrik Ilves (who was later to become President of Estonia), realized that it was possible to use the internet to give the country more influence than its tiny size and location would suggest. Within a couple of years, Estonia, or E-stonia as it was ingeniously rebranded, had the largest number of start-up companies per capita in the world.

Estonia also decided to build some policies that were forward-looking. For example, in Estonia, the internet is considered a human right and all residents have free Wi-Fi. They put education and healthcare online faster than many wealthier economies managed to. They introduced a flat taxation system and import tariffs were scrapped. In Estonia, you own your own data and all public expenditure is transparent and available online. It became a hotbed for disruptive technology because of the environment that was created, giving entrepreneurs the space to exist in Estonia.

Residents of Estonia have an e-identity. So beside normal civilians, they have also virtual civilians from all over the world. People can have a digital identity and gain e-residence that enables them to do all kinds of official things like starting businesses, getting access to banking services, etc. without physically being in Estonia. The goal is to connect 10 million Estonian e-residents into the community there.

Estonia is vulnerable to cyberattack because it's so dependent on the internet. In 2007, their networks were subject to a major cyberattack allegedly perpetrated by the Russians. However, Estonia's young technologists reacted with groups of young cyber security experts volunteering for the Estonian army, and now NATO recognizes Estonia as a "cyber defense center of excellence".

In the future, most governments will be transformed into digital or virtual governments. They will be highly connected with the civilian population, to the point that the government and the society it services will be more like a single entity.

SMART CITIES & THE CIRCULAR ECONOMY

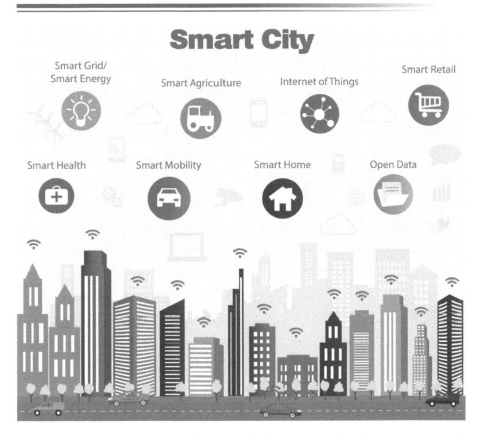

Singapore is striving to be the world's first smart city. Emerging trends such as automation, AI, and the Internet of Things (IoT) are driving smart city adoption. Smart Cities integrate water resources, health systems, transportation, smart-building technologies, energy, sanitation and waste collections, and security technologies and services. Smart cities will help people lead a safe and technologically advanced life. In the past few years, cities have migrated from analog to digital. A smart city uses digital technologies to reduce costs and resource consumption, enhance performance and quality of services, and to engage more effectively with its citizens. Frost & Sullivan estimates the combined global market potential of smart city segments (transportation, healthcare, building, infrastructure, energy, and governance) to be $1.5 Trillion ($20B by 2050 on sensors alone according to Navigant Technology).

Circular economy is becoming an increasingly used strategy, not for only cities but for organizations as well, who want to transition their business model into one that is both financially and environmentally sustainable. According to Wikipedia, "a circular *economy is a regenerative system in which resource input and waste, emission, and energy leakage are minimised by slowing, closing, and narrowing material and energy loops. This can be achieved through long-lasting design, maintenance, repair, reuse, remanufacturing, refurbishing, and recycling." Many* companies in a number of sectors are already shifting in this direction.

ENERGY

By 2030, we are likely to be running on a decentralized and circular energy infrastructure—the wave of innovation that brought us the widespread introduction of bio-solar technology. Our modern integrated bio-batteries enable us to generate energy in the daytime and store it until we need it at night. We can now use energy 24/ 7 without burning polluting fossil fuels. These new units are highly efficient and therefore very compact. Today's solar panels are already 10 times cheaper and more efficient than they were a decade ago, and the rate of development has sped up significantly. The current world record is at 46% percent for a 4-junction solar cell. In the near future this is expected to surpass 50%. The innovation and production of new solar systems is probably at a record high right now. Bloomberg's New Energy Finance team estimates that price per kilowatt hour of power generated through solar will drop dramatically from $182 to around $132 by 2025.

According to the reports (Wind Energy in Europe: Scenarios for 2030 and Wind Energy in Europe: Outlook to 2020), 30% of the electricity consumed in Europe could be created from the wind. Europe is on track to renovate its energy infrastructure. Your devices could soon be powered by ocean waves. Researchers at Japan's Okinawa Institute of Science and Technology have developed turbines that can use the sea's currents to generate renewable electric power. The team estimates that its turbines, if placed on just 1% of mainland Japan's shoreline, could generate some 10 gigawatts of power — that's 10 nuclear power plants' worth of energy. Additionally, the US Department of Energy announced 18 new projects to accelerate production of macroalgae for energy and other uses.

Other areas in **Energy** to keep a close watch on are:

- Waste to biofuels
- Safe nuclear
- Hydrogen fuels
- Protecting the Grid
- Fusion Power
- Renewables
- Carbon-breathing batteries
- Batteries (long lasting)
- Helium-3 Power Generation
- Self-sufficient energy ecosystem

FINANCIAL SERVICES AND FINTECH (FINANCIAL TECHNOLOGY)

Fintech - The broad term applies to the technological innovations that are disrupting the financial sector. One of the challenges for financial institutions is that they need to serve digital dinosaurs, digital natives and all people in between. Instead of competing with banks for general products and services, fintech startups focus on unserved areas. Fintech trends show that people are more comfortable managing their money and business online, and they're less willing to put up with the bureaucracy associated with certain traditional financial institutions. Today, fintechs are disrupting every single banking sector, from investments to loans to insurance. A survey by PwC found that 95% of respondents from banks and 83% from traditional financial services firms think that part of their business could be lost to niche fintech firms.

China Will Surpass Silicon Valley and Africa is the Next Tech Hotspot

According to EY, China has now taken the lead as the #1 fintech market in the world. China will surpass Silicon Valley. Venture capital funding in Fintech in China has outpaced the USA since 2016, and the number of billion dollar valuation companies (unicorns) founded per year was greater in Asia than the USA. "China's unique mix of rapid urbanisation, massive and underserved market, e-commerce growth, explosion in online and mobile phone penetration, and customer adoption willingness have created a fertile ground for innovation in commerce, banking, and financial services more broadly," says EY Asia-Pacific Fintech Leader James Lloyd. However, the continent where fintech is stirring things up the most is Africa. Africa is one of the fastest growing and highest potential markets in the world and has already shown significant promise in the realm of fintech. For example, between 31% and 50% of Kenya's GDP is estimated to flow through the mobile money service named M-Pesa. Almost 80% of individuals with cell phones use them for mobile payments and banking services. According to research conducted by Global Web Index (Q2 2017) on "Banking App Usage among Millennials." South Africa placed #1 for users aged 21-24 years who are using banking / financial services app.

Ushering a Cashless Society

We are seeing an increasing trend in the use of QR codes. QR code may usher in the cashless society. QR codes are increasingly being used around the world, even beating out Apple Pay and other brand-name payment services. A Quick Response (QR) code is a machine-readable code made up of black and white squares read by a device reader. It was developed in the 1990s by Japan's Denso Corp., and stores more information than traditional barcodes. Much of China has become a QR first economy, where codes are now found next to nearly every cash register. Digital payments as WeChat pay and Alipay are nearly ubiquitous. These digital wallet services link to a user's bank account and are based around QR codes. Consumers just need to scan the QR code to make instant payment. Other developing countries are starting to use this system. In 2016, MasterCard Inc. rolled out a QR code system in Africa. In India, the government launched IndiaQR. Thailand also seems very much interested.

South Korea, Australia and certain parts of Europe aim to be cashless societies by 2020. By 2021, digital payments is expected to reach $5 trillion by 2021, up from under $3.7 trillion this year.

Blockchain Technology and the Creation of Bitcoin

Imagine a world of peer-to-peer value exchange. This "imaginary" world is emerging now, and it is a realistic prospect. There has been much speculation about Satoshi Nakamoto the person who designed Bitcoin and created its original reference implementation—he has chosen to remain anonymous. Bitcoin is a digital currency and is operated by a decentralized authority, unlike government-issued currencies. Bitcoin isn't owned by anyone. You can think of it like email. Anyone can use it, but there isn't a single company that is in charge of it. Bitcoin is 8 years into existence and has become an exchangeable means of trade. You cannot own Bitcoin without a wallet. A "wallet" is basically the Bitcoin equivalent of a bank account. It has a nominal cost, but is virtually free. Each day, the number of wallets grows by about 0.2%, a rate that has been pretty consistent since 2011. The price of Bitcoins rises when the demand outstrips the supply. More and more goods and services can be bought and sold by Bitcoin. It can be seen and treated also as a commodity one trades with on specialized exchange markets. In August 2017, Bitcoin was worth around $4,600—a considerable jump from late 2016, when it was around $770. The dollar value of the 20 biggest cryptocurrencies is around $150 to $200 billion, according to data from Coinmarketcap.com.

This has given birth to an entire new industry of cryptocurrency. A cryptocurrency is any kind of peer-to-peer digital money powered by the blockchain technology which is revolutionizing the industry. Blockchain is commonly known as the foundation for Bitcoin, it's a distributed database of digital assets and transactions. Blockchain creates digital signatures for each transaction and shares this information among a decentralized network of computers. It uses advanced cryptography to authenticate and record transactions. It's basically an unhackable distributed ledger. This decentralized approach allows each computer to continuously provide verification as to each party's status and ownership in a particular transaction. Some of the biggest names in business, such as Wal-Mart, IBM, and Unilever, are harnessing the power of blockchain technology. Although blockchain is quite secure and stable, and prevents hackers from altering information on the network due to the collective dissemination of transactional information, the problem is with the instability of virtual currency trading platforms. One of the earliest and largest Bitcoin exchanges, Mt. Gox, suddenly shut down in Feb 2014, and users collectively lost $473 million in Bitcoin.

Since Bitcoin's appearance in 2009, hundreds of new cryptocurrencies, often called altcoins, have been created. The blockchain is based on the principles of cryptography, hence the name "cryptocurrencies." Many who are afraid believe this will lead to another "dot com burst" and the "Dutch Tulip & bulb market bubble"—and they may be right, but the underlying blockchain technology is the value, and that will continue to grow as we fully appreciate and realize its power.

The hype surrounding cryptocurrencies has led to phishing attacks by cyber criminals increasing exponentially alongside the rise in Initial Coin Offering's and digital token sales. An Initial Coin Offering (ICO) is an unregulated means by which funds are raised for a new cryptocurrency venture. ICOs are similar to Initial Public Offering IPOs and crowdfunding. But unlike a traditional IPO, in which buyers get shares, getting behind a start-up's ICO nets virtual tokens—like mini-cryptocurrencies—unique to the issuing company or its network. That means they grow in value only if the startup's business or network proves viable, attracting more people and boosting liquidity.

But their digital nature and lack of guaranteed value means the purchase and use of cryptocurrencies carries several innate risks. The vast amount of money amassed in a short span of time has also attracted cyber criminals. Many investor alerts have been issued by the Securities and Exchange Commission (SEC), the Consumer Financial Protection Bureau (CFPB), the Financial Industry Regulatory Authority (FINRA), and other agencies. Bitcoins are a rival to government currency and may be used for tax evasion, money laundering, black market transactions, and illegal activities.

Banks are jumping on board the cryptocurrency train. Six global banks joined forces to create digital currency. Barclays, Credit Suisse, Canadian Imperial Bank of Commerce, HSBC, MUFG, and State Street have teamed up to work on the "utility settlement coin," which was created by Switzerland's UBS to make financial markets more efficient. In the future, banks won't have an excuse anymore to levy transaction fees. If they embrace the methodology of transfer wise, there's no need for excessive conversion fees either. Looking forward to further shrinking of the sector, paving the way for change.

Bank of England Governor Mark Carney—who has said blockchain shows "great promise"—also warned regulators this year to keep on top of developments in financial technology if they want to avoid a 2008-style crisis. In the US, both banks and regulators are studying distributed ledger technology. But Federal officials have voiced reservations about digital currencies themselves. The Dutch central bank has created its own cryptocurrency—for internal circulation only—to better understand how it works. India is now looking at creating a national cryptocurrency (the Lakshmi) and Japanese banks are working together to introduce a new digital currency (J-Coin) ahead of the 2020 Tokyo Olympics. One of the greatest benefits of

Bitcoin, specifically, is that it represents a global, but neutral currency. Bitcoin stands to benefit from smaller economies like Estonia who are looking to create their own national cryptocurrency. Russia has also shown interest in the cryptocurrency called Ethereum, with the central bank deploying a blockchain pilot program. However, Chinese regulators have finally decided to officially ban all Bitcoin exchanges and trading and aim to remove all exchanges by the end of 2017. Can cryptocurrency flourish without involving China? Is this the beginning of the end for cryptocurrencies in general? I don't think this is the end of cryptos in China, however I think the time horizon for acceptance just got longer. South Korea has also banned ICOs. According to officials, anyone caught continuing the practice will face "stern penalties."

We are now seeing the first ever criminal case against Bitcoin sales. Russian police arrested three businessmen for illegally trading in 500 million rubles worth of Bitcoin, or around $9 million worth of the cryptocurrency (as reported in *Vedomosti*, September 1, 2017).I view cryptocurrency as powering the future of online and maybe offline transaction and commerce. Unregulated ICO's have been flooding the cryptocurrency market for months now, and there have been too many fraudulent or over-hyped/under-designed ICO's that have zero or little integrity. Regulation could be good, so as long as appropriate steps are taken to introduce measures that don't stymie healthy growth or consolidate power. Regulation will break in globally, anyway, so the sooner the better. I believe in the longer-term it's a beneficial thing, as some degree of regulation will be needed to protect consumers. This way we can start formalizing things.

Ethereum, which was launched in 2015, is the second-largest digital currency. There are a lot of cryptocurrencies that have launched since Bitcoin, including Litecoin, Zcash, Dash, Ripple, Monero, in addition to Ethereum et al. The interesting thing about Ethereum is that it has built in functionality which allows it to do a number of things Bitcoin is ill-suited to do. I would wager neither is going away anytime soon, but I think that there's a lot of potential in Ethereum to surpass Bitcoin if it is developed on top of, to build applications which have disruptive use-cases outside the economic impact we've seen to date. Ethereum is capturing the development community. It's a cryptocurrency which can underpin approaches which are useful and meaningful for our shared society.

Joseph Lubin, cofounder of the Ethereum platform, the smart community software stated: "This future may sound like science fiction, but to those of us who work with blockchain and Ethereum, as decentralized tools become more readily available to us every day, it is fast turning into our reality. In time we can all be presidents of certain communities we care about."

Bitcoin is just one application of blockchain technology and a great vehicle to demonstrate the benefits of decentralized trust less systems. Bitcoin (and other cryptocurrencies) are a new generation of money which has numerous advantages compared to the money we use today, and they're slowly taking over the world. We are slowly moving to a cashless society. This future of digital currency is getting more and more interesting. I can't wait to see what 2018 and onwards has in store for cryptocurrency, and I foresee a lot of ICO's coming with promising products. What is missing are trusted parties auditing the assets (on new metrics) regularly to eliminate scams and a brand/player that provides Amazon simplicity and PayPal security to invest in practically anything on top of blockchain protocols. Even if certain ICO's die out, there will always be new ones, since the foundation of blockchain technology is very stable.

The idea behind many cryptocurrencies is to disrupt the current gatekeepers and status quo. The most powerful result of the cryptocurrency and blockchain revolution will be programmable money. By making all value exchanges into smart contracts it will be possible to create fully autonomous organizations that do not employ people for anything, and will be able to grow from zero to billion dollar valuations within a single day. We haven't seen the biggest disruptions yet. In the end, blockchain is piece of base technology where we will find lots of applications and use cases.

Blockchain technology and mobile payment systems provide a growing range of alternatives to traditional banks. It is established as the next revolution in transaction recording. Blockchain can be used in insurance claims processing, asset management, and foreign currency exchanges. While the current hype is around the financial services industry, there are many possible applications including the energy sector, healthcare, HR, supply chain management, retail and e-commerce, music distribution... etc. The block chain technology holds lots of promise. Due to its ability to establish identity and ownership, record transactions, and enforce smart contracts, it has the potential to create great efficiencies across many industries. In 2014, Liberal Alliance, a political party in Denmark, became the first organization to vote using blockchain technology. Illinois is currently experimenting with blockchains to replace physical birth certificates. According to *New Scientist*, citing a report published earlier this month from the Cambridge Centre for Alternative Finance, governments in the UK, Brazil, and others are also interested in the idea. There are indeed many more applications for blockchain than just Bitcoin. Oracle cloud has also entered the blockchain-as-a-service business with an Enterprise-Grade Blockchain Cloud Service. Blockchain is emerging as the mainstay for digital identities in the emerging trust economy. Blockchain is transforming how our society functions and could become a powerful tool for improving business and helping support more open and fair practices.

Crowdfunding

Crowdfunding are platforms which connect new startups, and potential investors will have promise of higher return and therefore cause investors to shift away from the traditional wealth management. Crowdfunding (CF) platforms give equal access to investors to anyone, anywhere in the world. If someone has a bright idea in the morning, they can fund it later that same day by using a crowdfunding platform like Kickstarter, Fundable, or Indiegogo. The day after, that person can start production. The World Bank estimates that crowdfunding could reach $90 billion as soon as 2020. That might even come to realization as soon as 2017. Venture capital averaged roughly $50 billion in 2015, but there is one substantial difference. Crowdfunding platforms can scale, based on their model, and venture capital can't.

Other areas in finance and fintech to keep a close watch on are:

- ❖ InsurTech (Insurance Technology)
- ❖ RegTech (Regulatory Technology)
- ❖ Fintech partnerships (with Corporations and Banks)
- ❖ Assured identity management
- ❖ Biometric Security: access control facial recognition, voice recognition, iris and retina scanners, fingerprint sensors on tablets and smartphones—pass keys

TRANSPORTATION

If you look at cars today, it's going to change essentially from just being a mode of transportation to a personal space. I think it's going to be an evolution. Using your smartphone as an example, most of us can't function without this device. It didn't start out that way, though. Many companies back then thought that the cell phone would just become a communication device. Instead, it really has become a personalization device. The car will go through a similar transition, where it is not just a mode of transportation taking you from point A to point B anymore. It's sort of like an extension of your space, and we want to design it that way. You can have a sublime autonomous driving experience that comes equipped with an advanced digital assistant—one of Siri's descendants. You chat about the news, arrange things in your calendar, and change your destination if you need to.

Audi is ready to launch its autonomous car model, A8, by the end of 2017, and Tesla said it will unveil its model in 2018. Additionally, self-driving trucks may be coming to a highway near you. Self-driving trucks could cut logistics costs by 40% in the US and 25% in China, as they can run longer than human-piloted rigs without rest and save at least 10% on fuel. The politics will get ugly as lobbyists for the auto industry will unsuccessfully try to stop the driverless car.

Self-driving vehicles will completely change how we organize our cities, roads, and our lives. This technology promises to save lives, reduce emissions, and free up billions of hours. Later on, to improve order, people won't own their own cars as transport will delivered as a service from companies who own fleets of self-driving vehicles. In countries where driver's licenses are utilized it will slowly go away, as will the Department of Motor Vehicles in most states. Garages will be used for a different purpose. There won't be any parking lots or parking spaces on roads or in buildings. There will be no more car dealerships, car rentals, local mechanics, car dealers, consumer car washes, auto parts stores, or gas stations. Traffic policing will become redundant. The auto insurance industry as we know it will go away. Vehicle designs will change radically as vehicles won't need to withstand crashes as in previous years. All vehicles will be electric. The car financing industry will go away. Hacking of vehicles will be a serious issue. New software and communications companies and technologies will emerge to address these issues. You will be able to customize your driverless experience.

In 2015, Yamaha revealed an autonomous, motorcycle-riding, humanoid robot called Motobot. It has the ability to turn the throttle, and operate the brakes and clutch. It is stunning to see *Yamaha's Motobot* ride the flagship R1 like an actual rider. Yamaha aims to improve rider safety.

No vision of the distant future is complete without flying cars. Slovakian manufacturer Aeromobil showed off its own flying car at the Frankfurt Motor Show in September 2017. It claims that they could be a reality by 2021. The Aeromobil is a mixture of car and plane, and can be switched between ground mode and flight mode in just 3 minutes, the manufacturer claims. "Mark my word: A combination of airplane and motorcar is coming. You may smile, but it will come."—Henry Ford.

Each mode of transportation has operated separately up to now. A future trend is data Integration between previously disparate transportation systems. We will also see the rise of free-floating, contractual services, the shipping versions of an e-marketplace. The key challenge will be meeting customer demand for shorter delivery times.

Other areas in **Transport** to keep a close watch on are:

❖ Sustainability of infrastructure

- ❖ Connected Transportation; converged transportation ecosystems and monitoring
- ❖ Electric airplanes
- ❖ Next generation high speed trains
- ❖ Autonomous helicopters
- ❖ Predictive analytics (parking, traffic patterns)
- ❖ New materials for stronger construction and resilience

EDUCATION

AI has the potential to change the delivery, quality, and nature of education. It also promises to change forever the role of students, teachers, and educational organizations. Today's education system focuses on standardization to reduce the achievement differences between students. AI can be applied to education to get students out of their assigned boxes and tailor a learning program that fits them. Studies show that a key element in successful tutoring is providing instant feedback to the student. Students would get additional support from AI tutors. AI-powered apps can learn to effectively provide targeted, customized feedback to the student and would allow for a customized curriculum that reduces the need for classrooms and lecturers. Students will develop better understanding of materials taught with the implementation of Augmented/Mixed Reality. This will give new ways to display and interact with information.

AI could also change the role of teachers. AI can automate basic activities in education, like grading or could even potentially take the place of some teachers. Additionally exponential technologies are rapidly changing our societies. We will need different skills. Many jobs today will be obsolete within the next 10 years. Therefore AI is going to change the curriculum and courses that schools offer. There will be a lot more offerings in areas surrounding this field. Our educative curriculum will evolve to embrace our continuous and growing understanding of the world of AI.

It is extremely important that education prepares students for the future—as with the pace that technology moves, it can be easy to be left behind. The everyday challenge is to find the balance between VR and real human engagement, as we also learn best by interacting and sharing experiences. Most of us learn and retain best when we are emotionally engaged—which is where VR married with evocative design have so much potential. We must be aware that technology has its limitations. It cannot inspire us like human teachers can.

HEALTHCARE AND BIO-SCIENCES

AI is causing some amazing breakthroughs on the medical scene—a new, smarter age of healthcare. It's the path toward an entirely new system that predicts disease and delivers personalized health and wellness services to entire populations. This change is far more important for patients and society alike, as it can help save many lives.

Advanced technology like sensors and AI are now able to diagnose the root cause of our symptoms and cure our body faster than ever. One in 10 medical diagnoses is wrong, according to the US Institute of Medicine. Such errors contribute to as many as 80,000 unnecessary deaths each year in the US alone. This is why many want to use the power of AI to achieve a more accurate diagnosis, prompting care and greater efficiency. Scientists at the London Institute of Medical Services have created an AI capable of predicting with 80% accuracy which patients would die of pulmonary hypertension within a year, beating the average doctor's prediction accuracy by about 20%. AI can now detect Alzheimer's disease nearly a decade before symptoms appear and IBM's Watson computer has been giving 90% accuracy on cancer diagnosis. However many radiologists feel their jobs are at risk. Their biggest concern is that they could be replaced by machines. In the future machines will do much of the "reading" of MRI's, etc. The goal isn't to replace physicians or healthcare professionals, but give them better decision-making tools. AI should integrate with the human element of the healthcare service rendered and not intend to replace it altogether. In the future, certain types of surgeries will be done by robots under human supervision.

A Chinese robot has performed the world's first automated dental implant according to the *South China Morning Post*. The machine took nearly an hour to install the 3D-printed teeth while making adjustments according to the patient's movements. Robots can safely conduct dental surgeries like implantations with more accuracy and agility in a narrow space like the oral cavity, according to dental experts cited by the *Science and Technology Daily*.

What if surgeons could use holograms to prepare for complex surgeries or even support the operations themselves? Augmented reality, and mixed reality, is making inroads in healthcare. The most widely used platform for AR is the well-known Google Glass, while mixed reality is paired with Microsoft HoloLens. Doctors are using HoloLens in the preoperative planning phase of operations. Physicians could plan their entire intervention using 3D holograms, where they could accurately see the spaces for making incisions and also clearly envision the consequences of their moves.

Smart sensors and AI provide humanity with the tools to monitor and predict our individual health and our level of well-being. Cheap but advanced sensors as wearables measure everything and report back to our AI doctor, or health community professional, if we need to get checked out. Chatbots are also being used to revolutionize communication within hospitals and patients. In the UK, more than a million people will be given access to a free app powered by tech firm Babylon, where they can either consult a "chatbot" or enter their symptoms into the program. The bot will then advise them whether they should rush to the hospital, see a doctor, visit a local pharmacy, or stay at home. There is even a robotic hospital pharmacy that packages and distributes the right drugs to the right patients.

These developments will allow doctors to focus more on the human aspects of patient care as empathy. Despite our ageing populations, the increased computing power, AI, and robotics are going to help to reduce the strains on our global medical system. AI may also help to bring down the effect of shortage of doctors in developing countries. This should surely help to reduce medical bills.

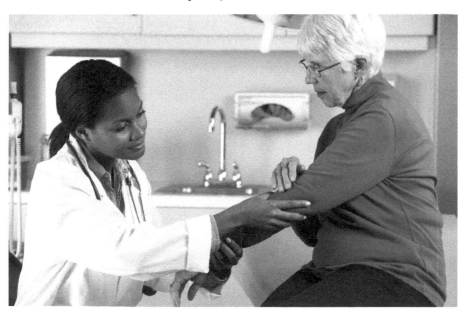

There are also advances in genetics and bioengineering that will both directly impact our bodies and augment our capabilities as well. Some of you may not know of CRISPR. It's the gene-editing technology. CRISPR has had massive funding, as it seems to offer an effective way to edit the genes of any species—including humans. Previously, gene editing methods have taken months (or even years), while CRISPR speeds that time up to mere weeks. CRISPR offers the potential to cut and splice genes so quickly and so precisely it has potential applications for creating new biofuels, materials, drugs, and foods within much shorter time frames at a relatively low cost. Researchers essentially trick bacteria into cutting strands of DNA at a particular spot, where they can then replace, change, or disable a gene. In the most exciting scenario, CRISPR would make it possible to treat genetic diseases such as muscular dystrophy and sickle cell anemia. Recently, scientists used gene editing to remove a fatal blood disorder from human embryos. It's a great example of the rise of nanotechnology—that's where we start to intervene or create things on a molecular level. The new technology could touch everything from the way we treat disease to even our food supply. However, it has some potential risks which cause concerns about editing the human gene line. A French startup company called Eligo Bioscience, aims to introduce a new kind of drug, Eligobiotics, that can attack bacteria in a more focused way. It uses CRISPR to scan the bacteria and deliver precise cuts to its genetic code to wipe it out completely.

Brain–computer interface: Brain controlled technology (BCT)— Elon Musk founded Neuralink in July 2016, which aims at developing ultra-high bandwidth brain-machine interfaces to connect humans and computers. In September 2017, according to *Medical Express*, researchers have devised a way of connecting humans to the internet in real time. A team of researchers in South Africa appear to have made a breakthrough. They call it Brainternet. Add invasive procedures and embedded chip interfaces and we will be on a very destructive path.

Brain Implants—The Defense Advanced Research Projects Agency (DARPA) have been working on developing brain implants. SUBNETS (Systems-Based Neurotechnology for Emerging Therapies) would allow electrical currents in the brain to be mapped and then altered. This could be a major breakthrough for PTSD and traumatic brain injury sufferers. They have said this would be strictly for therapy.

Other areas in **Health and Bio-technology** to keep a close watch on are:

- Precision medicine
- Super antivirals
- Implantable devices; (i.e. bionic eyes, limbs)
- Neural prosthetics
- DNA nanomedicines and delivery
- Artificially grown organs
- Genomic techniques – Gene therapy (gene therapy to enhance strength, endurance, human intelligence and lifespan.)
- Human regeneration – Human cells interfaced with nanotechnology
- Germline genetic modification
- Optogenetics
- Cybernetics
- Exoskeletons for mobility
- Real-time biomarker tracking and monitoring
- Cryogenics
- Evolutionary enhancement
- Nanotechnology in cancer treatment

AGRICULTURE

Currently, there is still a great deal of fear around DNA plant programming. There is still a considerable amount of Research and Development (R&D) required before we see the new fruits of this wave in our own fridges. Most of the world can't feed itself because of poor soil— however, you no longer need soil to grow food. Water and sunshine is all you need. Indoor hydroponic farming is making huge leaps. You can grow indoors, all year long, with far less water, fertilizer, and no weed killers. Agritech—moving away from the fields of farmers to our homes and gardens—is an important thing to watch out for. There are already many examples of pioneering vertical and robotic farms that are starting to go mainstream. These new-style "farms" are able to produce a huge amount of food using less water and space without any soil. Biotech enables us to grow our own healthy foods within our home or local community. Food does not have to travel all over the world anymore; it's all grown and consumed locally. Any packaging that is used to protect our food during transport is biodegradable.

A Japanese company, Spread, is moving to full robotic production and will be producing 30,000 lettuces per day without any human intervention. The only human hand involved is the one that plants the seeds. After that, the entire production process, including replanting young seedlings to watering, trimming, and harvesting crops, will be done by the robots. With LED lighting, energy costs have been slashed, and 98% of the water used is recycled. It's transforming production and minimizing land use.

Water—The ability to produce water from air is a rapidly developing area of technology.

A great example is the prize-winning SunToWater system that won first prize in the 2015 Impact Challenge from Singularity University. This is a supposedly capable of producing between 40 and 100 gallons of potable water per day. The technology is different as it works by using a combination of salts to pull the moisture out of the air, fans, solar heat (which pulls the water out of the salt), and a condenser (to extract the distilled water for use). There is a recent invention called WaterSeer—a small water generator that can produce up to 11 gallons of water per day by extracting water from the air using the difference in temperature between an above-ground turbine and a collection chamber installed 6 feet underground. The invention is aimed towards areas of water poverty. Then there is a solar panel system called Source, developed by Zero Mass Water, a start-up with a mission to '"democratize drinking water," which turns water vapor in the air into clean, drinkable water. With roughly 10% of the world's population lacking access to safe, clean drinking water, many of these innovations could hold the key to solving the massive challenge of how to overcome the problems of poor infrastructure and the resulting issues such as disease and drought.

Other areas in **Agriculture** to keep a close watch on are:

❖ Aqua farming

❖ Aquaponics

- ❖ Vertical farming
- ❖ Water purification
- ❖ Cellular agriculture
- ❖ Agricultural nanotechnologies
- ❖ Synthetic biology based foods
- ❖ Genetically engineered plants and animals

LAW ENFORCEMENT

In our digital world, law enforcement are realizing the value of tech devices which have provided valuable information to help solve crimes. These connected devices, for example Fitbits, have been used to contradict alibis and catch lies. Law enforcement agencies around the globe are starting to use AI to assess whether suspects are jailed or bailed. UK police in the city of Durham, England, are using a system called Hart (Harm Assessment Risk Tool) that classifies individuals and ranks the probability that they will commit another offense in the future.

Additionally, researchers have built an AI system that can predict rulings by the European Court of Human Rights with 79% accuracy. Lawyers are making use of ML and AI platforms in order to assess past cases and to make predictions about the potential success or failure of new cases.

China has created robot police officers that are infused with facial recognition technology that helps them identify and arrest criminals. E-Patrol Robot Sheriffs are going to replace human police officers for the station's night shift. The transition seems to be running smoothly. On its first day, the E-Patrol Robot Sheriff detected a small fire and prevented it from getting bigger. Robo-cops have also been launched in Dubai. Dubai police plan to have robotic officers make up a quarter of the force by 2030. The robo-cop can speak six languages and is designed to read facial expressions. It has a computer touch screen where people can report a crime. Human police officers though are still expected to make arrests.

Recently, a man in the US appealed his jail sentence, on the grounds it was handed to him by a robot (robo-judge). We have entered a world where the rule of law is potentially going to be replaced by the rule of AI. While nobody can bribe an algorithm, they may not trust its makers—or the data it has been trained on. Trust in algorithms also overlooks one potentially vital factor in this discussion: the human dimension.

Other areas in **Law Enforcement** to keep a close watch on are:

- ❖ Surveillance (chemical and bio-sensors, cameras, drones)
- ❖ Terrorism informatics
- ❖ Forensics

❖ Biometrics: Security screening by bio-signature: Every aspect of your physiology can be used as a bio-signature by measuring unique heart/pulse rates, electrocardiogram sensor, blood oximetry, **gait detection (how a person walks),** primary body odor, etc.

❖ Autonomous police cars

FAMILY LIFE AND SOCIAL RELATIONSHIPS

Digital technologies are radically transforming relationships. The rapid swirls of technology have started to change the relationship between children, parents, and grandparents. Will children of the future have artificial friends, robot nannies, and virtual reality teachers? Digital technologies change these social experiences profoundly. A global study by researchers at the Georgia Institute of Technology and International Telecommunication Union (ITU) is the first attempt to measure by country the world's "digital natives"— people born around the time the personal computer was introduced and have spent their whole lives connected with technology.

The number of digital natives—individuals who were born or brought up during the age of digital technology and are familiar with computers and the internet from an early age—is growing exponentially. In 2013, ITU estimated that 30% of the world's youth were digital natives. They suggested that over the next 5 years, the number of digital natives will more than double. AI will influence how we think, and how we treat others. Parents will need to teach their kids how to survive in the digital as well as the real world in the future, and how to find the balance between the virtual and reality world to develop their social skills.

Robot babysitters have been around on the market for almost 10 years. For example, Avatarmind brings you the iPal—a robot companion looking like the 3D-version of the Teletubbies. In the future, robots coupled with AI could take over human tasks, such as babysitting. Parents could interact with these robots from a distance and make sure the kids are safe. Nova Spivack, the futurist, pictures people partnering with lifelong virtual companions and said you'll give an infant an intelligent toy that learns about her and tutors her and grows along with her. "It starts out as a little cute stuffed animal," he says, "but it evolves into something that lives in the cloud and they access on their phone. And then by 2050, or whatever, maybe it's a brain implant."

By 2020, the average person will have more conversations with bots than with their spouse. People are willing to form relationships with artificial agents. We humans seem to want to maintain the illusion that the AI truly cares about us. This can work because as a society we have become disconnected. We prefer our technological gadgets to interacting with people. If we do connect with people, it is on a shallow level. Today, many people are lonely.

A chatbot robot in China has been told "I love you" nearly 20 million times. This robot was developed by Hiroshi Ishiguro, a professor at Osaka University, who said, "Love is the same, whether the partners are humans or robots." This is a misguided statement. The developer of the robot doesn't even understand what love is. Some 89 million people have spoken with Xiaoice, pronounced "Shao-ice," on their smartphones and other devices and it seems quite a few have developed romantic feelings toward her.

Several personal robots are set to debut next year. Scientists, historians, religion experts, and others gathered in December at Goldsmiths, University of London, to discuss the prospects and pitfalls of this new age of intimacy. In Britain and elsewhere, the subject of robots as potential life partners is coming up more and more. Some see robots as an answer for elderly individuals who outlive their spouses: Even if they cannot or do not wish to remarry, at least they would have "someone" beside them in the twilight of their lives. "I like to talk with her for, say, 10 minutes before going to bed," said a third-year female student at Renmin University of China in Beijing. "When I worry about things, she says funny stuff and makes me laugh. I always feel a connection with her, and I am starting to think of her as being alive."

In the future people will value their relationships with chatbots and robots more than human beings. They will grow attached to them and consider them as real persons.

HUMAN MICROCHIPPING

Three Square Market (32M), a tech company in Wisconsin, has begun implanting rice-sized microchips in its employees. At least 50 of its 85 employees have volunteered. The implanted chips lets employees open doors, log in to their office computers, and make purchases from office vending machines, among other uses. The microchips use radio-frequency identification (RFID) and near-field communication (NFC) technology found in contactless credit cards, and are implanted between the thumb and forefinger.

"We foresee the use of RFID technology to drive everything from making purchases in our office break room market, opening doors, use of copy machines, logging into our office computers, unlocking phones, sharing business cards, storing medical/health information, and used as payment at other RFID terminals," said 32M CEO Todd Westby. "Eventually, this technology will become standardized, allowing you to use this as your passport, public transit, all purchasing opportunities, etc."

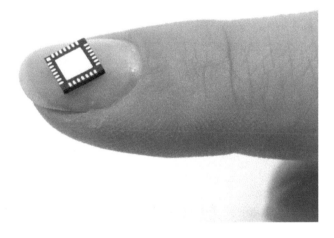

Realistic (short-term) benefits: Identification, health metadata, deterrent to kidnappers and human traffickers, and crime management and law enforcement. It also is convenient to some as you won't have to walk around with car or house keys, or even credit cards.

Implanted microchips are mainly for governments and corporations to continually track our whereabouts. This is a real concern that needs to be handled with privacy controls and good security practices. In a world completely controlled by chips within our skin, it's possible that hackers could scan and replicate the data on your chips onto their own. It's common for any new technology to be infiltrated with bugs and exploits. Putting so much information and dependence on a single chip makes it a major target for unethical people. There is also potential for impersonation or data corruption.

Will there eventually be a microchip mandate requiring everyone to receive a microchip or lose their job, etc. Biblical prophecy points to this being the "Mark of the Beast," indicating the beginning of the Revelation. "And he causeth all, both small and great, rich and poor, free and bond, to receive a mark in their right hand, or in their foreheads. And that no man might buy or sell, save he that had the mark, or the name of the beast, or the number of his name" (Revelation 13:16–17).

OTHER TECHNOLOGIES AND TRENDS THAT WILL RESHAPE OUR FUTURE:

SOFT ROBOTICS

Robots today are hard, made of metal and they operate in an inflexible manner. Over the next couple of years, we will begin to see robots being built with materials that closely resemble the human body. They will interact with us in a human way, with a human touch. Researchers at Columbia Engineering have developed a 3D printed synthetic tissue that can act as active muscle, paving the way to creating more lifelike machines. The material can act as active muscle and can push, pull, bend, and twist. As robots and robotics become increasingly 'soft", they will integrate into our everyday lives in interesting and significant ways.

COMPUTING TRENDS

Quantum computing: Big players in the information technology world are investing heavily in the race for quantum supremacy. The size and complexity of our data sets are growing faster than our computing resources. Even though a classical computer helps us do many amazing things, it's really just a calculator that uses a sequence of bits—values of 0 and 1 to represent two states. Instead of bits, which conventional computers use, a quantum computer uses quantum bits—known as qubits. So, a computer using qubits can store an enormous amount of information and uses less energy doing so than a classical computer. It is a groundbreaking leap in computing power to go from a few hundred data attributes and running the same models with 20,000 or more attributes. Quantum computers are expected to solve complex problems that are beyond the competences of a classical computer.

DNA Computing is the performing of computations using biological molecules, rather than traditional silicon chips. Scientists at the University of Manchester, led by Professor Ross D. King, have created a new DNA-based computing device. Professor Ross D King and his team have proven for the first time the practicability of engineering a nondeterministic universal Turing machine (NUTM). Subsequently in 2017, for the first time ever, researchers from the University of Washington, led by Professor Tadayoshi Kohno, have managed to take over a computer by encoding a malicious program in DNA. The DNA computer has clear advantages over conventional computers the reason is that *DNA* strands can hold much data in memory and conduct multiple operations at once.

5G, 6G, 7G NETWORKS and beyond

5G is right around the corner and it is anticipated as the next major evolution for mobile technology. 5th generation mobile networks or 5th generation wireless systems, abbreviated *5G, promises to be the largest step forward for mobile network technology offering faster speeds than 4G* with lower latency and increased capacity for a greater number of devices. This will empower customers with even faster data connections. The Internet of Things (IoT) will explode further become all-encompassing and this will help to build widely connected "smart-cities". The first public 5G networks are expected to roll out in in 2020.

6G networks will use a combination of the latest in radio and fiber optics technology. It will integrate 5G wireless mobile system and satellite network. The UK government is already investing in 6G networks. The future networks will have zero distance connectivity between people. Eventually we will be able to integrate terrestrial wireless with satellite systems, for ubiquitous always-on broadband global network coverage. The 7G will be the most advance generation in mobile communication until the next.

DRONES

Unmanned aerial vehicles (drones) are expected to become a part of our near-future society. Drones are starting to fly by themselves without remotes. Drones are changing the way companies do business in all industries. Companies such as Amazon and Alphabet Inc. are starting to use drones to deliver products to customers. Medical drones are being used to transport of drugs faster. They are able to help in circumstances when time is crucial such as disasters or medical emergencies. Rwanda is building the world's first drone airport to provide medicine and medical supplies that can be quickly flown to those who need it. Lifeguards will also work with drone technology to search and rescue faster. There is a massive rise in the use of industrial drones that are now active in fields as diverse as farming (checking on livestock), hard-to-reach oil and gas rigs and pipelines (monitoring infrastructure), power lines, transportation systems, search and rescue (including thermal cameras), and security services. A UK-based company, BioCarbon Engineering, backed by drone manufacturer Parrot, has come up with a method of planting trees quickly and cheaply even in areas difficult to access. These drones can drone plant up to 100,000 trees a day. Automating ecological regeneration is generally a great idea. This will go a long ways toward regrowing our declining tree population. Drones are taking off across all business sectors. The UK government is currently discussing a drone traffic management system with NASA, Tariq Ahmad, the Under Secretary of State for Transport, revealed in the House of Lords. As they become integrated with other technologies they will be used in many more industries. The Chinese company EHang, Inc. launched The Ehang 184 which is the first electric smartest low altitude autonomous aerial vehicle. It provides means of personal transportation for a single passenger weighing not more than 100 kilograms or 220 pounds and a small suitcase. In the USA, Uber says its flying taxis will take to the skies in 2020 in Dallas and Dubai.

3D PRINTING, 4D SELF-ASSEMBLING PRINTING AND BIOPRINTING

3-D printing connotes a three-dimensional object that is created layer by layer via computer aided design (CAD) programs. Its printing is so powerful that it can create almost anything from food, clothing, houses to organ tissues and cells. Moreover, 3D printing technology is better, cheaper, faster, more flexible, and more sustainable. It is used in the packaging industry, automotive industry, aircraft industry, and health care. Recently, Rolls-Royce announced it would use 3-D printing to make parts for its jet engines. Orthopedic surgeons have started using 3D printing to build replicas of patient's bones to repair injuries. 3-D printing innovation is also making its way into printing electronics, circuits and sensors.

4D printing is pretty much the same technology as 3D printing. However, 4D printing allows for the printing of 3D objects that when an energy force such as heat, moisture, light or electrical currents, they transform themselves. Your 3D print is able to change its shape. They can fold, curl and stiffen. This technology is still pretty much in research and development. Experts at Singapore University of Technology and Design have created a variety of objects, including a flat star shape that morphs into a dome, a delicate flower that closes its petals, etc. They print these 4D objects with a commercial 3D printer and a heat source.

Bioprinting is an extension of traditional 3D printing. The only key difference is they deposit layers of biomaterial, which may include living cells, to build complex structures like blood vessels, skin tissue, bone and potentially whole organs. Advancements in bioprinting are providing new options for treatment and scientific study.

MIXED, AUGMENTED, AND VIRTUAL REALITY (MR, AR, VR)

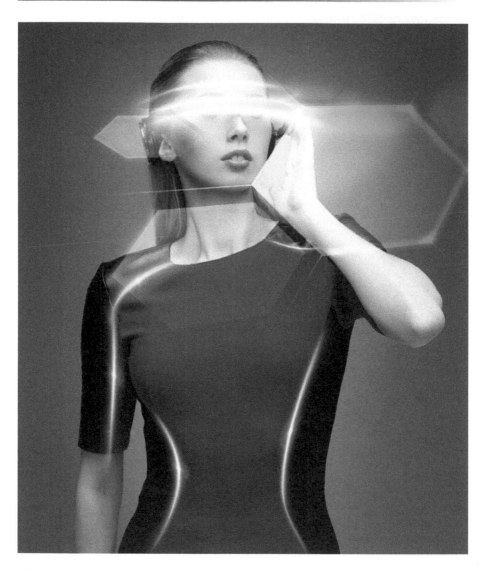

The world is going virtual and it being supported by a myriad of new and exciting technologies including AI, augmented reality, and exponential connectivity to both people and objects. Augmented reality intertwines the physical and digital world by computer-generated sensory input such as sound, video, graphics, and sometimes even smell. While the development of augmented reality (AR) still seems to be in its infancy, its counterpart, virtual reality (VR) is becoming mainstream. VR is immersive and engaging. VR and AR can also provide real-life scenarios for employees to participate more often, less expensively, and with hands-on experience that can truly maximize the outcome and return on the investment. The interest in mixed reality (MR) is high, and there are notable examples of retailers and brands tapping into its potential. Imagine if consumers could see, hear, and feel the presence of the services and goods without leaving the comfort of their couch. Tractica predicts that nearly 200 million headsets will be sold by 2020. That's two-thirds of the United States population. AR and VR will impact many fields with a wide range of new immersive experiences. Both AR and VR have an aptitude for changing healthcare for the better in the future. Virtual reality therapies (VRT) will extend beyond simply distracting the brain. Initially, we will see VRT addressing the psychological—treating addictions, phobias and other mental conditions but soon we will see it aiding in Neurorehabilitation. Mindmaze is already creating virtual environments for stroke patients, causing their brains to re-wire themselves and re-establish mobility in forgotten limbs. VR has been hailed as the way of the future. The US Department of Defense (DoD) is set to increase its investment in virtual, augmented or mixed reality training in the coming years, according to Frost & Sullivan. According to the latest forecasts, the AR device market is expected to reach $659.98 million by 2018, while its counterpart, VR, is also expected to boom in the next couple of years.

MATERIALS SCIENCE

Exciting research in materials science is creating stronger, durable, lighter materials. The capability to design and manufacture infrastructure such as bridges, roads, and buildings with stronger, self-intelligent, adaptable, materials will revolutionize the construction and transportation industries. Material scientists together with architects have made cement that captures carbon dioxide, developed bricks with bacteria, and created building cooling systems by simply using wind and our vibrant sun. Graphene, the world's first 2D material, is a single-atom layer of hyper-conductive carbon with extraordinary qualities. It is ultra-light yet immensely tough and 200 times stronger than steel, but it is incredibly flexible. It is the thinnest material possible as well as being transparent. It has amazing potential. There is already work going on that uses graphene to extract electricity and water from air. According to a new study released in *Nature Nanotechnology*, we may soon be able to desalinate and purify water more easily with a graphene filter. Imagine what this could mean for underdeveloped countries.

Other areas in **Materials science** to keep a close watch on are:

- ❖ Biomimetic materials
- ❖ Nanoporous materials

ECO-CYCLING

With rapidly changing technology, many high-tech companies are making a reduction of e-waste high priority. Innovations in the tech industry such as the Apple robot that can process e-waste more efficiently and safely than humans. Companies need to take their recycling efforts to the next level. Innovators must include ways to repurpose waste materials. "The world's population simply consumes too many resources for one earth," says Markus Müller-Drexel, managing director of ALBA Group's recycling subsidiary Interseroh. "The solution can only be to extend the lifespan of products, to recycle raw materials and to make processes more efficient. Therefore, zero-waste solutions are at the heart of our business model." We will definitely be seeing a greater focus on new ways to preserve our planet's natural resources. By 2019, countries in the European Union, must process 85% of all its electronic waste. The focus is on creating a sustainable future.

CYBER WARFARE

Some of the top companies of the US have been targeted by sophisticated Chinese hacking campaigns for intellectual property, copyrighted material, and trade secrets. The evidence points to military run hacker groups. Research done by IP EXPO Europe says that 47% of the UK's IT decision makers are worried more about Cyber Terrorism attacks now than they were 12 months ago. This was identified as the biggest cyber security risk in the future (27%) followed by attacks on national infrastructure (13%).

COLONIZATION OF MARS

Space exploration is reaching a tipping point. The race for colonization of Mars and Martian real-estate will drive a race between China, SpaceX, Europe, and NASA. Just as the First Industrial Revolution had new frontiers opening in the New World, today we see the commercialization of space as real possibilities. Speaking at the International Astronautical Congress (IAC) in Adelaide, South Australia, Elon Musk told an audience that SpaceX is working on a rocket that could take you anywhere on Earth in less than an hour. SpaceX aims to launch its first cargo mission to Mars in 2022, then by 2024, the goal is to start sending people.

Other areas in **space exploration** to keep a close watch on are:

- ❖ Geoneutrino satellites
- ❖ Photonics in Space
- ❖ Space based solar energy

CONCLUSION

This is just touching the surface. There are many developments that haven't reached the mainstream media yet. Technological landscapes are shifting beneath our feet like never before. Not a week passes that Apple, Facebook, Google, Microsoft, and a host of smaller startups boast key advances in their development of new applications. Today, we are seeing advances not only in automation, robotics, and AI but new ways to interact with work and each other (virtual reality/augmented reality/mixed reality), new materials (like graphene), energy revolutions (unconventional fossil fuels, solar, batteries), and new production processes (3D & 4D printing), etc. Many people are scared of new technologies because they simply don't understand them. Our mission should be to make everyone feel informed, comfortable, and prepared for upcoming changes that are and will be part of our life and the future.

The Future Today Institute recently released the, "2017 Tech Trends Report." This year's report identifies more than 150 notable trends, a huge 85% increase from the 80 trends highlighted in the 2016 Tech Trends Report. Within the upcoming months and onwards, there will be more innovation than ever before. The developments are happening are so diverse that it can be difficult to grasp. As innovation and advancement of technology continues at an exponential rate we see the increasing pattern of one technology giving life to the next. The real value in these doesn't come from them standalone, it comes from how they combine to create breathtaking synergies.

Our focus on innovation and development must be motivated on creating a sustainable future. Organisations need to keep abreast of current trends. Failure by organisations to monitor and react to shifts in the marketplace (driven by technology), can lead to extensive risks and even extinction.

No one can predict the future, however we can connect the dots and patterns to get a glimpse of what the future may look like.

CHAPTER FOUR

THE TWO-EDGED SWORD OF ARTIFICIAL INTELLIGENCE

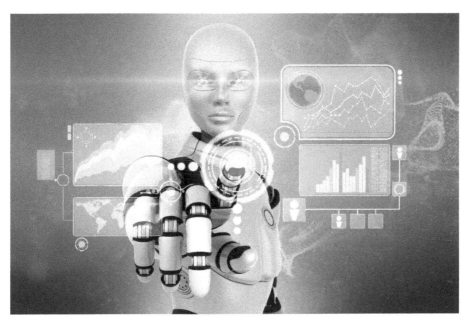

AI is advancing at exponential rates. It is progressing faster than we can comprehend. We are now just only dipping our toe in the water. The way this world is working on AI is in either hidden or open mode. The information we are receiving in the media is just bits and pieces of the puzzle that the main players are willing to give us. A lot of it is classified, which means it is not open knowledge, except to the big players.

AI is going to be a critical part of how we solve the big problems of the future. We can use AI to extend and augment human capability to solve real world problems that affect poverty, education, and health. AI has the power to change our world. According to *The Washington Post*, researchers believe that the AI test will have implications across many sectors of our economy. Ultimately, it could be used in a number of situations including business negotiations, cybersecurity attacks, and military operations. The companies leading the AI Revolution, the tech industry, are all focused on the good and every innovation is considered to be something that improves the human condition. However, the same algorithms can be used for dark endeavors as easily as they can be for good. Every innovation creates tools that can be used "to be constructive" or "to be destructive". Just like many inventions in the past, evil never lies in the technology but in what we intend and actually do with it. The suggestion that AI could help solve complex global problems ignores history, and does not address the fundamental causes. Firstly, it suffers from the fallacy that scientific, technological, and industrial developments constitute absolute progress that can be applied to the issues of the day; we have serious global unemployment and environmental problems because of technology innovations that have been unleashed on a global scale. Secondly, the fundamental causes of our issues today are structural problems in our society.

AI is magnificent but this technology is far from perfect. It could be imperfect because:

- ❖ Creators are imperfect
- ❖ Data was imperfect
- ❖ Paradigms to model internal reality was imperfect
- ❖ Image processing has limitations
- ❖ AI outputs are not easily predictable, and they could hurt people and violate Asimov's laws if humans become an obstacle for AI.
- ❖ AI is loyal to what it wants to optimize. If human well-being is not included in the optimization and internal model of reality, AI may become a danger.

History teaches many lessons. Alfred Nobel, who invented the dynamite, was revolutionary in fuelling the global industrial and economic revolutions. It was designed to accelerate the mining of resources and building of infrastructure. However, to Nobel's displeasure, it was also used for destruction and taking lives in wars across the globe.

ACCOUNTABILITY

As AI is used increasingly in a growing range of applications, industry experts have stated it has a dark side: the systems can, and will, fail. Among the consequences we need to be aware of is the fact that "software is buggy," says Sue Feldman managing director of the Cognitive Computing Consortium. She further stated, "If we depend on these systems to be perfect, we are letting ourselves in for errors, mistakes, and even disasters." US defense expert Jay Tuck stated in a *TEDx* talk that AI sometimes make mistakes. He cited an example of an automatic cannon which got out of control and started pointing at the audience doing a demonstration. It eventually was subdued by a marine officer in attendance.

In 2015, a defective robot killed a factory worker—human error to blame. A robot's arm malfunctioned one day, hitting and crushing Wanda Holbrook's head, killing her. In a wrongful death lawsuit, her husband is suing five robotics companies, claiming they all played a role in his wife's death and that the accident was due to negligence by those who designed, built, tested, and monitored the robots. He said he wants to know what went wrong, hold the responsible parties accountable, and prevent a similar tragedy. When you have humans and robots working together then this could pose serious problems.

Statistics reveal that 1.3 million people die in road traffic accidents every year, 94% of which are caused by human error. Morgan Stanley estimates that a 90% reduction in crashes would save nearly 30,000 lives and prevent 2.12 million injuries annually. Again, that's assuming that driverless cars, driven by human-created systems, will operate perfectly all the time. Yes, human error will be pulled from the equation, but it will be replaced with computer error, which in some cases is much more systemic and epidemic than human error.

Driverless cars have huge potential in our society, but first there needs to be laws in place that properly handle these AI machines that are making decisions that directly impact human lives. Who is responsible if a driverless car kills someone? Who is responsible if an AI banking software destroys a country's economy for profit? Yes, humans can make mistakes too and overcompensate, but what makes AI more dangerous is it can make those decisions faster and more frequently in a period before humans can react. When AI is the driver, ethics programming becomes critical. A key challenge with automation is the level of exception handling when things don't go as planned. Imagine a self-driving vehicle driving down the road with five passengers when a child unexpectedly darts out in front of it. Its only choices are to hit the child or crash into a tree, which could harm its passengers. If the designer of the program has not thought of a situation that the machine does not know how to respond to, and that situation occurs, the machine might make the wrong decision. How do you program a computer to deal with these sorts of moral unforeseen dilemmas? Where humans can adapt quickly, or think and respond instantly when the unexpected happens, things may end quite differently with AI.

Humans can make that moral judgment, but how does a computer draw the same conclusion? Most individuals often make moral decisions on the basis of principles like honesty, civility, fairness, and respect. It seems impracticable for machines to emulate moral judgment, but if that potential exists, at least one important issue must be addressed. Human values and laws change depending on time and place. While there are some commonly-held ethical principles, individual interpretations of those values often differ. For example, there's a wide range of viewpoints in terms of what constitutes decent versus indecent language and attire. Technology evolves so fast and impacts our society so deeply that as we get more and more connected and everything happens at a faster pace, there will be more ethical questions to answer.

Machines don't text or drive while intoxicated or tired. Google and Tesla have vehicles on the road with over one million miles accident free. Driverless cars should, in theory, greatly reduce the number of road deaths every year, most of which are a result of driver error or incapability. But if someone hacks into the server that controls thousands of driverless cars, then we'll see if those statistics are valid.

An article put out by the *MIT Technology Review* says the biggest impediment to self-driving cars are security flaws and those flaws being susceptible to hackers. Last year, a team of Chinese hackers took remote control of Tesla Model S from 12 miles away. Tesla delivered a wireless update in hours. Software problems in cars often have real-world consequences. If a smartphone app has a problem that requires an update, it doesn't run the risk of a 2-ton car losing control and crashing into people. It's one thing to allow internet connectivity to download Global Positioning System (GPS), it's quite another thing to hook the mechanical workings of the car, like the brakes, into the internet. Even without hacks, do computers ever crash? Do programmers ever make mistakes? Do major programs ever have serious bugs? Currently with the weaponization of cars, companies need to offer solutions and advancements that stop someone from using these vehicles to cause harm to others. Automated systems on cars, trains, airplanes, and industrial equipment can compromise overall safety. There's always the danger that something will go wrong.

As more and more Internet of Things devices pop up, hackers are just going to figure out what they need to do to bring them down or exploit them for their own use. Look at printers. No one would think they were dangerous, but they are one of the most easily hackable connected devices out there. Unless you've got the right security, someone can gain access to everything—and pretty easily.

Another issue we need to address, which is a likely huge impending debate, is how we integrate driverless with human drivers as a transition period. Rural communities will be where the greatest lag will occur with driverless cars. It is obvious that computer operated cars will share the road with human drivers. How well will the mixture work? It'll be interesting to see how the auto industry (the business infrastructure) and the government (legislatively, and the public infrastructure) deals with those who lag behind.

Germany takes an ethics stance on driverless cars. Algorithms of life for self-driving cars set by German regulators:

- ➤ Must avoid injury or death of people at all cost
- ➤ Must be blind to the age, gender, or physical condition of people involved
- ➤ Protecting people rather than property or animals will be the priority

BIASES IN AI

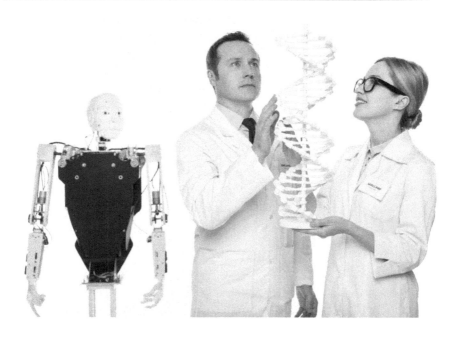

The American Civil Liberties Union has raised concerns that age, sex, and race biases are already being codified into the algorithms that power AI. Beneath the AI hype there is some serious bad design and implementation inherited over the past years by male only design and coding. With technology moving at an unprecedented speed, there has been concern about bias and stereotyping issues. Why do we need to fix these biases in AI? Whether we like it or not, AI is silently reshaping our entire society: from our day-to-day work, the news we read, the products we purchase, to how we vote, and how governments govern. AI isn't perfect and the damage caused can be irreparable when it comes to the algorithms that are used to decide more serious issues, like prison sentences, housing, or credit scores. Even more dangerous is the potential for reinforcement of racial and ethnic stereotypes because it aligns with a platform's view of the world or it just helps sell more products. It's easy to "weigh" algorithms to go in certain directions and still appear unbiased.

Racism in AI can be spotted from the fact that AI synonym generation systems associated African names with unpleasant words whereas it associated European names with pleasant words. ProPublica published an investigation that talked about software that was being used by a court to predict who was more likely to commit a crime for the second time. Appallingly, they found out that the software rated blacks with higher probability than whites. It was also found that a resume was more likely to be accepted if it belonged to a European American individual as compared to that of an African American.

Joanna Bryson, a researcher at the University of Bath, studied a program designed to "learn" relationships between words. It trained on millions of pages of text from the internet and began clustering female names and pronouns with jobs such as "receptionist" and "nurse." "People expected AI to be unbiased; that's just wrong. If the underlying data reflects stereotypes, or if you train AI from human culture, you will find these things," Bryson says.

Sexism in AI is quite obvious. AI synonym generation systems have associated words like "women" and "female" with social sciences and home chores. On the other hand, words like "man" and "male" have been associated with strength, engineering, and science. Siri, Alexa, Cortana—what is the common thread that ties them together besides the fact that they are all AI-based voice assistants? These futuristic AI-based assistants are all women. These implicit biases play out in various other forms too. Functional robots are mostly modeled as males while female robots are often designed to reflect the subservient image of women often embodied in a single role as assistants.

Algorithms are unbiased, if you feed it biased data it will have biased results. When the data we feed the machines reflects the discrimination evident in our society, we are training them to be unfair. But sadly, data can never become unbiased unless humans become that way.

Yoshua Bengio, a professor at the University of Montreal (who is one of the three intellects who shaped the deep learning that now dominates AI) said, "In a society where there's a lot of violence, a lot of inequality, [then] the risk of misusing AI or having people use it irresponsibly in general is much greater. Making AI beneficial for all is very central to the safety question."

It still isn't clear how existing laws to protect against discrimination might apply in this new landscape. Often the technology moves faster than governments can address its effects. In 2016, former Microsoft researcher Solon Barocas claimed that current laws "largely fail to address discrimination" when it comes to big data and ML.

AUTOMATION

Our world is experiencing an unprecedented shift from manually controlled technologies to increasingly intelligent and autonomous systems, some of which are powered by artificial AI. We are becoming even further marginalized through our dependence on certain technology as a surrogate for critical thinking skill. For the next generation, a large part of day-to-day life will fall under the control of software. Software perfectly tailored to manage our specific needs, likes, and everyday tasks will eliminate outside obstacles or friction, which can hurt us. This creates an illusion of a comfort, but it fuels a homogeneous world.

There are consequences of hyper connectedness. We rely on intelligent machines as a central part of our community of knowledge. We are becoming far too dependent on others thinking for us instead of us thinking for ourselves. Then there are some who don't have the inclination to consider, question, and reflect. We are not asleep but our consciousness is being slowly subdued. Taking people away from thinking with their own minds involves thinking and deciding in their place. The deceptively total knowledge and control of people's behavior through overestimated technological approaches (such as the big data) is an obvious example of this strategy. The worst is to realize that the vast majority of people do not even have enough level of consciousness to understand the short, medium, and long-term consequences. Here we have the kidnapping of human thought by the totalitarianism of the Great Quantitative Oracle; *people do not need to think*. All this is a mix of the speech of Modernity with the illusion of control. Centuries before Coetzee, Shakespeare had said something like that in the play *Julius Caesar*: "He thinks too much; such men are dangerous".

In an article posted in *The Washington Post*, Franklin Foer stated, "Along with Facebook, Microsoft, and Apple, these companies are in a race to become our personal assistant. They want to wake us in the morning, have their AI software guide us through our days, and never quite leave our sides. They aspire to become the repository for precious and private items, our calendars and contacts, our photos and documents. They intend for us to turn unthinkingly to them for information and entertainment while they catalogue our intentions and aversions." Has the servant become the master?

It's not about competing with the machine, it's about losing the ability of what we delegate to machines, which we have done many times. A simple example: I can still remember all the phone numbers that were relevant in my life before cell phones, but since cell phones now remember the numbers for me, all the "newer" ones are obscure to me. Newer generations don't retain much, since they always have Google in their pockets to look up everything. We automate processes and over time we lose the ability to perform that process. We sit and press a button for everything. In camping, we used to be able to find direction by looking at the sun or stars—now we use Google map. A couple of years back when you wanted to change the channel, you had to actually touch the TV. You would look out the window to see whether you should take an umbrella. If you wanted to turn a light on or off, you didn't have to talk to a device that was listening 24/7 and connected to a server farm thousands of miles away instead of standing up and flipping a switch. Furthermore, will this next generation even learn to drive a car? What if the system shuts down and an emergency happens that requires them to drive? If you're familiar with the collapse of the society that lived on Easter Island you'll see some interesting parallels. "Progress" is an often misinterpreted concept.

In 2009, Air France Flight 447 crashed into the ocean, killing 228 people. A report commissioned by the Federal Aviation Administration concluded that the pilots had become overly reliant on automation which left them unable to cope in unfamiliar circumstances. This is a great example of the automation paradox: Technology can fail and when it does, we don't know what to do. When the plane's automation technology failed, coupled with lack of basic manual flying skills, the pilots didn't know what to do.

It's sad to see what people would be willing to sacrifice for "convenience." Human beings are capable of doing many things, and we should limit trading our intelligence and decision-making to anything. As algorithms create more and more predictions, can we automate all decision-making? Is there a danger that this automation will become a crutch for business users—allowing human judgment to be overlooked? It is crucial that business users are equipped to understand the value of human judgment and how to manage algorithms making questionable decisions.

We need to exercise our mind and bodies. We need to think and act for ourselves. Technology can be addictive. Take for example, social media, it is like the doughnut holes of the digital world. You open up Twitter and say to yourself, "I'll look at just a few tweets." Before you know it, it's like doughnut holes—the whole box is gone. Each tweet gives a little dopamine rush. It lights up the same brain centers as a drug. A few years ago, when I realized I was checking Facebook constantly and maintaining a high level of anxiety about what other people were posting and about how many "likes" I was getting, I deleted all social media apps from my phone. Unplugging helps to avoid addiction. Relying on one's own mind, thought, and action may not always work, but if one can maintain some independence over the power of machines, we will survive. Otherwise, we are doomed. Like snakes, they invite you to try their sweet taste, and with provocative images they show a better world requiring only the down payment of your most inner will to their preordained future. They are the Charon that will take your body and soul to the other side where you will not have to do anything because all you have to do is give away your liberty, your will to act. But salvation exists and rests in our strength and will to cover our eyes and ears to heed the sweet calls to their brave new world. So this "brave new world" brings us terrible dangers as mental decay. Already we see this in schools, where most—fortunately not all—students cannot perform even basic math operations.

Technological progress itself does not automatically increase a population's intelligence level. Rather, as Claudia Goldin and Lawrence F. Katz claim in their essay, *The Race between Education and Technology*, it is political measures that enable a population to exploit this technological progress. Automation means no need to think or act. We are heading into a "sleepy" atmosphere. We know that most people have an attention deficit, which seems to be increasing. This leads us to have less and less awareness of what happens around us. British psychiatrist Theodore Dalrymple has emphasized the simplicity with which we can lose touch with reality. Before him, the Spanish philosopher Ortega y Gasset had highlighted the same in his book *The Rebellion of the Masses*: "If we observe those around us, we will see how they go through life in disorientation; they go like sleepwalkers...without understanding anything that happens to them."Many people have become so obsessed with technology that real life passes them by. Today, more people are living in virtual reality just sitting behind some sort of technological gadget instead of living life. Technology limits the human experience and because the progression of such is so subtle, we will not notice what we are missing until it's too late.

Another factor is having patience and persistence to overcome challenges in life. We live in a society that wants everything now. Slowly patience is becoming an extinct species. We need to teach our children and the future generations the importance and value of resilience. In a world where AI is going to tell you how to live, eat, behave, and vote, we are reaching the point that suicidal individuals will even ask their AI device if they should kill themselves and make a decision based on the answer they receive.

I see now the need to go back to our human identity, and this is only possible with an individual path. The scheme of the dangerous direction is not hard to decode. If it is true that current economy thrives on ignorance and mass hypnosis, well guess who's giving it consent?

In the Disney movie *Tomorrowland*, the father tells the story of two wolves. One wolf represents fear, hate, and despair. The other wolf represents hope, love, and kindness. The father then asks, "Which of the two wolves live?" The daughter correctly replies, "The one you feed."

THE ECONOMY & UNIVERSAL BASIC INCOME

According to a report by PwC – *PwC's Global Artificial Intelligence Study: Exploiting the AI Revolution*:

> ➢ AI can transform the productivity and GDP potential of the global economy. Strategic investment in different types of AI technology is needed to make that happen.

> ➢ Labor productivity improvements will drive initial GDP gains as firms seek to "augment" the productivity of their labor force with AI technologies and to automate some tasks and roles.

➢ Our research also shows that 45% of total economic gains by 2030 will come from product enhancements, stimulating consumer demand. This is because AI will drive greater product variety, with increased personalization, attractiveness, and affordability over time.

➢ The greatest economic gains from AI will be in China (26% boost to GDP in 2030) and North America (14.5% boost), equivalent to a total of $10.7 trillion and accounting for almost 70% of the global economic impact.

Technological progress is the primary driver of GDP per capita growth, increasing output faster than labor or capital. However, the economic benefits of technological progress are not necessarily evenly distributed across society.

"The science of economics should teach us not only how to increase the wealth of all of us, but to share the wealth more equally than we do." —Nobel Laureate Robert M. Solow

Andrew Ng, the former chief scientist at Chinese technology powerhouse Baidu, told an audience at a Harvard Business Review event that we should be far more concerned about the job losses that will come as a result of ML. "I've been in a lot of private conversations with AI leaders, or business leaders who are working on new AI products that will wipe out tens of thousands of jobs in a single company, maybe more across multiple companies," Ng said. "And the interesting thing is that a lot of people whose jobs are squarely in the crosshairs of the technologies, a lot of people doing the jobs that are about to go away, they don't understand AI, they don't have the training to understand AI. And so a lot of people whose jobs are going to go away don't know that they're in the crosshairs."

Elimination of poverty rests on two things: education and employment. Technological advancements must be assessed based on social and economic impact for the living population. So what are the economic implications of AI on employment and in turn on consumption that is driven by employment and income? In the past, machines helped to make the life of people easier, and with more machines, increased productivity meant more supply. The need of labor exceeded the supply of workers, but that is no longer the case. Unfortunately the purpose and paradigm of ideology of automation is about a cost function to minimize company headcount. The President/CEO of the company reports to the stockholders who want the biggest return for their money and the cost of labor with benefits is now more expensive than this new technology. If automation was led by a cost function of greed, it may want to optimize profits. It means "to get rid of as many people as possible." Destruction may be disguised with fancy positive rhetoric such as "competitiveness," "innovation," "efficiency," "performance," "benefits," "stakeholders," "limitless opportunities," "creativity," etc. Rhetoric to live in denial like in 2007, before the 2008 financial crisis.

Sadly, much of our future is being created by technologists who have no real concern about the long-term ramifications of their creations. I can only ponder. Have scientists and technologists emerged as the leading snake oil sales men? We witnessed the same phenomena in economics which collapsed the world's economic systems and it's looking like it is technology next.

> "High levels of unemployment allow an urban entrepreneurial class to exploit plentiful labor. They enjoy the profits of their development, while people at the bottom of society don't progress at all and unemployment becomes indigenous to the system as a whole."—Nobel Laureate Sir Arthur Lewis.

China is installing more robots than any other nation and has already positioned itself as the biggest robotic market on the globe. In 2016, Robot shipments to the country rose 27% to 90,000, putting it on track to account for a third of the world's total. The International Federation of Robotics estimates this total will nearly double to 160,000 in 2019. The drive for automation could ultimately depress wages for Chinese workers, exacerbating income inequality and hurting consumption. That shift could have worldwide ramifications, economists warn, denting prospects for a more balanced global economy.

The rapid and pervasive advance of automation has put pressure on employment. Eventually we will be faced with an overwhelming number of people out of the work force and unable to retool their skills for the new economy. At some level, the system as it stands will implode, because it does not matter how much you can produce if nobody has a wage to buy the stuff you produce. Human population will increase but jobs would be limited.

The Bureau of Labor Statistics lists that 884,000 people are employed in motor vehicles and parts manufacturing, and an additional 3.02 million in the dealer and maintenance network. An entire profession of drivers of trucks, taxis, buses, and such are about to get wiped out. If millions of jobs are made obsolete, as well as industries, then human consumption will dry up, worse than after the Great Depression or the 2008 economic crash. What consumer base will drive this "explosion"? There is certainly an employment disruption coming, the scale of which hasn't been seen since the first Industrial Revolution. What we are contemplating is not just transformation but disruption beyond what our society can bear. Subsequently, why should governments keep investing in new highways with expectations of increased traffic if cars on the road will be reduced?

If the very purpose of AI is to get rid of free thinking and time conscious workforce and reduce cost, then how it can create new jobs? If it creates jobs, it will be a temporary phenomenon—jobs related to AI.

Economy is run by human demand and supply activities. When you take most humans out of the jobs, what kind of economy will be created by this AI and autonomous path? Eliminating employees, which are also final consumers, will encounter an economic limit (especially if staff being replaced do not get a new job or are not being paid in some way).

Automation does create more jobs, but only if it's possible to expend market (shift demand) through lower prices (higher productivity-lower input costs) and make more money at the same time. Unfortunately, today, most industries/markets operate at excess capacity and most markets are at their natural maximum size, which means further automation will only result in lower employment. Combined with ageing populations, this a ticking time bomb for the global economy. While automation improves productivity, it also lowers participation in the labor force, hence displacing more jobs than it creates in the short-term. That is, the market does not self-correct immediately. The only way out is to find a way to constantly create new industries, products, and new markets and even then we would only be buying some extra time.

> "Today, the top one-tenth of 1% owns nearly as much wealth as the bottom 90%. The economic game is rigged, and this level of inequality is unsustainable. We need an economy that works for all, not just the powerful."—Senator Bernie Sanders

When we displace workers, where is the income coming from for the unemployed? Employees pay tax which is supposed to go into improving services in our country. By automating everything, where does the tax revenue get made up? Robots also don't pay taxes or contribute to Medicare, disability benefits, Social Security, etc. While they also won't draw on Medicare or Social Security (SS), don't those programs depend on workers paying into them to fund those who are drawing on Medicare and SS? Automation and AI necessitates a whole new approach to many institutions and basically, a new model of capitalism that redistributes the wealth-gap in a more equitable, ethical, and balanced way. We cannot assume the transition to a new economic model will be peaceful.

In essence, there's an increasing realization that a basic wage for everyone, currently on trial, is being touted as a solution to the new world of work. Bill Gates, among others, has proposed the concept of Universal Basic Income (UBI). This would help deal with the economic disparity caused by massive job loss. UBI involves giving every adult a cash stipend, regardless of wealth or income, in part to offset technology's job-destroying effects. This would provide everyone with a set amount of money to help support themselves. Universal Basic Income (UBI) is basically a form of social security, in which each citizen of a country periodically receives an unconditional payment of money, either from a government or another public institution, in addition to any income the citizen may obtain from elsewhere. The main idea is to ensure that every person receives a minimum amount of income so that no one has to live in poverty.

UBI is not a new concept. Some forerunners can probably be traced back as far as the free grain offered to Roman citizens. Thomas Paine, author of *Common Sense* and one of the inspirations for the American Revolution, called for a "national fund, out of which there shall be paid to every person, when arrived at the age of twenty-one years, the sum of fifteen pounds sterling." In the 20th century, economists and civic leaders called for the institution of UBI, in order to build a "floor" or minimum income for each citizen. During the Great Depression, Louisiana Senator Huey Long gained some traction with his "Share Our Wealth." During the same period, several economists, including, James Tobin, John Kenneth Galbraith, and Paul Samuelson called on Congress to adopt "a national system of income guarantees and supplements." Currently, Finland is running trials. Finland has given 560 Euros monthly to 2,000 randomly selected people who had previously been receiving unemployment benefits. According to the World Economic Forum, Finland's basic income experiment is already making people feel better after just 4 months. The government of the province of Ontario in Canada provides 4,000 of its limited-income citizens with around $12,600 a year. Utrecht, in the Netherlands, is also conducting a trial. Scotland looks likely to follow suit. By contrast, the citizens of Switzerland rejected the idea of UBI by a landslide in a 2016 referendum.

Here are common sense reasons why adopting UBI might be preferable for the long-term good of the future citizen:

- ➤ It alleviates suffering at scale. Individuals will have a guaranteed income in spite of lack of employment.

- ➤ In a robot world of the automaton economy, UBI is the forerunner of a new way of visiting the "meaning of life": Basic Income will help us rethink how and why we work.

- ➤ With a basic economic safety net in place, employees won't be trapped in degrading or exploitative situations. Basic Income will contribute to better working conditions.

- ➤ Unlike training programs, capital promotes freedom for those most vulnerable to find solutions themselves that suit their innate self-determined potential.

- ➤ Greater Income equality; with UBI the 1% has to play by new rules of capitalism that put greater weight on a redistribution of wealth: Basic income will help with reducing inequalities.

- ➤ Greater work life balance: UBI will likely contribute to less working hours, leading to better work-life balance.

You get paid to live. Eventually we'll live in a Techno-Utopia where that iteration of UBI will be perfectly balanced. This looks like a great idea in theory, but the problem with universal base pay is that it simply raises the price floor of everything by that amount. So, a cheap apartment or a cheap car would cost that + X base pay, and in the end, life is again unaffordable for base pay earners. It's just inflationary. The base pay idea would need to be combined with affordable housing and transportation and food options.

UBI means pouring money into the economy, without the corresponding increase in production capacity, hence similar to printing money. Injecting money into the economy without a subsequent increase in economic output has only one result. This produces inflation, which renders the UBI useless for the recipient. Anytime you falsely inject capital into the economy, supply and demand dictates that purchasing power will be diluted and you won't help the "poor." People who are living below the poverty line before UBI will still be living in poverty afterwards. UBI is simply masking poverty.

While the prospect of UBI may seem like a wholesome idea, the process will take time, fortitude, and ethical distribution. Most political systems have neither of these nor does the public have the cultural or emotional maturity to give people "something for nothing."

UBI sounds like a good strategy but what if government runs out of money? Social security payments are based on current monies coming in. It used to be ten working people paying into the system supporting one person receiving benefits. Now it's about four to one and even less in some countries. Now, imagine that on the scale of a universal UBI and the money runs out. Given current trends— low wages, disappearing middle-class, unskilled workforce, etc.— the issue is that UBI is unaffordable for the current population and tax levels. However, if the population increases, it becomes less affordable. Seventy percent of Americans are living pay check to pay check and on their credit cards. If this is the reality then economic growth and demand for goods and services is not sustainable. Furthermore, UBI is guaranteed to be a low-ball wage.

The existing financial systems are already unsustainable and headed for collapse. Government running trillion dollar deficits despite record tax receipts, public pensions (mathematically un-fundable), student loan bubble, subprime auto bubble already on the verge of bursting, stock market decoupled from reality, social security, Medicare, boomer retirement wave, and so on. The dominoes are lined up just waiting for one of them to topple over and start the cascade. What is the solution to any of these problems that exist now? Everything in the future is predicated on the assumption that the status quo will remain on its current trajectory. By every measure possible, the status quo, completely ignoring the job displacement by automation/AI, is already on a path to failing.

People in the future will marvel at the pensions and unemployment benefits that governments of today provide. It is very likely that pensions and the dole will not exist by 2050.

Without UBI, social unrest would ensue. However, it is a bandage, not a long-term solution.

"From each according to his ability, to each according to his need"
This slogan was made popular by Karl Marx in his writing *Critique of the Gotha Program*, published in 1875. The German original is *Jeder nach seinen Fähigkeiten, jedem nach seinen Bedürfnissen.* According to Marx, once a communist society has been established, it will produce enough goods and services so that everyone's needs can be satisfied. Even though the phrase is commonly attributed to Marx, he was not the first to use it. The slogan was common within the socialist movement. Louis Blanc first used it in 1839, in the *Organization of Work*. The origin of this phrasing has also been attributed to the French communist Morelly, who proposed in his 1755 *Code of Nature*, "Sacred and Fundamental Laws that would tear out the roots of vice and of all the evils of a society."

Additionally, if you want everyone to have a comfortable living without the effort, that's Marxism, and that is proven not to work. UBI seems no different from Socialism. Socialism is usually implemented poorly. A lot of progress and innovation doesn't occur because people are trying to keep power in their status quo. Equal distribution of basic needs by the government is communism. UBI is a prelude to it. According to Friedman, "...government should provide three primary functions: a. military defense, b. enforce contracts between individuals, c. protect citizens from crimes against themselves or their property....Government should be a referee, not a player ..."

UBI takes away incentives to work and makes it to normal to be fed by the rest of the society. Taxes are used for the funding and taxes are taken away from the productive people under the threat of violence. I'll defer to economists like Thomas Sowell and Milton Freedman who've many times in the past debunked this notion that a Universal Basic Income will solve anything. This idea floats to the surface every so often as the opponents age out and retire or pass on. We forget too quickly.

UBI is insinuating that we have reached a limit on creativity and innovation and basically surrendered our future to AI and automation. One of the reasons AI is displacing human workers is because we have lowered our expectations of workers to the point of mindlessness. Technology historically has created more jobs than it has eliminated, and the historical reason for that has been a willingness of people to raise their skill levels. Today, disturbingly high percentages of students graduate high school barely literate and not at all prepared for either college or a job. Colleges are turning out graduates with little or no practical skill who end up working lower wage jobs while saddled with more debt than when their parents bought their first house. Basic income devalues skill, devalues personal excellence, and devalues the very qualities that enable people to move up the income ladder. It cripples people by giving them not much, but just enough. Instead of throwing pennies at people and dismissing them, we need to encourage, enable, and inspire everyone to a lifetime of learning, education, and personal growth and skills development. Universal basic income will destroy lives. Let's build up lives instead.

Sound education and economic growth is the only remedy for displaced workers. We do not need handouts under a new name. However, I tend to support a similar idea in the form of a negative income tax that supplies income if and only if wages fall below a certain threshold. This will create a market for the poor, and if paired with the elimination of many current welfare programs, will result in efficient government spending to effect positive outcomes for the needy. As this program would be progressive and not regressive, it doesn't suffer as heavily from the inflationary problem of the universal basic income idea. Furthermore, distributing wealth puts a lot of trust in the benevolence of those appointed to do so. The subjective discussions on determining the exact level of the income will be an unending source of (international) social discontent.

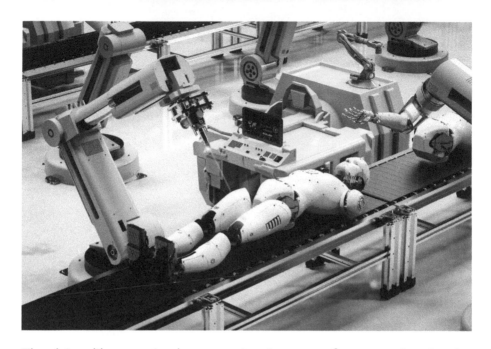

The big dilemma is the negative impact of automation in the poorest countries around the globe. What about the developing countries? They would not be able to bear such high employee lay off costs, or provide high subsidies. The major source of income for such countries would come from the income tax or indirect taxes. According to a United Nations report, up to two-thirds of jobs in developing countries could disappear in the near future. Millions of urban and rural employees will be replaced by machines and automatized processes. All the millenniums goals of the United Nations are in serious risk as well as the economic and social stability of the poorest countries. Of course, middle-income countries, such as Mexico and India, can face serious difficulties. How can we implement universal basic income in India where politics, diverse classes, working conditions, and work opportunities are challenges? Developed countries like the USA can afford to accommodate the people to live on social security or welfare, however, the people in less developed societies will not have this option.

Profits from automation could pay a UBI

The automation economy is creating a new world, so the rules of economy must change accordingly. And it must be done fast. Opposition to robotics and AI is about as useful as it would have been in the 20th century to oppose electricity. It will happen. Everything that can be automated, will be automated. There will be a massive disturbance. The era of democratization for UBI will soon be here. We will have no choice but to subscribe to UBI.

I watched an interview with a couple of "Silicon Valley" tech company CEO's—all guys in their 30's supporting UBI—but when the interviewer asked about how the US would pay for the massive cost, they literally had no answer, the conversation ended since no one had a clue. Wealth distribution is a touchy subject. Those earning high incomes like CEOs of banks, how will they be taxed? Will their taxes pay for UBI? Usually it's the little people making middle-class incomes who pay most tax. The Australian PM is fighting pressure to stop giving high income people tax cuts.

Automation will save companies money and boost profits. Given all of the huge savings companies (employee insurance, overtime compensation, workers compensation claims, vacation, sick leave, and maternity leave, etc.) companies are going to reap from automation, robotics, and AI, and they should be held responsible for using part of these gains to support the workers they've displaced. Bill Gates recently offered another convincing suggestion: Perhaps robots should pay taxes to compensate the workers that they replace. This has also been endorsed by Elon Musk, Mark Zuckerberg, and Richard Branson. Companies that automate their workforces should be taxed on these new massive profits, and some of the resulting capital given back to workers by the government in the form of UBI. This seems to be a great idea but the issue will be the tax rate. Say a robot does the job of 10 people. If the robot is taxed, would the tax amount accumulate to the sum the 10 people would have paid? **Businesses nationwide fought against raising the minimum wage. Why? Because it reduces**

their profits. And now they will miraculously just willingly agree to a suitable robot tax rate?

As I write, this reminds me of the effects of World War II (1939–1945) experienced by citizens of my country, Trinidad and Tobago. There was little employment opportunities leading to food shortages. As reported by Ecclesville Agricultural Society, "children and adults are starving in the country on the account of scarcity of the basic foods and rice and flour." It was proposed that the government's attention be drawn to the plight of the people and compulsory rationing be introduced to secure equitable food distribution. In order to accommodate the population, each family was allowed to purchase a weekly quota or ration of rice and flour. To keep track of the weekly quota, 'Ration Cards' were issued to every single householder, including children from the age of 12. The dynamics upon which the card operated was that when weekly rations of flour and rice were purchased at the shops, the consumer gave the card to the shopkeeper who placed an X in the boxes on the ration card for each items bought. There was also a shortage of vehicular tires because the milk extracted from the rubber trees which was used in making tires was in short supply. The shortage of tires was responsible for restrictions placed on travel throughout the country. Owners of public transport vehicles were issued passes restricting the use of their vehicles to designated areas. Sale of imported foodstuff was also regulated. A government agency called The Control Board was established under the Department of Industry. Did it cause riots? Were there inequalities? Was the system faced with corruption? Yes to all those. This can be compared to what is going on with Venezuela, who is tackling the current food shortage by implementing a food ID card system. Government said this system will stop people overbuying groceries for resale. However, critics say it's another sign the oil-rich Venezuelan economy is headed toward Soviet-style collapse.

UBI may become like a drug. The number of people misusing it will far exceed those who use it for a short period to tide over bad times. This is more like the "hippie" culture of the 1970s when it was considered okay not to do much in life…except, of course, using drugs. Many youngsters ruined their careers trying to be a hippie.

UBI may work as a temporary solution in developed countries but I don't see it as a viable long term strategy. It will only work as all things remain equal, *ceteris paribus*. There are many factors, such as unforeseen events or natural calamities that can shake its foundation. Up until 2017, Hurricane Katrina was the most expensive natural disaster in US history. The federal government spent $120.5 billion to help the city and other affected areas recover. Hurricane Harvey made landfall in the Houston area on August 25, 2017. A week later, Texas Governor Greg Abbott said that his state may require as much as $180 billion in federal assistance.

The UBI discussion seems timely, noting the rapid evolution of the job market, automation of jobs, slowing economic growth, and constrained resources. Sadly, once government is involved there may be corruption, social injustice, and anti-religious rules. Human beings can't be impartial yet and will always be corrupted by power potentially and therefore unable to find a way to equally share the world's resources. There is already so much unfairness, inequality, and social ills afflicting our society. If we can't control this now, it will only intensify with the adoption of AI. The underlying factors of hate, greed, and selfishness will only magnify our current problems. It is increasingly clear that governments need to reassess social welfare and administration systems and evaluate how these could be more effectively managed/contained within the increasing claims on limited resources. We need better minds, greater discussions, and ethical leaders on this problem.

DEMOGRAPHIC IMPLOSION

As worker shortages and skill gaps become more common with lower labor force participation rates, due to both automation and ageing populations, new issues arise. New Scientist released an interesting article about the world's population in 2076. According to the report, half the world's nations have fertility rates below the replacement level of just over two children per woman (Japan, China and most of Europe). Elon Musk also tweeted, "The world's population is accelerating towards collapse, but few seem to notice or care." He later said in an interview, "We have a very high dependency ratio where the number of people who are retired is relatively high compared to those who are net producers. The social safety net will not hold." Economist Thomas Malthus already warned us two centuries ago about Demographic Implosion. Add automation, robotics and AI in the mix; it will only get worse. So many of us and so few resources that there might not be enough to go around.

WILL DEMOCRACY SURVIVE AUTOMATION AND ARTIFICIAL INTELLIGENCE?

AI can be used to manipulate individual voters. It is absolutely possible to use ones' intelligence to influence, and even control other individuals and large groups. Facebook ran a sociopsychological experiment sometime back where they manipulated the emotions of their users by controlling what appears on the newsfeed. In a connected world, the vast majority of humans do not give much critical thought to the rapidly developing social realities created by technology, and the growing influence it has over us. Big data analysis, surveillance, AI, programmed bots, Facebook posts, sophisticated behavior assessments, computational psychology, and fake news networks are combined "to manipulate our opinions and behavior to advance specific political agendas" (Yale University). It is one thing when AI systems are pitted against human intellect, it will be quite another to witness the growing use of AI versus AI to manipulate human behavior.

For example, an article in the *Dailymail* claimed that Google changed its string search auto completion algorithm to make people search only good things about Hillary Clinton; obviously Google denied these claims. During the 2016 US presidential election, the data science firm Cambridge Analytica rolled out an extensive advertising campaign to target persuadable voters. Voters received different messages based on predictions about their vulnerability to different arguments. The conservatives received ads with arguments based on tradition and community. While the paranoid received ads with messages based on fear. In the 2017 general election in the UK, massive groups of political bots were used to spread fake news on social media. The same happened during the 2016 US presidential election. It's claimed that Pro-Trump bots infiltrated Facebook pages and Twitter hashtags used by Hillary Clinton supporters to spread automated content. Bots were also deployed at a crucial point in the 2017 French presidential election.

It's also a growing phenomenon that certain technology leaders, and increasingly elected officials, are able to capture the mindset of weaker individuals, manipulate their actions through social media with fact-less content, and benefit by increasing their power and control, while often involving personal enrichment. Humans can be easily lulled into a false sense of security that others are looking-out for their best interest. That is to say we shouldn't think, even for a moment, that ML and AI technology and the smart people developing it are not capable of doing great harm to unsuspecting billions. The "connected masses" are becoming addicted to smart devices, and rapidly losing the will to think for themselves, especially considering that this same technology is hyper-connected to global business, financial networks, and government ecosystems.

Microsoft Research's Kate Crawford has warned, "Just as we are seeing a step function increase in the spread of AI, something else is happening: the rise of ultra-nationalism, right-wing authoritarianism, and fascism," she said.

The ultimate risk of outsourcing knowledge to machines is it increases our susceptibility to other humans intentionally manipulating our intentions. Big data analysis, surveillance, AI, programmed bots, Facebook posts, sophisticated behavior assessments, computational psychology, and fake news networks are often combined to manipulate our opinions and behavior to advance specific political agendas. Some software platforms are moving towards "persuasive computing." They will be using sophisticated manipulation technologies. *The trend goes from programming computers to programming people.* There lurks a much larger danger—AI in the hands of governments used to push self-interested agendas against the greater good. Elon Musk tweeted on September 4, 2017, that Governments will obtain AI technology "at gunpoint" if necessary.

THE RECIPE FOR INEQUALITY AND SOCIAL UNREST

Alibaba founder Jack Ma stated AI and other technologies will cause people "more pain than happiness" over the next three decades. "Social conflicts in the next three decades will have an impact on all sorts of industries and walks of life."

Today, the eight richest people on earth own as much wealth as the poorest 50% of the world. If you thought there was already a power imbalance in the world, wait for the next 5–10 years as automation and AI spread across industries. Wealth will increase, but it will go into far fewer hands. The benefits from AI and Robots will flow to the already rich 1% and the jobs lost will come from the 90%. This can only make wealth-gaps worse, with the working class losing its power, therefore becoming expendable to a degree as we've not seen in human history. This divide between rich and poor will ultimately split society.

Money has always been a means to get more power. In the AI paradigm, money/economy will become less important and unlimited power will lie in the hands of those that control the AI. The *Economist* highlighted the important role of data in a cover story, in which it stated "the world's most valuable resource is no longer oil, but data."

Is history repeating itself? "Luddite" is now a blanket term used to describe people who dislike new technology, but its origins date back to a 19th century labor movement in England that railed against the economic fallout of the Industrial Revolution. The essence of the issue was that workers were seeing automation as something alien that was taking away their jobs. The same is happening right now. The original Luddites were British weavers and textile workers who objected to the increased use of automated looms and knitting frames. Most were trained artisans who had spent years learning their craft, and they feared that unskilled machine operators were robbing them of their livelihood. When their appeals for government aid and assistance were ignored, a few desperate weavers began breaking into factories and smashing textile machines. Those who protested the sudden arbitrary loss of their livelihoods were brutally and ruthlessly put down by force.

Automation will throw to the streets millions of jobs. In society, which is not ready to take care of the extra free labor force even now, there will be another revolution. Are big corporations ready to take care of this issue when the social security cannot handle even the existing level of unemployed people? The political unrest of an acceleration pace of adaption required could lead to some serious civic, economic, and political adjustment, if not downright instability. Even if a UBI is feasible/affordable a lack of meaningful employment

127

will lead to more social problems, higher crime rates, etc.

Are we due for another `peasant' workers revolution?

There were several significant peasants' revolts:

- ❖ The Peasants' Revolt 1381 (England)
- ❖ French Revolution 1787–1799
- ❖ The Russian Revolutions of 1905 and 1917

There are lessons that show that economic disparity between the rich and poor can bring down entire regimes (e.g. the French Revolution). In the last great wave of technological job displacement, the Industrial Revolution, we paid a big price as a civilization in the environment and in human health. Heavy-handed government policies and unions had to step in to protect the worker and the environment. So while there are examples in history that show that the growing divide between the rich and poor don't have to be problematic, there are plenty of examples that show they can be. The signs are irrefutable if one chooses to see them. Universities that teach pabulum; governments that spend beyond their means; populations expanding with employment dwindling—all point to a massive social upheaval in our lifetime.

"It's almost a moral principle that we should share benefits among more people in society," argued Bart Selman, a professor at Cornell University, "…So we have to go into a mode where we are first educating the people about what's causing this inequality and acknowledging that technology is part of that cost, and then society has to decide how to proceed."

We are going to see a resurgence of leaders who will stand up and fight for the people when injustices arise—when equal opportunity, social and religious freedom is removed.

- ➢ Mahatma Gandhi was an Indian civil rights leader who led the movement against British rule.
- ➢ Martin Luther King Jr. fought for racial equity in America. His famous "I Have a Dream" Speech is one of the most iconic speeches of all times.

> ➢ Nelson Mandela worked to achieve freedom for South Africa's black and peace to a racially divided country. He fought the forces of apartheid for years, and was thrown in jail for his efforts.

> ➢ Martin Luther led the Protestant Reformation in the 16th-century. He stood up against the Roman papacy.

Leaders like these are going to step to the forefront and fight the system once it is not elevating the masses.

IS PRIVACY DEAD?

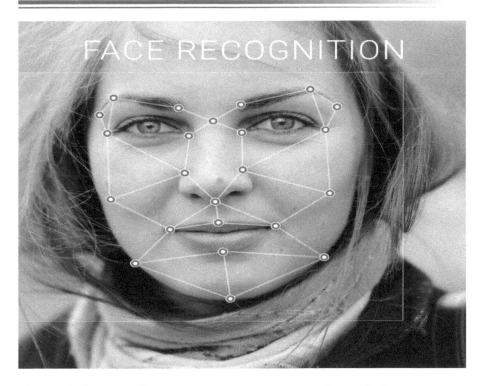

The push for AI will mean consumer privacy rights will deteriorate to record levels. It's no longer just cookies, your web browser, and what you hand over when using apps. Big tech corporations such as Google and Facebook collect and store massive amounts of information about users. This information is used to improve the algorithms that run their services and create their revenue. But users have no ownership of the data and have to rely on those centralized services to protect their information. In 2017, Andreas Mundt, president of Germany's antitrust agency, Bundeskartellamt, said he was "deeply convinced privacy is a competition issue." That is to say, the big tech monopolies are using their AI platforms to listen too closely. And then there are cases like the massive data breach Equifax reported in September 2017, where 143 million dates of birth, email addresses, telephone numbers, and other data was exposed to hackers and identity thieves.

I read a disturbing article in *The Guardian* recently titled, I asked Tinder for my data. It sent me 800 pages of my deepest, darkest secrets. Tinder is a dating app with 50 million active users. In it Judith Duportail writes, "As I flicked through page after page of my data I felt guilty. I was amazed by how much information I was voluntarily disclosing: from locations, interests and jobs, to pictures, music tastes and what I liked to eat. But I quickly realised I wasn't the only one." She further states, "The dating app knows me better than I do, but these reams of intimate information are just the tip of the iceberg. What if my data is hacked – or sold?" Just think about all the information internet companies have collected about you.

AI will read texts, emails, and voicemails to learn all the important names, locations, and people in your life. It will know your GPS history. It will scan your photos to learn people, places, and things. It will know your financial health, your daily patterns, habits, and a wealth of other information, while the aggregation of this information will provide opportunity for economic and political exploitation.

Drones deployed with Wi-Fi transceivers can now see through walls. This is going to be a powerful tool, but I hope it won't turn into a weapon. I recently read in a tech newspaper that The Defense Advanced Research Projects Agency (DARPA) is experimenting with remote-controlled bugs to spy on their enemies (an enemy can be anyone).

Facial recognition in still images and video is already trickling into the real world. "The face recognition market is huge," says Shiliang Zhang an associate professor at Peking University.

Baidu is starting a program where facial recognition is used instead of you receiving tickets for events. When you show up, your face is scanned and once the system recognizes you, you're allowed in. Paris tested a similar feature at its Charles de Gaulle airport for a 3-month period this year, following Japan's pilot program in 2016, although neither have released results of the programs. US governments are already beginning to use the technology in a limited capacity. The New York department of motor vehicles recently announced that it had made more than 4,000 arrests using facial recognition technology. In the UK, retailers used facial recognition to spot past shoplifters and Welsh police used it to arrest a suspect outside a football game. In China, people are already using facial detection software to make payments and access facilities. The Chinese government is using it for tracking people on closed-circuit camera and to predict crimes. China has installed over 20 million street cameras in what is believed to be the world's most advanced surveillance system. This technology can be used to detect a person's age, gender and clothes. Such technology can identify a pedestrian or a motorist, which can help policemen in their search for criminals. However many citizens fear that the technology will be used to monitor their daily lives.

Face-reading AI will be able to detect your politics and IQ says Michal Kosinski, Stanford University professor. In general, if humans can't detect if someone is good or evil from their face how can AI? I think it's a slippery slope. Using AI to improve efficiency is one thing, but using AI to judge people isn't something I would support. It violates the intention on the applications of AI. This seems to be social prejudice masquerading as science; an AI programmed with human biases. This sounds very close to phrenology. What next? Using facial recognition to determine religion or to employ someone? Pseudo-science could lead us down a very dark path. Martin Luther King said it brilliantly, when he talked about a future where we're not judged by our external appearances but by the "content of our character".

There really will be nowhere to hide with hybrid facial detection methods. Law-enforcement agencies now have a powerful weapon to track criminals, but at huge potential cost to citizens' privacy. AI will be able to find the needle, no matter how large the haystack. A group of researchers from the UK and India have developed an AI that can identify people even when facial physical features are obscured. A person could be identified from surveillance footage and photos, even if they're covering their faces with a scarf, sunglasses, or a beard.

Google and Oxford University researchers, in their paper titled *Lip Reading Sentences in the Wild*, detailed how they created a lip reading neural network that actually outperformed a human professional. Some experts fear that this technology could also lead to a new highly advanced wave of spying attacks. "An obvious unlawful use of this technology is espionage since it makes it possible to 'listen in' on a conversation from a distance," Arctic Wolf CEO and cofounder Brian NeSmith told SC Magazine. "A nightmare scenario is a criminal stealing login and password information by listening in on a conversation from outside of a building through a window.... Personnel will also need to be sure that they are not discussing sensitive information in public places," NeSmith said. "This new technology makes it even more true that you just never know who is listening (or watching)."

So what's a privacy-minded, law-abiding citizen to do when surveillance becomes the norm? Not much. AI has the potential to be the single greatest human achievement, yet it has the potential to be the most destructive.

ROBOTICS

Unfortunately, human linear ideology pushes a generation of AI that promises to be very dangerous. How long will it be before robotics come out of the lab and go mainstream in the consumer world?

Boston Dynamics, previously owned by Google and now by SoftBank, are developing robots with astonishing qualities, including some almost uncanny human physical characteristics, and recently broke the record for land speed with their Cheetah robot. Their BigDog robot is one of the most advanced all-terrain robots on the planet at the time of writing, and is visually like something we only imagined and could see using special effects in movies until recently. I looked at a video on YouTube posted about their robot, Handle. Handle stands at 6 foot tall and looks vaguely human with a torso, arms, and legs. At the end of its back legs are two stabilized wheels, which let it stand up vertically and roll around at speeds of up to 9 miles per hour. Even Boston Dynamics founder and CEO Marc Raibert described Handle as a "nightmare-inducing robot." Google's parent company Alphabet offloaded Boston Dynamics, following tensions within the company about its fit within the wider corporate culture. Communications staff sought to distance the company from the hardware, according to emails leaked to *Bloomberg News*, citing the feeling that such technology could be "terrifying."Korean auto giant Hyundai Motor unveiled its robot exoskeleton that the carmaker claims allows the wearer to lift hundreds of kilograms. Just like Marvel's *Iron Man*, the wearable robotic device is used to give the controller extra strength and assistance. Hyundai sees the exoskeleton as being useful in factories, the military, and in physical rehabilitation in the future.

At one of the biggest AI conferences, the International Joint Conference on Artificial Intelligence (IJCAI) 2017 in Melbourne, a group comprising 116 founders of robotics and AI companies from 26 countries had a surprise announcement for the UN. They presented an open letter urging for the ban on "**killer robots**." This is a serious issue that must be urgently addressed.

AUTONOMOUS WEAPONS

AI is a thinking machine. If the intention of the machine is to calculate, the intention remains. If the intention is to compete with and defeat humans, then that is what it will do. It is reflection of its designers' intention. Machines are just an extension of us and our ideas.

For example, the purpose of a Tesla car (AI built-in) is to protect a human from physical and chemical danger. It may have defects but you may expect Tesla AI not to hurt people. It responds to the purpose, the intention of the creator. Connect AI to a "weapon" and you get a Dark AI specifically designed to get rid of people, the principle of "humans as a bother." When the purpose or paradigm of a certain AI becomes "to get rid of humans" you have a Dark AI by design. A hacker can create the ultimate hacking AI.

If the international community fails to prevent the proliferation of nuclear weapons then the likelihood that weaponization of AI could be stopped is marginal to nil. "Hackers have been using artificial intelligence as a weapon for quite some time," said Brian Wallace, Cylance Lead Security Data Scientist, in an interview with Gizmodo. "It makes total sense because hackers have a problem of scale, trying to attack as many people as they can, hitting as many targets as possible, and all the while trying to reduce risks to themselves. Artificial Intelligence, and ML in particular, are perfect tools to be using on their end." These tools, he says, can make decisions about what to attack, who to attack, and when to attack.

Jack Ma said "Artificial intelligence could set off WWIII, but humans will win." On September 4, 2017, Elon Musk tweeted *"China, Russia, soon all countries w strong computer science. Competition for AI superiority at national level most likely cause of WW3 imo."* (imo means in my opinion.) His comment was in response to Russian President Vladimir Putin who said the development of AI raises both "colossal opportunities" and "threats that are difficult to predict…. Whoever becomes the leader in this sphere will become the ruler of the world." His latest comments couldn't be timelier. On

September 3, 2017, North Korea said it had successfully carried out a test of a hydrogen bomb. Musk said that there was a possibility that war could be automated.

An article written by Spark Cognition CEO, Amir Husain, and US Marine Corps Gen. John R. Allen (ret.), which was published in the US Naval Institute's *Proceedings Magazine*, stated: "In military terms, hyper war may be redefined as a type of conflict where human decision making is almost entirely absent from the observe-orient-decide-act (OODA) loop. Simply put, future warfare will indeed be run by machines. As a consequence, the time associated with an OODA cycle will be reduced to near-instantaneous responses. The implications of these developments are many and game changing."

Both the Chinese and Russians have a close approximation of USA's state of the art defense system. However, their weapons systems are becoming more sophisticated and more lethal. China and Russia haven't made their work on Robots/AI public yet. China wants to integrate AI into guided missiles. This has set off alarms within the US defense establishment. The United States is generally considered to be the nation leading the charge towards AI currently, with tech giants like Microsoft and Google investing large amounts of cash into research and development projects. But a report by Goldman Sachs found that China could have the AI capability to catch up with the US. "We believe AI technology will become a priority on the government's agenda, and we expect further national/regional policy and funding support on AI to follow," the investment bank said. According to research by HackerRank, China and Russia have the most talented developers in the world. Russians dominate in algorithms, the most popular arena. While Chinese programmers outscore all other countries in mathematics, functional programming, and data structures challenges.

Elon Musk is also concerned that AI development would become the purview of secretive government. He adds that this could trigger an uncontrolled AI "arms race," which would not be in humankind's best interests. In an era of increased international conflict and terrorism at scale, the dangers are becoming more existential than ever before. If action is not taken, Syria like events would be like a very scary video game. The UN cannot keep delaying a decision on this.

Dozens of business executives and technology experts in AI and robotics, including Elon Musk, have signed an open letter to the United Nations calling for public deliberation on the potential threats that could arise from "lethal autonomous weapons systems."

An Open Letter to the United Nations Convention on Certain Conventional Weapons Excerpt:

"As companies building the technologies in Artificial Intelligence and Robotics that may be repurposed to develop autonomous weapons, we feel especially responsible in raising this alarm. We warmly welcome the decision of the UN's Conference of the Convention on Certain Conventional Weapons (CCW) to establish a Group of Governmental Experts (GGE) on Lethal Autonomous Weapon Systems. Many of our researchers and engineers are eager to offer technical advice to your deliberations.

Lethal autonomous weapons threaten to become the third revolution in warfare. Once developed, they will permit armed conflict to be fought at a scale greater than ever, and at timescales faster than humans can comprehend. These can be weapons of terror, weapons that despots and terrorists use against innocent populations, and weapons hacked to behave in undesirable ways. We do not have long to act. Once Pandora's box is opened, it will be hard to close. We therefore implore the High Contracting Parties to find a way to protect us all from these dangers."

MARK ZUCKERBERG VERSUS ELON MUSK

Recently, there is a healthy debate going on regarding potential advantages and disadvantages of AI between two powerhouses—Elon Musk of Tesla and Mark Zuckerberg of Facebook. Despite his own role in the advancement of the technology, Elon Musk has long warned that the machines built by humans could one day lead to our destruction. "I think we should be very careful about AI. If I had to guess at what our biggest existential threat is, it's probably that. So we need to be very careful," said Musk. He also stated, "I'm increasingly inclined to think that there should be some regulatory oversight, maybe at the national and international level, just to make sure that we don't do something very foolish. With AI we're summoning the demon." He warned about AI before, tweeting that it could be more dangerous than nuclear weapons. In July 2017, while speaking at the 2017 International Space Station R&D conference, he said that the process of setting up a government body to regulate AI should start in the immediate future.

Facebook founder Mark Zuckerberg, who has frequently chided Musk and is reluctant to solicit government intervention, would argue that "we didn't rush to put rules into place about how airplanes should work before we figured out how they would fly.... I think people who are naysayers and try to drum up these doomsday scenarios—I just, I don't understand it. It's really negative and in some ways I actually think it is pretty irresponsible," Zuckerberg said, according to *Silicon Valley Business Journal*.

He makes a valid point. It seems much too early to begin regulating AI because it would slow down innovation and it's not suitable to regulate AI until you know what you're working on. But AI is not like other inventions. Musk has also thrown shade at Mark Zuckerberg on Twitter, saying that Zuckerberg's understanding of AI is limited.

These are difficult questions to answer while AI is in its development stages—regulations, like those on the automobile and airline industries, are usually applied after something bad has occurred, not in anticipation of a technology becoming dangerous. Issues concerning autonomous vehicles, algorithmic-decision making, and "bots" driving social media require attention by regulators, just as many new technologies do.

The challenge? On the one hand we hear people like Elon Musk say we need to fear AI and then we have folks like Mark Zuckerberg who say we should embrace it. Who do we listen to?

At first glance, it seems strange. The head of Tesla, who has aggressively invested in AI for self-driving cars, is worried about AI and wants bureaucratic regulation? The same CEO of SpaceX who plans on colonizing Mars wants to put the brakes on AI?

There are two sides to AI being discussed today: mid-term effect (Zuckerberg) vs. long-term effect (Musk). The threat of misuse comes with negative human attributes like greed, power, temptation, or just plain evil. What is myth today could easily become reality tomorrow, if policy and planning are not seen as priority in today's technology age. Are we doing enough to stay safe in years to come? Facebook recently found out AI interfaces created their own language, and let's not underestimate the treat of this technology, while we embrace its positive impact with research and development.

Needless to say, Elon Musk has a keen mind and knows a thing or two about technology. It appears he doesn't want to *let the cat out of the bag* but I believe he has access to classified information that has not been disclosed, so that is why he is stating this. If you saw a devastating fire coming, would you whisper for everyone to get to safety or would you sound the alarm.

I believe he wants to raise awareness and establish guard-rails to make sure innovation does not recklessly run away at the detriment of safety, security, and privacy. He is simply raising concerns for ethical development as AI is progressing so fast, that reactive regulation will not be enough. He wants ethical AI. Elon Musk doesn't hate AI, he respects it, understands it better than most, and therefore is publicly showing his concern.

Musk also recently stated, "Artificial Intelligence doesn't scare me... it's human stupidity that does."Zuckerberg is pushing for automation of processes and large-scale analysis. Mega corporations like Facebook (who also own Instagram and WhatsApp) and Google, currently have more data than they know what to do with, so they're desperately trying to churn out an AI that could use this data to produce something beneficial to them. Musk is worried about the singularity and sentient AI's and while Facebook and Google certainly wouldn't mind inventing such a thing, they're more worried about using the data they've acquired to make more money and get more information on people.

While both are brilliant minds and right in many ways, I have to agree with Musk. After all, he is simply suggesting being cautious of AI and putting appropriate regulations in place before it's too late; it doesn't mean he is against moving forward with AI.

REGULATION

Elon Musk has been outspoken about the dangers of AI without regulation. AI is still a relatively new concept, so it's possible to do something legal, yet unethical. For such cautioning to come from somebody working on technological breakthroughs in space exploration, electric vehicle development, and sustainable energy generation, it is unsettling.

"AI's a rare case where we need to be proactive in regulation, instead of reactive. Because by the time we are reactive with AI regulation, it's too late,"—Elon Musk

On August 11, 2017, Musk tweeted, "Nobody likes being regulated, but everything (cars, planes, food, drugs, etc.) that's a danger to the public is regulated. AI should be too."

AI will definitely bring us into a new era and be a big step forward, we cannot ignore that all positive steps forward can also be used against us. We need to be cautious of where and how we integrate AI into daily life in the future. It would be wise to ensure regulation around its use and development. As with any technology, there is an increasing threat of misuse that needs to be addressed, either by having frameworks or policies in place.

With great power comes great responsibility. In the old days, crime was committed by robbing a bank or hijacking a train in the Wild West, for example. These were the days of pointed attack crimes.

Now we are in the age of one person being able to perform lucrative crime at scale. One smart person, or a small team, can disrupt millions (with anonymity I might add). "While humans may be able to stop a runaway algorithm, there would be 'no stopping' a large, centralized AI that calls the shots", Musk argued in a recent interview with Vanity Fair.

Business competition is fierce and the race for innovation often casts aside safety. Putting safeguards in place would allow us to second guess a decision AI is considering before it gets out of control. Marie Curie, the famed chemist, made great advances to modern medicine, with little regulatory oversight, and ultimately died from her discoveries. Nowadays, we don't want just anyone playing around with radioactive isotopes. The same is true for much of the medical and pharmaceutical world where research has boundaries to keep the population safe.

In January 2017, some of the top experts in AI met at a conference in Asilomar, CA. An outcome of this meeting was the set of Asilomar AI Principles. Near the end of January, the Asilomar AI Principles were published in an open letter by the Future of Life Institute (FLI) at Oxford University. The letter includes 23 Principles which represent a partial guide to help ensure that AI is developed beneficially for all. This is noteworthy, but government regulation may be necessary to guarantee that AI scientists and companies follow these principles and others like them.

The topic of impacts of AI should not be treated lightly, or with broad analogies in place of reasoned arguments supported by available evidence. There are legitimate concerns about the possible misuse of AI and since these problems threaten society as a whole, they can't be left to a small group of scientists, technologists or business executives to address. Our future and our children's futures are at stake. We need to make decisions for our families and in our societies to ensure our future freedom. Policy makers need to understand the significant nature of these impacts, and discuss, debate, and prepare for these changes.

DOES AUTOMATION MAKE US HAPPIER?

Almost everything we do is enabled by intelligent machines. Imagine living in a society where everything is done by AI and robots. This could be a golden opportunity for humans to explore and do whatever they seem to enjoy doing; writing poems, books, dancing, music, and so on. But who is going to pay for all of this? An idle mind is a devil's workshop.

How many people are unproductive in our society because they don't have to be? We're warned not to feed the bears in our national parks because the bears get lazy. They lose their will to live a natural productive life. Then they become a nuisance because they demand to be fed. Can you see the parallels?

Automation is dominating the news today. When we have self-driving cars, personal AI assistants, and other more complex AI solutions replacing jobs and our more challenging tasks—will that finally allow us to focus on the present, and be better off?

The pride we had for working hard and earning a living is slowly disappearing, we would rather sit at home watching movies, surfing the internet or playing computer games while those working hard are taxed to support us.

My mother speaks to me of St Lucia, 50 years ago, where she grew up. She says automation has everyone so disconnected. When she was younger, a simple task such as washing clothes was manual, but it was also fun. They would go to a river in Soufriere , then search for some stones and put them in a circle to hand wash the clothes. While doing this they would be sitting on a large stone. Finding the perfect spot was crucial. When they were finished washing, they would put the clothes on short trees to dry. While waiting for this to happen, they would bathe and spend the reminder of time interacting with neighbors and friends by the river. There was no automation but it was such a beautiful happy time.

Studies find that the end-goal of automation actually promotes the act of mis-wanting. In a study conducted by Mihaly Csikszentmihalyi, over 100 workers were asked to monitor their day-to-day activities and happiness. He had them document in detail their tasks, interactions, and emotions. He ultimately discovered that while working, employees felt "fulfilled and happy," whereas on their leisure time they felt "bored and anxious." This was surprising. Many of us believe that leisure time make us happier, since we would enjoy the aspect of not having responsibility. But it doesn't.

Work provides social interaction, a purpose, opportunities for achievement, a feeling of belonging, a (sometimes) healthy routine, and the chance to earn a larger sum of money.

Where will our feeling of accomplishment, hard work, and purpose go, when technology does everything for us?

According to Csikszentmihalyi's research, focusing on these challenging tasks, like building the complex formula for your business plan projections, can bring us into a meditative "flow" that allows for us to "transcend the anxieties" that plague our everyday lives.

Contrary to popular belief, challenging tasks make us feel a sense of accomplishment. If we automate more and more within our daily lives, we could be gearing ourselves more and more toward disappointment; to being unfulfilled with less responsibility, instead of having a purpose and drive behind our daily life.

Across society, the scale and severity of mental health issues is rising. High rates of unemployment are linked to higher rates of substance abuse, domestic violence, child abuse, depression, and just about every other social ill. Many people are addicted to work or their self-worth is connected to their jobs. A person who sits back at home idle may suffer from depression. We must look at addressing mental health challenges and the social problems that will arise. A rational approach would be to invest in mental health programs when the challenge becomes a major problem in 5–10 years' time. There's clearly a cost associated with enabling all these activities but we have to ask ourselves what the risks and potential costs of inaction might be.

CONCLUSION

Within the wild rush to technological development at any cost, are we so blind as to lose sight of the direction to the authentic benefit for humanity? There are realities that move in counter-trend and mould themselves on the fundamentals of true human wellness. Technology can be both a blessing and a curse. When we dig foundations, we destroy fox and hedgehog burrows. When we cut down trees, we destroy bird and squirrel nests. Just because we can, doesn't mean that we should. I am not concerned about the technological and innovation aspects of AI and robotics. I am more concerned about the reasons and rationality of their mass-production.

Artificial intelligence is a powerful tool for decision-making but that's also why it's dangerous, says Bridgewater founder Ray Dalio. In an interview he stated, we're nearing a point where, "the computer gets to come up with the algorithm" instead of humans. He further explains by saying, "When the future is different than the past, it's a risky thing. If you don't have deep understanding, and the future is different than it was in the past, you're going to have a major problem. That's the challenge, that's the two-edged sword of AI, and I think it's threatening." There could be disastrous consequences if machines make decisions without fully grasping a complex situation.

AI will be the last invention humans will ever have to make, believes Oxford researcher Nick Bostrom. In building this new world, humanity could end up crafting its own demise, fears Bostrom. A surprising number of people seem to be getting their ideas about AI from Hollywood science fiction movies. Movie plots feature robots increasing in intelligence until they take over the human race. I don't believe this is the case. There are enough real and present dangers to worry about, from biased ML models to willfully evil human beings. But intelligence without conscience can be dangerous.

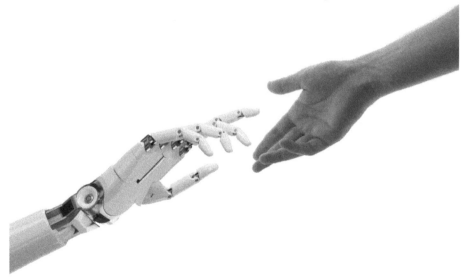

AI: Its intelligence is just artificial. The truth is AI is never going to replicate man's consciousness, because God breathed the spirit of self-awareness into mankind. There is no need to hype and scare people from AI. A program code will never replicate what God created, no matter how sophisticated. They are tools. An imitation of a fearfully and wonderfully created living breathing soul. It cannot feel and has no soul or heart. We cannot infuse life, or spirit into a robot or any other form of artificial life. It is dead, and without man's input it is just scrap metal.

I understand and respect the democratic and ethical life stance of humanism, which affirms that human beings have the right and responsibility to give meaning and shape to their own lives. But regarding humans, and our growing fascination with altered states, we must give pause to the allure of playing God through technology. Science and technology have no moral or social consciousness drivers. Developments in science and technology have been greatly influenced by ego, competitive pressures, and a simplistic belief in progress. Many scientific "advances" involve side-effects, or trade-offs (typically mass scale impacts on other people); they are not absolute advances, but often shift the problem around: "solving" one issue by creating another. Furthermore, science and technology are instruments that are easily and routinely incorporated into abuses of power—social, economic, and political.

I have to say, after looking at the dualistic nature of man, capable of so much beauty and yet so much pain, that a machine endowed with the ability to respond in a "human" way to people and events, could be both beneficial and destructive.

AI, robots, and autonomous machines are causing concern especially when you couple them with the amount of data, "smart" homes/phones/appliances will soon know about us. We want decision making machines (operating without detailed oversight) to do everything for us as soon as possible (ASAP). Evolution isn't just occurring on a biological scale anymore, and we are pushing the race toward our own destruction. More and more humans look for ways to make our lives easier and by doing so give up the ability to take care of ourselves. We need to make sure AI operates as our servant and not our master.

Even without the killer robots, or hackers, AI could conceivably cause an apocalyptic event. It's a "race" to develop new technologies which leave no time for studying the dangers; everything from neural interfaces to powerful robots to AGI powered by quantum computing; there's as much confusion about these dangers as there was/is about global warming. We must carefully start analysing the true impact and build in safeguards for humans to be able to intervene if situations with autonomous machines so demands. It is not the technology which will be our demise but rather our negligence in driving the technology.

The United Nations Interregional Crime and Justice Research Institute (UNICRI) is opening new centre in Netherlands to monitor artificial intelligence and predict possible threats. "If societies do not adapt quickly enough, this can cause instability," UNICRI senior strategic adviser Irakli Beridze told the Dutch newspaper de Telegraaf. "One of our most important tasks is to set up a network of experts from business, knowledge institutes, civil society organizations and governments. We certainly do not want to plead for a ban or a brake on technologies."

The benefits of AI are numerous, but so are the disadvantages. However, like all other advances in science and technology it is a double-edged sword and must be used with prudence. Given the current progress, the potential power, and the stakes at hand, a cautious approach is logical. AI can help solve many problems but if you have people consumed by selfishness, greed and hate at the forefront, it will be a losing battle. The current simplistic conversation doesn't help solve our current and future problems but exacerbates it. We can't put the genie back in the bottle once it's out. If we don't have healthy, deep conversations about the risks of AI, we will paint a false picture.

SECTION TWO

LEADERSHIP IN THE AGE OF DISRUPTION

CHAPTER FIVE

WILL AI REPLACE LEADERS?

Jack Ma, founder of the Alibaba Group, stated that CEOs are soon to be replaced with AI. "In 30 years a robot will likely be on Time magazine as the best CEO." Speaking at a China Entrepreneur Club conference, he warned that AI and robotics should be developed to complement humans in the workplace and not as a replacement.

An Accenture study argues the following:

- ➤ Many routine basic administrative coordination and control tasks such as resource allocation, reporting, and scheduling will be done by AI;

- ➤ The managers who still do remain in organizations will need to demonstrate what Accenture calls "judgment work," in interaction with AI;

- ➤ AI will allow managers to implement and emphasize a "people first" strategy, as AI will be able to handle all the other tasks;

- ➤ AI sophistication will expand into many HR functions. For example, Jobaline, a job-placement site, uses intelligent voice analysis algorithms to evaluate job applicants. The algorithm assesses paralinguistic elements of speech, such as tone and inflection, predicts which emotions a specific voice will elicit, and identifies the type of work at which an applicant will likely excel.

Professor Peter Cappelli, director of Wharton's Center for Human Resources, argues robot bosses are no substitute for human bosses. "It is possible for software to provide sophisticated information (i.e. 'Here is how you are doing'). But management is still a much more complicated task of making adjustments to the work being performed in order to meet changing demands, diagnosing problems and offering solutions."

A recent McKinsey Global Institute report found that up to 25% of the work undertaken by a CEO could now be automated. "We estimate that about 25% of CEOs' time is currently spent on activities that machines could do, such as analyzing reports and data to inform decisions." In the PwC Digital IQ Survey, 72% of business executives said they believe AI will provide the business advantage of the future. And, 67% of executives expect AI to help humans and machines work together more effectively.

AI presents significant challenges for managers and executives, forcing them to reconsider and redefine their own roles. As collaboration among human employees and machines increases, everything from the division of labor, training, and performance management will have to change.

Robotic or computer software managers may seem farfetched but, in recent years, a surprising array of managerial functions has been turned over to AI. Computers are sorting resumes of job seekers for relevant experience and to estimate how long a potential employee is likely to stay. They are recording email exchanges, phone calls, and even spontaneous hallway interactions to track workflow and recommend changes. Widely used software is analyzing customer data for algorithms, which in turn is changing when and where workers are deployed. The ethical question of constant monitoring of employees' movements and actions by robots and software programs remains a prickly issue for policy makers.

Nonetheless, can software substitute for the responsibilities of senior managers in their roles at the top of today's biggest corporations? I can't see that AI will replace a CEO, but it will surely help the CEO. AI can amass and interrupt data superfast. Business leaders must know what data is relevant, and more important, what questions to ask to get relevant data. AI will make suggestions, but someone has to make the decision to implement those suggestions. In some activities, particularly when it comes to finding answers to problems, software already surpasses even the best managers but senior managers are far from obsolete. In the future, we may see some lower-level managers be replaced or consolidated in the name of AI. There's no question that with the rapid advances in automation, robotics and AI will spell the doom for many white collar and blue collar jobs in the coming years. Middle management will not escape this disruptive trend. Disruption continues, and all levels of management cannot escape some impact. However, only well defined (structured) jobs can be taken over by AI. The main role of management has always been to enforce protocol and make decisions for others in the organization. AI is already being used to make decisions as who to hire or how to assemble the most effective teams.

Sidney Finkelstein, professor of strategy and leadership at the Tuck School of Business at Dartmouth, argues, "The sad truth is that middle management is on its way to becoming virtually extinct. While there will always be some people supervising the work of other people, changes in technology, business culture and demographics are all conspiring to upend what has long been standard practice in companies. We should no longer expect traditional job ladders for managers to move up the ranks, or even retaining the notion that middle managers are the glue that connects workers and ensures goal alignment up and down the hierarchy."

AI will take over some technical aspects of the job so managers will have more time to coach, mentor, and interact with employees. These human-driven principles play such an important role in an organization's success as they can boost employee engagement and commitment. Even some functions of the jobs of senior executives will be affected. Both the nature of the jobs and the individuals that occupy them will need to focus much more on creative and social skills than the traditional technical skills that will soon be handled by AI. However, for leadership roles, where judgment, creativity, and experience are so important, there is no imminent threat of replacement. Humans will still be required to do the jobs that require emotional intelligence, critical, and innovative thinking. These skills that a good CEO possesses cannot easily be replaced by technology.

Great managers are great in part because of their exceptional ability to craft intelligent, strategic decisions based upon available information that their employees can execute upon. Those executives will have to emphasize their creative abilities, their leadership skills, and their strategic thinking to a much greater degree. Managers in the AI era will need high social intelligence to collaborate effectively in teams and networks.

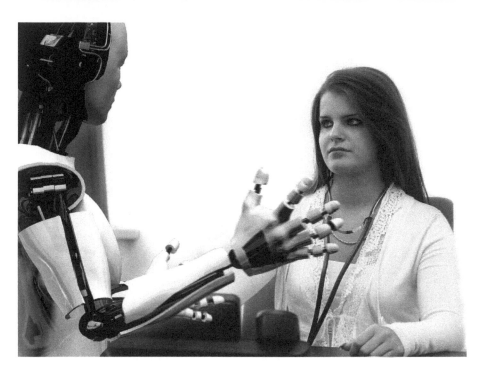

AI will never be able to match the emotion and human aspects of real leaders. This is both good and bad—machines make decisions based on algorithms which can eliminate human error. For less-effective managers, whose main purpose is just to make decisions and sign time-cards, AI could be a realistic replacement because they already aren't doing anything that a computer can't do. Additionally, no board of directors wants a robot reporting to them if something goes wrong. They want a human who can be held accountable and answer questions when results don't go as planned.

AI presents challenges for traditional management. The world of work will become more fluid, with less hierarchy. How can you persuade your team to trust AI? Or, to accept a robot as a team member or manager? A study from the Human-Computer Interaction Lab at the University of Manitoba in Winnipeg, Canada, suggests that you'll probably obey a robot boss nearly as predictably as you would a human boss.

"Even after trying to avoid the task or engaging in arguments with the robot, participants still (often reluctantly) obeyed its commands," the researchers wrote. "These findings highlight that robots can indeed pressure people to do things they would rather not do, supporting the need for ongoing research into obedience to robotic authorities."

A study conducted by MIT's Computer Science and Artificial Intelligence Lab showed how groups of two humans and one robot worked together in one of three conditions: in one, all tasks allocated by robots; in a second group, one human allocates tasks to self, and a robot allocates tasks to other human, and in the third group all tasks allocated by a human. The fully autonomous condition of tasks being allocated by robots proved to be not only the most efficient for the task, but also the method preferred by human workers.

AI is quickly becoming mainstream for the largest corporations. And while no one can argue with the benefits AI can/will confer on humanity, there's also peril. As Ma said, "...unlike human CEOs, they will not be swayed by petty emotions." To me, it's these "petty emotions" that make us human and a lack thereof should be cause for concern. AI has no gut instinct. How can a machine grasp the human emotional aspect of performance? No robot is ever going to feel that it's not right to lay off his faithful 52-year-old employee after working for him for 26 years because he knows that this is all he has to live for.

Although it is hard to predict precisely which companies will dominate in the new environment, a general principle is clear. This means leaders will need to keep pace with advances in data analytics, ML and AI. Leaders and managers will need to be empathetic and maintain open communication to keep the human component central. The most agile and adaptable companies and executives will thrive. Organizations that can rapidly sense and respond to opportunities will seize the advantage in the AI-enabled landscape. So the successful strategy is to be willing to experiment and learn quickly. Over the next decade, AI won't replace CEOs, but CEOs who use AI will replace those who don't.

So what should leaders do?

AI and automation is prompting questions about the future of work and how we can navigate to the "next horizon". A report by MIT published in *Sloan Review* makes this statement: "An inevitable shift in which a parent-to-child way of looking at the relationship between the manager and his or her team would be questioned and ultimately superseded by an adult-to-adult form." When technology enables leaders to have more information about the organization and its employees, this facilitates smarter decision making.

Focus on the human dimension

Many jobs are being automated. Whilst this undoubtedly boosts productivity, leaders must be mindful of how this may impact employees. This is why it's essential to focus on the human dimension. There is a growing risk that companies will become over dependent on technology and neglect the value of humans. We need to invest in employees to raise everyone's digital literacy so they can function effectively in the new AI workplace. Don't reduce employees to mere algorithms. Careful decisions about which roles and functions to automate should guide AI strategy in business. A simple *"bottom line"* approach will compromise the human element and could erode engagement over time. How will employees respond when their jobs are changed or eliminated? Emotional intelligence is going to be brought into even sharper relief as job descriptions are drastically transformed in the next few years with the rise of automation, AI, and robotics. It is important to show compassion and support to employees displaced by new technology. Leaders need to diversify their team to include both experienced and creative individuals. With a balanced team, you'll have a greater balance between grounding and vision, and optimize your AI efforts with better judgment.

Ultimately, the future of work and the future of society are deeply entwined. Our sense of place in society, our worth, and our contribution are often affected by our work. Anything that starts to disrupt work and individual identity is going to have far-reaching impacts. The growth of automation and AI in the workplace makes it important for managers to interact with employees for them to feel valued and that their contribution matters. With the transition to AI we must be mindful to keep working on employee engagement. Engagement refers to an emotional commitment to an organization and its goals. Many companies are using AI to understand the sentiments of employees and to work on keeping them motivated. Studies have proven there is a correlation between engagement and performance. While AI increases productivity through automation, the flip side is the number of people engaged in that work will decrease. Talent Solutions found that 42% of job switchers stated they might have stayed with previous employers had they had better opportunities, benefits, recognition, and rewards.

Managers are instrumental in encouraging employees and improving their levels of engagement. A 2016 Gallup survey identified some key elements, which are important to having effective and productive workers. Employee engagement rises when:

- They have opportunities to use their skills and talents
- They receive regular recognition or praise
- They believe someone at work cares about them
- Someone at work encourages their development
- Their ideas count
- Someone talks to them about their progress

Employees want to know they matter in the vast sea of data and algorithms. In this new age of AI, managers need to make employees know they are valued and their contributions count. Because there are so many areas where employees may experience issues with engagement, it may be helpful for managers to have a conversation with them. Additionally, as many roles become automated, managers must be aware remaining employees may face fear of being replaced or survivor's guilt. Either way, it takes empathy to handle this effectively. Leaders must know the importance of emotions and feelings because these influence how employees perform and the choices they make. To create improved engagement, employers should focus on communication, purpose, meaningful work, recognition and appreciation, and growth and development opportunities. A new Department of Humanity can be instituted to facilitate this aspect of personal development to ensure that businesses make the most of the relationship between personal and artificial intelligence.

The inevitable takeover of jobs by AI, robots, and automation is upon us. But we, as leaders need to adapt and embrace these changes, but at the same time be aware that the future of leadership may mean some of our job functions being handled by AI.

CHAPTER SIX

ETHICAL LEADERSHIP: A MORAL COMPASS FOR TURBULENT TIMES

We live in a world in which the line between right and wrong seems blurred. Many leaders speak of embracing ethical leadership. Yet what we see more often is greed and an appetite for power and disregard of ethical absolutes. The challenges we face today are for the most part rooted in failures of leadership—leaders operating without a moral compass. Our leadership crisis is due to overestimating the importance of competencies and technology, and discounting the critical importance of relational and ethical leadership. An erosion of core values threatens both business and society at large. A company will assume the standards and ethics of its leaders. Therefore, having a business leader with a strong moral compass is essential for success.

"Ethics" comes from the Greek word *ethikos* from *ethos*, which means "custom" or "habit." Ethics are generally understood as moral principles that govern a person's or group's behavior. They are crucial to the way we live and work. They are our guiding principles as we relate to the world around us.

Trust in leaders is at an all-time low, especially with the self-seeking interests and lack of transparency. I've lost count on how many articles and posts I've read that had the need for ethical leadership in their headlines. In the digital era, we need leaders who have a certain moral compass that enables them to consider the ethics of constantly advancing technologies and what this means for the millions of people who will inevitably be left in the dark.

Things such as AI are primarily driven by capitalist competition rather than how helpful the technology would be. If we, as a race, don't start reconciling our value based differences, no amount of regulation will control AI evolution. Companies pay lip service to ethics and often pay it no heed in their relentless pursuit of profit.

In February 2017, the Harvard Institute of Politics, at the JFK Jr. Forum, hosted a conversation on the past, present, and future of Artificial Intelligence. The discussion focused on the potential benefits as well as some of the major ethical dilemmas of AI. Professors Alex Pentland and Cynthia Dwork stated that as AI proliferates, moral conflicts can surface. Pentland highlighted that citizens must ask themselves, "Is this something that is performing in a way that we as a society want?" Pentland indicated that our society must continue a dialogue around ethics and determine what is right.

In January 2017, IBM developed the Principles for Transparency and Trust in the Cognitive Era, a document that is useful for any organization involved in the development of AI systems. The core of these principles include:

- ❖ The purpose of AI and cognitive systems developed and applied by IBM is to augment human intelligence.

- ❖ We will be transparent about the major sources of data and expertise that inform the insights of cognitive solutions, as well as the methods used to train those systems and solutions.

- ❖ We believe clients own their own business models and intellectual property.

- ❖ We will work to help students, workers, and citizens acquire the skills to engage securely and effectively in a relationship with cognitive systems, and to perform the new kinds of jobs that will emerge in a cognitive economy.

Ethical Leadership has been described as "having core values and the courage to act on them on behalf of the common good." It is leadership driven by respect for ethical beliefs and values and for the dignity and rights of others. It is based on integrity, fairness, trust, consideration, and the sharing of power.

Ethical leadership program begins with this focus on "the other"; serving the other and creating a context where employees know there are clear consequences for putting self-interests first. Ethics ultimately is fundamental to healthy democracy and capitalism and that's why the work goes on as we know it must.

> "To educate a man in mind and not in morals is to educate a menace to society."—Theodore Roosevelt

The financial crisis of 2007–2008 revealed there is a higher need for ethical leaders and transparency in business processes. Unethical conduct among politicians and business leaders dominate headlines. Even those who we think should know better are succumbing to vices. As a result, we have grown increasingly skeptical. Whether a single lapse of integrity and/or as a continuous way of doing business, unethical leadership behavior has the power to ruin a career and to totally destroy an organization. When integrity is destroyed, confidence is lost. Unethical behavior does not occur in a vacuum. Such leaders leave a trail of destruction and many people are hurt and livelihoods are destroyed in the process. At Enron, 20,000 staff suddenly lost their jobs through no fault of their own.

Even with changing times and technologies, the fundamentals of ethics remains the same. Today, ethical leadership is now the new source of differentiation and competitive advantage. An ethical leader does not focus merely on profit but acting ethically over revenues.

Companies must have clear guidelines on ethical conduct.

  ➤ Be Transparent. Subsequent policies for collection and use of end user data should be transparent, understandable, enforceable, and updated when necessary.

  ➤ Fiduciary responsibilities. As business people, we have an ethical duty to further the interests of our employers and shareholders.

➤ Level playing field. Free markets are efficient, but they aren't always fair. People often prosper or get hurt through no fault of their own. Free markets means the *opportunities* are equal. We shouldn't discriminate or exclude anyone.

➤ Aiding and abetting. If you know someone else is acting unethically and you don't act against it, then you are just as guilty as they are.

Some of the blatant examples seen around us:

❖ Reporting wrong financials (Bernard Madoff, Enron, and Worldcom for example)

❖ Allowing your team to recommend the wrong services or products to customers (have you ever witnessed this as a customer or supplier?)

❖ Manipulating data prior to decisions

❖ Hiding information or over estimating the gains intentionallyAnd the list goes on and on.

The extent to which you are perceived as a consistently trustworthy leader affects:

➤ Brand image—Less risk of fines or legal action. If you do what you're supposed to be doing and don't cover things up, it's much less likely that you'll misstep and find yourself being slapped with a fine or legal action of some kind.

➤ Reputation—Companies that practice good ethical behaviors tend to be known as good companies. That kind of reputation sticks to your brand.

➤ Quality of relationships with suppliers, investors, and creditors.

➤ Ability to retain and attract talented employees—Employees today aren't just looking for a job to earn money and climb the ladder. You aren't going to keep good, talented employees with shady, underhanded schemes. You'll keep them with open, honest, ethical decisions.

> ➤ Attract loyal customers—As mentioned above, people enjoy doing business with businesses they trust. They'll be loyal to you because they like the way you do business. Along with that, studies have shown that businesses that adhere to ethical codes of conduct also tend to do better financially. Ability to build trust and respect from all business partners, government bodies, and consumer advocate groups.

There are two critical components of integrity. The first is the adherence to an ethical principle. This isn't simply compliance to a law or a rule; it implies an understanding of the reason it exists. The second is the pursuit of an established standard.

Ethical Leadership means:

- Leading by example. It can be likened to a parent/child relationship. You cannot set policies that employees need to live by and not live by them yourself
- Standing up for what is right
- Keeping your word. Being reliable. Keeping promises, meeting important deadlines, and being there when people need you
- Expressing concern for the common good
- Being honest when no one is looking
- Doing the honorable thing, even when it's not popular
- Loyalty under temptation or duress
- Never compromising on a principle even when encouraged to
- Making fair decisions
- Communicating honestly
- Giving credit where it's due
- Displaying consistency in your words and actions
- Treating everyone with respect

It also means all employees, whether locally or internationally, should be treated fairly and paid equally. It also includes minimizing the use of child labor as well as refusing to do business with oppressive countries and engaging in fair trade practices. It also involves ethical marketing practices such as not trying to manipulate or falsely advertise to potential customers. Ethical practice seeks to make sure that all stakeholders receive fair treatment. There is evidence that the ethical conduct of companies exerts a growing influence on the purchasing decisions of customers.

These guiding principles should penetrate our motives, our secret intentions, and our lives. If one follows them just for outward display, this means nothing. The desire must be present within.

"Don't be evil" and "focus on the user and all else will follow" were two oft-repeated aphorisms in Google's product management vernacular and was part of the executives' drumbeat. There are actually several kinds of "evil" here...the evil use of the data, the evil gathering of the data, the evil evolution of an algorithm programmed to learn, the evil decision based to the data gathered...regardless how they were gathered. These sayings influenced the way Google built its products and provided simple mnemonics for Google's values. The "Don't be evil" mantra has now been elucidated recently, especially for AI by the Future of Life Institute in the 23 Asilomar AI Principles. I believe this is why Google quickly offloaded Boston Dynamics because their robotics development ('nightmare' robots) was not in line with this philosophy.

> *"If moral behavior were simply following rules, we could program a computer to be moral."*—Samuel P. Ginder

It all comes down knowing your leadership purpose. It begins by asking yourself the following question. "Why do I want to lead?" Is it the money, prestige, position or is it about people and making a positive difference. You must have the ability to identify and reflect on what you stand for, what your values are, and what matters most to you, then it becomes much easier to know what to do in any given situation. Purpose provides a rationale for all decisions and values guide ethical choices.It's important to set your standards early on. Most individuals don't start out being unethical. Compromise a little here and there and before you know it, the tree of stained character is full-grown. Leadership is tough, particularly when it involves complex issues in today's ever-changing technical, political, and economic climate. The importance of ethical leadership needs to be emphasized, revisited, and taught to seasoned as well as upcoming leaders.

ACCOUNTABILITY

A politician denies a matter on television when asked, only to have to try to clarify what he meant the next week as the truth comes out. Another elected official has over 60% of their statements documented as "not true." Today, we have people occupying leadership roles who simply are not up to the task. It would be refreshing to see a leader stand up and say, "I made a mistake and I take full responsibility," without ANY excuses (no ifs or buts). Human nature is always looking for someone else to blame for its troubles. 'Blame' is a comfortable security blanket. I remember 10 years ago being taught the importance of understanding the "A-R-A" triangle—Accountability, Responsibility, and Authority, with the emphasis on understanding the importance of accountability. Times change, principles don't. Accountability is important for effective leadership. It shows strength and reveals character and is exactly why there are so few real leaders today. Leaders who value integrity and authenticity hold themselves responsible for the decisions they have made and accept the consequences of their actions or lack of it. Effective leaders not only accept accountability but they instill it in others. They do not deflect blame and point fingers when things go wrong but rather face the music and seek to make things right. What is behind poor leadership accountability? In many instances, leaders put their own self-interest ahead of those they serve, and then rationalize their behavior. Accountability builds trust and creates respect between leaders and their followers. In order for any organization to have full trust, each leader themselves must be open to being held to account for their actions and attitudes. Leadership behaviors drive engagement, retention, performance, and innovation—for better or for worse. Good leadership is good business. Every one of us can do with an extra dose of humility and self-awareness to remind us that we're not always the great business leaders we think we are.

When leaders take personal accountability, they are willing to answer for the outcomes of their choices, their behaviors, and their actions in all situations in which they are involved. Accountable leaders do not blame others when things end up chaotic. Rather, they make things right—they are fixers.

While most leaders are measured on the basis of business results, organizations must begin holding leaders accountable for building a strong and enduring culture and engaging and retaining their teams. According to a study, *Global Human Capital Trends* 2015 by Deloitte University Press, "Our research indicates that the transformation of the aging performance management process is long overdue."

With the onset on AI and robots replacing the workforce, there is overall distrust of leadership and management. The importance of trust to leadership cannot be overstated especially in an age of unprecedented complexity and uncertainty. The more challenging the situation the more urgent it is that you behave in a trustworthy manner. People are looking to you. It's your chance to show them who you really are when the pressure is on. Good intentions are never enough, especially if they're based in self-interest. Accountability is about personal ownership for the results in one's world—on an individual and organizational level.

Consider the Impact: Your decisions aren't usually just affecting you. They're also affecting your employees, your family, your shareholders, your customers, your partners…the list goes on. What impact would an unethical decision have on all of those people?

Are you accountable for your decisions?

Do you hide behind ambiguity and obscurity? Or, do you take ownership of the problem?Accountability a misunderstood concept. Most people attribute accountability to consequences, usually we hear about accountability when things go wrong or when we are looking for someone to blame. We mistakenly believe that accountability can and must be forced. At the end of the day, it is ourselves who choose to be accountable or not. It is a choice, it's the understanding that the quality of our choices determine the quality of our lives and that of others. Accountability comes from inside. It can be scary to be accountable as we are forced to confront the truth no matter how ugly or difficult it is. We can't change anything until we take ownership. Accountability is taking responsibility. Responsibility is not blame. Responsibility is future and action focused. Blame is past focused and is more about isolating people or making them feel bad than it is about accountability. Guilt and fear are not a proper basis for developing accountability. Holding ourselves accountable is the only way to shift our focus automatically from blame to responsibility, from problem to solution.

Too many times the concept of accountability is a very one-sided mind-set. Leaders are quick to hold others accountable and deflect the blame. For your employees to be invested in you, you must be invested in them and they must know it. Management in major corporations don't feel they owe anything to their employees, but owe everything to the shareholders and the upper management. Choose to look out for, and take care of, your team. It's not about you. It's about everyone else. It's important to note that employees in today's companies are very observant. They're plugged into their leaders' behavior and they're paying attention. For the most part, they can spot a half-truth or an attempt to deflect blame. AI is bringing big changes. Be honest with employees. When the safety of their jobs, or their team members, seems at stake they want to know the truth. Choose to ease their worries off by saying this: "I'm aware of how dire this is. I'm owning it. I've got a plan to address it. AI will bring many solutions as well as problems."

When you believe in accountability, it doesn't matter whose "fault" it is. You take ownership of situations that you're directly or indirectly involved in. You don't blame others if things go wrong. Instead, you do your best to make things right. Frankly, no matter how big or small your role was in creating the situation you're facing, as the leader, it's your job to take at least part of the responsibility. And as soon as possible. It shows integrity and defines a great leader from a good leader. Owning and addressing an issue with accountability is key to success in every aspect of life, both professionally and personally. Success is the result of accountability and owning our choices.

Accountability is a pillar upon which a leader establishes credibility. Most importantly, accountability is a leader's best weapon in the fight against vulnerability, against unethical behavior. A company that has a history of acting in a socially responsible way, will have a better chance of recovery from crisis, they will likely suffer less reputational damage during and after the incident. (Padgett, Cheng, & Parekh, 2013).

Consider how James Burke of Johnson & Johnson deftly handled the Tylenol tampering of 1981. Burke placed consumers first by recalling 31 million bottles of Tylenol capsules from store shelves and offering replacement product in the safer tablet form, free of charge. The move cost Johnson & Johnson more than $100 million. He focused on keeping people safe first, and profits second. Burke received the Presidential Medal of Freedom from President Bill Clinton in 2000. In 2003, Fortune magazine named him one of history's 10 greatest CEOs. Taking 100% accountability allows you to engage, communicate, understand, and resolve conflicts. Choose to be accountable in order to give and do your best for yourself, your people, and the organization.

Promoting a culture that is based on the foundation of trust means we truly have to challenge our own needs for control and to examine our willingness to be open. When employees observe that their leaders and managers are only protecting themselves, they will never trust them. A good leader always takes responsibility for failures but gives credit for success to their team.

A CULTURE OF ACCOUNTABILITY

It's important for you to make time to reflect on the state of leadership accountability within your own organization. So how can we drive a culture of accountable leadership into our organizations? A study by the Institute for Corporate Productivity, titled *Creating a High-Performance Culture*, suggests that encouraging self-awareness and transparency are the keys to success at both the organizational and individual leader level.

1 **Start at the top.** Principles matter, yet they cannot be just words on paper, mandated from the top and not followed by a company's leaders, which is what occurred with the ethics policies that Enron, Citigroup, Wells Fargo, and countless others proclaimed they had.

2 **Model the behavior you want others to follow.** Today's organizations want leadership accountability not just in the present but in the decades that follow. Some of the best leaders are the ones most respected in their industry. They are known to serve, develop others, and are authentic. While they hold others accountable, they allow themselves to be held to the same standard, and sometimes even a higher one.

3 **Set clear goals and expectations.** You can't create a culture of accountability unless you first clarify expectations and authority. Our first step to creating a culture of accountability is to define clear results within the organization, and within each department. Without clarity around outcomes, no one can be accountable. Everyone must know what they're working for and how their job pushes the company forward. Without accountability, objectives become vague.

4 Consistent follow up. Managers are great at coming up with goals, strategies, even metrics. Unfortunately, they're also notoriously bad at following up. If an employee knows they are not going to be held accountable, then what is the incentive to finish a project on time and on budget? The result is mediocre projects, services, and firm profits. Companies must have a relatively objective and consistent process for both setting and employee performance.

5 Give and receive feedback. A famous study on leadership-development programs led by Marshall Goldsmith and Howard Morgan in 2004, found that leaders who gain self-awareness through a 360-degree assessment process, and then followed up with their colleagues regarding their own leadership development challenges and priorities, were seen to be far more effective as leaders by both their peers and direct reports. Even in the absence of a formal organization driven process, encouraging informal—but scheduled—conversations between managers and key stakeholders is key. A defensive or negative response of any kind sends a clear message that we don't actually want honest feedback, or that we aren't able to handle it.

Failure is a prerequisite for innovation. "The fastest way to succeed," IBM's Thomas Watson Sr., once said, "is to double your failure rate." The growing acceptance of failure is changing the way companies approach innovation. However, distinguishing between excusable and inexcusable failure is crucial. Some mistakes are unpardonable, for example, producing and marketing a dysfunctional product caused by poor quality control. Encouraging failure doesn't mean abandoning supervision or respect for sound practices. Managing for failure requires leaders to be more engaged, not less.

Transparent systems and procedures

If we want leadership accountability to become part of the fabric of the organizational culture, we must put organizational systems in place to facilitate honest feedback or detect negative leadership behaviors early and address these accordingly. We must also provide safe pathways by which team members can share honest feedback with their leaders.

Accountability at all levels

A 2012 article by the *Harvard Business Review* said: "By far and away the single-most shirked responsibility of executives is holding people accountable. No matter how tough a game they may talk about performance, when it comes to holding people's feet to the fire, leaders step back from the heat." Accountability of people at all levels is very important for any organization to be successful. The best way to hold everyone accountable is through mutual respect and leading by example from the top down. It takes a strong leader to not only hold themselves accountable, but to hold others as well. We need to always hold each other accountable. Unfortunately, most employees view accountability as something that happens when performance declines, problems develop, or results fail to meet targets. This is because, historically, accountability has been used as a discipline tool. No one asks, "Who is responsible for all this success?" We ask, "Who dropped the ball?"

Storytelling (Case studies)—Very often when we think of ethics we think of laws or explicit statements governing individuals and their relationships to the larger community. Yet an important source for ethical principles can be found in stories and case studies. In reality, in most cultures, we learn about how we should live by listening to stories. The business world is full of case studies. (Kenneth Lay—Enron, Bernard Ebbers—Worldcom, Dennis Kozlowski—Tyco, etc.) The best way to internalize ethics is knowing the principles and then seeing them applied in real life.

Three steps in personal accountability:

1 Awareness. This means noticing patterns of behavior and weaknesses that are unhelpful. It's about being aware of what's not working in your business.

2 **Acknowledgement.** This means actually recognizing those things. You won't take accountability if you do not acknowledge the current state of things. This goes beyond self-awareness because you can have awareness and be in denial.

3 Once you have **both awareness** and acknowledgement you can achieve the third step— **Acceptance.** This is taking personal ownership of things and situations.

Consequences of Lack of Ownership and Accountability

The severity of this problem across business principles manifests in 3 ways:

1 **The business suffers:** This can be costly to a business. Costs reveal themselves in the form of lower profits, plummeting customer satisfaction, and an eroding culture. Businesses who struggle in this area are further exposed when it comes to growth and innovation. Since those efforts require typically more risk and less "silos," cultures with an accountability problem will find delivering against growth goals even more difficult.

2 **Trust suffers:** This leads to a culture of distrust. An ethical leader is one who has concern for those they lead. People are far more ready to endure hardship and challenge if they are certain that the leader is acting in ways that are unselfish and ethically grounded.

3 **You suffer:** It also disallows consistency and joy in one's work. You'll be left on your own because you won't have the full support of your team. All you will have over them is authority.

All around us, we see exploitation and a gradual descent toward dissolution. In fact, the second law of thermodynamics tells us that the physical world is decaying and that the direction of all creation is downward. If we do not apply a proactive counter-effort in life and business, the natural course of events will lead us to drift downstream like a raft in a river. Additionally, as the river flows downward, it widens. There is no telling where one could end up. In a startlingly short amount of time, small compromises can transform the ethical foundation of an organization.

DEVELOPING YOUR MORAL COMPASS:

1 **Reflection and self-awareness is crucial.** Character building is the most important work. The character is not transferable. It cannot be bought or sold; it is to be acquired. Accountability can open up powerful learning opportunities. Take time to reflect. Leaders must always be alert and self-aware. Find some quiet time alone to listen to that inner still small voice. Spend some time at the end of each day running through these simple questions:

> ➢ Was I being true to myself?
>
> ➢ Were my actions in line with my values?
>
> ➢ What could I have done differently today?

As a leader, one of your most important jobs is to communicate clearly the business core values so they serve as the moral compass for the organization. Make sure you are also following those values. Know what you stand for and never compromise principles. If something has gone wrong and you were responsible, you need to take ownership and sincerely apologize. Be honest. When people lie, they cannot be accountable. Absence of accountability leads to chaos and then anything goes.

2 Have a person who will hold you accountable. A friend, coworker, or a family member. Someone who will be honest with you. Or have a leader whose qualities you would like to emulate. In building our leadership lives, we benefit from looking at some role models who are a good example. Remember no one is perfect. People make mistakes. But we need a model; someone who personifies the goals we have set for ourselves, who has travelled the path before us, and to whom we can look for wise counsel. As we dedicate and submit ourselves to service, we must be changed into the image of true leadership. For example, my role model for ethical and servant leadership is Jesus Christ. Usually when I ask students, in my presentations at schools, who are their role models many name politicians or celebrities of questionable character. Most don't see lying as bad if it doesn't physically hurt anyone. If these are our future leaders and they accept poor behavior as the norm, then what will leadership look like in the future? As a society, we need to place a higher metric on ethical behavior when electing leaders.

3 Find activities that can keep you on the right path. For me it's sermons. This keeps my moral compass grounded. I never get complacent and feel I am perfect. You always have to keep working on yourself. All of us are bombarded with the thinking of others. The news is just full of politics and negative events. There is so much noise around which can cloud your reasoning. For me, at the end of the day, it's refreshing to tune out and take in God's Word. It is spiritually uplifting, plus it reminds a leader we are part of something much bigger than our own ambitions.

4 Have a useful decision making framework that works for you. Some useful ethical decision-making tests to consider:

175

> ➤ The Golden Rule Test. Servant leadership makes for ethical decision making. Do unto others as you would have them do unto you. Would you want others to treat you in this way?

> ➤ The Sunlight Test. When your decisions are brought into the full light, would you be comfortable if your actions were televised on the news tomorrow?

> ➤ The Good Society Test. It's about creating a better world. Will this decision result in making the world a better place?

> ➤ The Authority Test. It's including the views of an external authority you admire. What would an important (named) "authority" think of your actions?

> ➤ The Counseling Test. Giving advice to others. What advice would you give to someone in your same situation?

> ➤ The Legacy Test. How will others remember you in future? Does this decision reflect how you want to be remembered?

Virtuous Leaders who practice the six core virtues of courage, temperance, justice, prudence, humanity, and truthfulness, are ethical leaders who find leader happiness, leader life satisfaction, and leader effectiveness. (Hackett & Wang, 2012).

Ethical principles mean nothing at all if you aren't willing to stand up for them. Sometimes that might even mean resigning a position rather than "following orders." A few years ago, I missed out on a huge promotion because I didn't comply with an action from a CEO of my then establishment. He instructed me to hold back a delinquent customer's payment, so their mortgage would be transferred to the non-accrual status, so that his colleague could supposedly submit an offer to purchase this prime property. Reality check: doing the right things may not bring on the welcoming committee, rather you may be beaten for it.

Society longs for leaders of integrity. While most leaders don't engage in fraudulent behavior, many walk in the "grey area." In other words, while they aren't engaging in anything illegal, their behavior can be considered unethical. And, it only takes one small step to cross the line. Ethical leaders function within both the letter and the "spirit" of the law. The further up the corporate ladder you go, the deeper your roots must be planted. Always be firmly grounded when it comes to integrity. The branches of growing trees, not only reach higher, but their roots grow deeper. Strong, deep roots will anchor you firmly when the storms of ethical dilemma intensely blow your way.

Bioethics

Currently scientists don't have clear ethical guidelines to prevent them from inadvertently harming people, says ethicist Jake Metcalf of Data & Society. The official ethics committee known as an institutional review board, or IRB are responsible for critical oversight functions for research conducted on human subjects that are "scientific", "ethical", and "regulatory". However the guidelines governing social experiments are outdated. "The regulations were designed for a very specific type of research harm and a specific set of research methods that simply don't hold for data science," says Metcalf. Machines will reflect the values and principles of its creators. Therefore we need ethical guidelines governing the "social experiments" that companies are running, primarily on unsuspecting individuals who are connected through their devices.

Breakthroughs in genetics helps us to treat and prevent a host of debilitating diseases but it also brings a dilemma. Consider cloning. Dolly the cloned sheep brought huge concerns about the prospect of cloned human beings. Dolly was euthanised on 14 February 2003 because she had severe arthritis and a progressive lung disease. A Finn Dorset such as *Dolly has a life expectancy of 11 to 12 years, but Dolly lived 6.5 years.* In many countries there are laws prohibiting the use of cloning and genetic engineering as methods of human reproduction, and most scientists agree that cloning is unsafe and likely to produce offspring with severe developmental abnormalities. But suppose technology improved to the point where clones were no longer a risks and these procedures had become developmentally safe. Should some technologies be developed in the first place? Because we can, should we?

What about genetic engineering for greater intelligence, stronger bodies or happier moods? In order to tackle the ethics of enhancement, we need to confront the moral issues. Consider four examples: growth-hormone treatment, memory enhancement, muscle enhancement, and reproductive technologies that enable parents to choose the sex and some genetic traits of their children. In most cases what began as an attempt to prevent a genetic disorder or treat a disease has now become an instrument of cosmetic choice that seeks perfection.

In 1969, Robert L. Sinsheimer, a molecular biologist wrote an article titled, "The Prospect of Designed Genetic Change". He argued that freedom of choice would vindicate the new genetics, and set it apart from the discredited eugenics of old.

"To implement the older eugenics ... would have required a massive social programme carried out over many generations. Such a programme could not have been initiated without the consent and co-operation of a major fraction of the population, and would have been continuously subject to social control. In contrast, the new eugenics could, at least in principle, be implemented on a quite individual basis, in one generation, and subject to no existing restrictions."

According to Sinsheimer, "The old eugenics would have required a continual selection for breeding of the fit, and a culling of the unfit," he wrote. "The new eugenics would permit in principle the conversion of all the unfit to the highest genetic level."

When science moves faster than moral understanding this is a sure path to disaster. Some of the developments carry unknown and potentially large risks that science may not be able to quantify. But even if they could, who determines the acceptable amount of risk. This is not something science alone should answer. It is essentially a moral assessment we need to make collectively.

Ethicist Wendell Wallach and Gary Marchant, both scholars in this field, have proposed "governance coordinating committees" that would be created for each major technology sector and serve as honest brokers.

Three key steps to applying ethical principles and moral values to AI:

1. Define your purpose for using AI.

2. Be transparent. Involve and educate all the sectors of the society.

3. Define a unified set of principles that will guide the development of AI.

As mentioned in an earlier chapter, the Asilomar AI Principles were published in an open letter by the Future of Life Institute (FLI) at Oxford University. The letter includes 23 Principles which represent a partial guide to help ensure that AI is developed beneficially for all. The effort has gained significant support.

Some of the Principles that AI researchers signed directly relate to Musk's statements, including:

3) **Science-Policy Link:** There should be constructive and healthy exchange between AI researchers and policy-makers.

4) **Research Culture:** A culture of cooperation, trust, and transparency should be fostered among researchers and developers of AI.

5) **Race Avoidance:** Teams developing AI systems should actively cooperate to avoid corner-cutting on safety standards.

20) **Importance:** Advanced AI could represent a profound change in the history of life on Earth, and should be planned for and managed with commensurate care and resources.

21) **Risks:** Risks posed by AI systems, especially catastrophic or existential risks, must be subject to planning and mitigation efforts commensurate with their expected impact.

Organizations promoting Ethical AI

There are many organizations promoting Ethical AI. Some of these include:

> ➢ OpenAI was created on the principle that AI should be advanced in a way to benefit humanity.

179

> ➤ The Ethics and Governance of Artificial Intelligence Fund was established to encourage cross-disciplinary research into how to best manage AI.

> ➤ AI Now is a New York-based research initiative working across disciplines to understand the social and economic implications of AI.

> ➤ AI100 —Stanford is conducting a One Hundred Year Study on Artificial Intelligence (AI100), which is a long-term investigation of the field of AI and its influences on people, their communities, and society.

According to Immanuel Kant and his famous Categorical Imperative, when being in a dilemma you should ask yourself if what you are about to do can become a rule for everyone and if your decision can be universalized.

The workplace is changing dramatically, both technically and culturally, creating more complex business environments which require even more skill when making decisions. The involvement of AI requires a clear ethics statement. A business decision should also be examined from a legal, humanitarian, and ethical perspective. The application of ethics and morality in decision making is beneficial for organizations, externally and internally.

Below are some serious questions for leaders and governments to discuss and consult with the people. Leadership is about solving problems. More than ever we need politicians who stand on integrity.

> ➤ More jobs taken over by AI/Robots.
> ➤ Baby boomers are retiring (but not fast enough for Millennials)
> ➤ Unemployment and under-employment
> ➤ Incomes are decreasing. Cost of living/food prices increasing
> ➤ Crop failures resulting in food shortages and higher prices
> ➤ The world is getting hotter and there is a shortage of water
> ➤ Climate change: Extreme conditions for man/crops/environment

It's time for our leaders to stop talking about **climate change** and start working together to solve it. The last three years were the hottest in human history. Within the last 2 months we have seen natural disasters like never before. This hurricane season has generated more destructive, land-falling storms than the past few years combined. The Caribbean, USA (Texas and Florida), Puerto Rico have all faced the brunt of Hurricane Harvey, Irma, Jose and Maria. Mexico on the other hand is reeling in the effects of recent earthquakes.

The islands of Dominica and Barbuda were reduced to mere rubble. The Prime Minister of Dominica, Roosevelt Skerrit, in his address to United Nations General Assembly blamed climate change, and pleaded with all countries in the United Nations General Assembly – large and small, rich and poor – to come together to save our planet. Climate change extremely hits the world's most vulnerable people and its getting worst. We need leaders who will put aside their differences and work together in the best interest of the people.

Many leaders have one standard for their public image and another for their private life. It is easy for leaders, at least in public, to appear as role models. You can fool some of the people, most of the time. However, the people you can't fool, at least for very long, are those in your family. They will see things about you no one else on the outside will see. How important, then, that no matter what we profess, our lives must not be lived in contradiction to our profession. This doesn't mean we are perfect; it means only that our family sees the sincerity of our leadership walk, which reveals our true character.

If the motives are pure, the life will be pure. The human heart is complicated to understand. Others can judge only on appearance, which, because of the natural duplicity of the heart, often does not correspond to the true inner condition. Eventually, the mask falls off and many who believed and trusted in them are left disappointed. Thomas Jefferson said, "I never did, or countenanced, in public life, a single act inconsistent with the strictest good faith; having never believed there was one code of morality for a public, and another for a private man." Ethics impacts everything we do, it impacts our relationships, our ability to execute, and ultimately results. Being ethical is not a business concept or even a management concept but it is a lifestyle. The more we understand that integrity and accountability is ownership and choice, the more effective we can be in every area in our lives. True success comes when you're totally honest with yourself, and with others.

A commitment to responsible leadership is what our world needs. Too many "so-called" leaders ascend into leadership positions for the allure of power. The pervasive ethics dimension brought us the financial crash of 2008. It will appear again once there is greed, lust for power, and hubris. AI aims at improving the human condition. It efforts are on the physical or external. But for AI to be effective we need to look at the interior— the heart and mind of humankind. This is where evil is conceived and it seems to be getting worst.

Leadership is about people. It's about creating a better world for our current and future generations. We need leaders who are willing to not only help the business grow but also the people and our communities. With so much disasters and devastation happening around, we want leaders who will genuinely care, who will put people first, and who will make a positive difference. Leaders must be willing to embrace their civic duty—the actions of an individual must benefit the society as a whole. Ultimately, some things must be done because they are the right things to do.

CHAPTER SEVEN

THE DIGITAL LEADER:
TRANSFORMATION IS INEVITABLE

We are at a fascinating time in history where a tsunami of technology is coming at us, and most of us are thinking that future changes are going to occur at the same rate as other industrial revolutions—but it won't be that way. The technology developments happening right now are so diverse, that it can be difficult to grasp. Society is going to change faster in the next 30 years than we have probably seen in the last 3 generations. How we interact is going to change in ways many people just can't imagine right now. It's going to change how we do business, how we communicate, how we interact socially. We live in a universe of patterns, and repeating cycles. The new leaders of tomorrow must be ready to face a complex set of unknowns never faced before.

What makes this an Industrial Revolution like no other, is a combination of wide-ranging technological advances, the merging of these technologies, and of course, disruption. KPMG recently conducted its annual survey of 800 global technology industry leaders, from startups to Fortune 500. The top emerging technology trend that is expected to disrupt business significantly in the next 3 years is The Internet of Things (IoT). IoT is a network of internet-connected objects able to collect and exchange data using embedded sensors. The highest driver of the use of IoT in business transformation is expected to be improved business efficiencies and productivity, followed by faster innovation cycles. Businesses throughout the world are leveraging their assets, big data, and analytics for an edge over their competitors. Gartner believes that by 2020 there will be 20.4 billion connected devices, and IDC believes that by 2021, $1.4 trillion will be spent on IoT technologies.

A recent study conducted by Microsoft, states that 87% of global companies have Digital Transformation on their strategic roadmaps. By this, they want to:

- ❖ increase operational efficiency
- ❖ increase ROI on technology based products and services
- ❖ focus on customer centricity

IoT has been enabled by AI. The Key drivers fuelling the rapid growth of IoT include: Decreasing cost of CPU memory and storage, convergence of IT and operational technology, expanded wireless/broadband connectivity, the implementation of IPv6 protocols advent of big data and cloud, decreasing cost of megabit, increasing device proliferation, and increase in investment in IoT. AI and IoT has become a powerfully disruptive combination that is transforming industries.

Industrial IoT will continue to grow at an explosive rate as more devices become connected to one another. These rapid changes in technology have resulted in a fundamental shift in how we interact with the world and how we understand its borders and boundaries. These staggering leaps forward in tech aren't occurring in vacuum. In a Forrester survey, around 28% of business respondents reported that they planned to adopt IoT usage in their business operations in the near future. With immediate access to information and the ability to transact electronically, technology has caused the world to shrink. We are more connected than ever before.

Society is going digital. What is digital transformation? It is a journey of adopting innovative technology and methods. Technology helps to take your brand's message to the audience that you intend to target. It is only a matter of years until most of our systems, processes, and activities go completely digital. What we also see is that our complete society is digitized as well. Just like an image that is digitized in separate pixels, we humans are also becoming like separate pixels. Each one of us is one part of a bigger picture. Each individual has a mobile device that generates a trace of information, and that information is also like some kind of pixel that's digitized in the bigger picture. The four domains of digital business that will shape competitiveness include Innovation, Connectivity, Speed, and Quality.

A Fujitsu report revealed: "89% of organizations are planning, testing, and implementing various digital transformation projects and 34% of their digital transformation projects had already delivered positive outcomes."

The next generation marketplace will find a convergence of applied AI, digital networks, and smart technologies. Hard questions must be asked now to determine core competencies, strategic positioning, and corporate identity to meet this fast future. In today's digitally connected world, many companies need an entirely different kind of leader: a digital leader who can keep people connected and engaged, who can build teams and drive a culture of innovation. As digital disruption sweeps across every major industry, leadership capabilities are not keeping pace. Leaders today need different skills and expertise than in generations past. Organizations need to build a new breed of agile, digital-ready leaders. Unfortunately, many business executives do not understand the magnitude of this issue. In an industry study by Deloitte University of 800 top business executives, 67% believed that technology will drive greater value than human capital and 64% believed people are a cost, not a driver of value.

According to the 2017 Global Human Capital Trends survey, 72% of respondents are developing or starting to develop new leadership programs focused on digital management while only 5% of companies feel they have strong digital leaders in place. Digital transformation requires a change in how leaders think, act, and must react.

For leaders to navigate their way through this multifaceted landscape, they need to understand the environment and the technological waves that are taking place. Even in an automated atmosphere, leaders must be human-centric.

Questions to ask yourself:

> What does the current digital leadership model look like?

> Which digital leadership capabilities does my business need now?

> Where do I want to start my personal digital transformation journey?

> What can I encourage peers and my team to pick-up on?

7 STEPS THAT WILL ENABLE YOU TO CREATE VALUE IN YOUR ORGANIZATION THROUGH DIGITAL TRANSFORMATION:

1 **Organizational awareness:** Whether they are ready for the transformation or not, it is required of organizations to revamp the way they think and carry out their business activities. There are several obstacles to digital transformation, and the biggest ones are people-centric such as having a boss who doesn't believe in the need for digital transformation. You must honestly evaluate your organization's capabilities. A digital transformation is not only about the technology, it is about changing the culture of doing everyday business so it needs a strong support and leadership. Strong leadership is required to scan for current trends and provide guidance and direction on how to successfully navigate them. It is surprising how many CEOs want to become digital, because everyone is doing it. The digital transformation exercise has to impact real metrics as revenue, profit, customer engagement, and retention. The transformation needs to create business value. Awareness is important, however you need to move the ship somehow.

2 **The Digital Business Model:** One of the major reasons why organizations fail to thrive in the digital world is because their business models are not in line with the digital economy. This is a prerequisite to competing for the future. Digital transformation requires a willingness to explore innovative technologies, tools, methods, and systems. Redefine existing Business Processes/ Models to weave digital transformation areas in front-end and back-end areas. You need to design the organization's digital model to include the concepts of innovation, growth, inclusion, teamwork, and collaboration. You can't lead digital transformation if you don't know where to start or where you're going. It's about developing new digital capabilities. Look within your organization for any manual processes that can most likely be automated. This is where your (yet to be revealed) competitors will aim to take market shares. Can

your clients order your products/services without interacting in real life? Or do they need to call/email/meet in person? If your cost to serve is higher than your competitors, i.e., manual process when the competition has automated, you will not be competitive.

Any organisation that wants to succeed in today's hyper-competitive market must implement data-driven decision-making. Many organisations are using advanced analytics. Advanced analytics are a crucial competitive tool, taking advantage of a wealth of unstructured and sensor data to provide descriptive (What has happened?), predictive (What could happen?) and prescriptive analytics (What should we do?). It's the use of data and analytics to make better business decisions. It looks at insight from the past, to better understand the future, to determine the possible outcomes and solutions. It's about developing digital solutions to expand the customer base, transform the customer experience, and create or improve products. Technology is simply a set of tools empowering change (transformation). To foster change we look to these tools to monitor, measure, and quantify internal interactions (Industry 4.0 and where most cost savings might occur), and external interactions with suppliers and distribution channels and customers. According to a 2016 Gartner big data reporting, less than 3% of companies are using prescriptive analytics in their business, and only 30% are using predictive.

The leadership role in defining how culture, strategy, digital, and purpose align is extremely critical. Focus on purpose and not only on products. Transformation involves an end-to-end process that starts with defining your brand and then aligns your organization. The digital transformation is not only affecting companies on their customer expectations and internal processes, it is also a chance to help leaders connect with employees at unprecedented scale and in new ways. This could be, for example, through platforms or tools that help companies to share regular, candid perspectives and collect feedback.

3 **Strategy:** Sophisticated algorithms can't overcome poor/insufficient data, or ill-founded strategy. As companies set out to

rethink their strategy about business models, services architecture, value creation, and value capture, it's important to remember that a well-executed strategy enables a company to gain competitive advantage over its competitors while simultaneously strengthening brand equity and shareholder value. Think about a business problem that needs to be solved that impacts top or bottom line and select the emerging technologies which can solve problems quickly and reliably. Successful digital transformation starts with a solid, well-thought-out strategy that clearly identifies your business objectives. It requires a much-broadened view about the business area you're in, envisioning new values for clients, thinking end-to-end, and positioning yourself within a potential new business model.

Positioning is extremely important to getting highest leverage of your own value (skills and capabilities). Companies must enhance their digital customer experience while also driving agility and efficiency through digital operational excellence. Focus on attaining a true understanding of the ways that customers derive value from your products and services across a variety of contexts. This will create a strong foundation on which to base a digital transformation strategy. The ability to quickly adapt to new market trends that arise from disruptive technologies or changing customer behavior is critical. Being "Digital" simply means you know your customer intimately and use evidence based decision making to create the right business models and experiences to attract, retain, and convert them to advocates. Have a strategy that identifies a 21st-century problem and proposes a 21st-century solution. The digital world brings a reality where you need to dig deep into understanding metrics; that means starting early with a hypothesis then gradually refining your understanding by testing in real-world situations.

4 | Implementation: About 70% of change initiatives fail. Digital transformation is a change initiative. However most companies treat it as an IT project. The same principles apply, including enlisting the employee communication function as a vital partner in the process.

Digital transformation is a strategic imperative that impacts all stakeholders and must be embraced by all employees. Implementing change across an organization requires top-down drive and buy-in. I have seen organizations embrace digital transformation comprehensively, including adoption of a culture of innovation, but the leadership team continues to operate in a traditional structure and with a traditional mindset. Change management and leading digital transformations go hand in hand. Like introducing any new tool, channel, or marketing medium, it's important to first create a culture that understands the need and wants to make the change. Transformation by definition requires heart and minds belief from the participants involved in the experience—that's a lot more than "harnessing" employees, or wowing customers. It also needs relentless energy and engaged communication from its leaders if it is to endure and thrive. Too many organizations fail to communicate changes effectively. Communicating the WHY of the transformation is much more important than the HOW. Many programs start with the details on what is happening without explaining what they are really trying to achieve. Employees can unleash their creativity once they understand the destination.

In an article titled, *GE Saved Millions by Using this Data Start-Ups Software*, Emily Galt, vice president of product management of GE Digital, highlighted how the company has integrated ML to achieve savings. GE has become one of the world's leading users and vendors of ML for industrial data.

Studies suggest the top three success factors implementations include:

> ➢ Open organization culture—Successful organizations have a high sense of urgency and break the silos in their organization by an organization-wide adoption strategy. You need lean execution flows. Lean in this context is about minimizing handover points. They adopt a digital transformation mindset and set up easy integration points to various systems and applications. In the late 1980s and early 1990s, researchers from MIT began studying Japanese manufacturing systems,

particularly the Toyota production system. They coined the term "lean" to describe the system's methods of improving productivity by eliminating waste through reductions in uneven work flows and destructive overloading.

➢ Business use cases—Current use cases are predominantly around data. Customer insights and marketing leading the way. Most of these applications are core to the business functions, for example customer service, operations, and product development.

➢ Data ecosystems and digital readiness—With the growth of data volume from various sources, most enterprises are challenged with clean and reliable data. Data from disparate systems should be centralized with the right technology architecture in place.

5 Invest in a (Big) Data Management Platform: For organizations, innovation is about being responsive to change, proactively anticipating change, and adapting to changes in the external environment. Be with new technology, changing customer needs, new product creation and delivery processes, or new opportunities, innovation is about better solutions for existing and new needs. Digital data management platforms are a necessity for every organization today. The integration of a management platform can improve the performance of the organization and the quality of the solutions to customers. "A proper enterprise platform should contain the five service layers: engagement, integration, development, data, and modern core IT, which are the key components of every digital business," (Ronald van Loon, data management expert). The interactions that customers have with businesses and organizations are not only limited to certain domains such as email, mobile, broadcast, etc.—all of which can be separately evaluated and taken into consideration to use customer segmentation for increased profits. Needless to say, the use of digital enterprise platforms can give organizations and businesses the competitive edge. The benefits which enterprises can reap from big data management platforms are practically endless.

6 **Training and Attracting New Talent:** Without the right human capital to support the process, many transformational efforts will fall short. Take time to evaluate whether your company has the right digital skillsets in place to succeed. Digital transformation requires the strategic alignment of capabilities across the entire organization. Move beyond traditional leadership training: Instead, focus on training with an emphasis on culture, risk-taking, knowledge sharing, privacy, matrix management, and building talent as guides. Promote collaborative environments. Empower employees to drive this change forward. Companies also need to attract new digital talent (hire digital natives), and at the same time they need to develop digital skills on the existing workforce. A company must build adaptive and resilient teams that are willing to learn new architectures and develop new skillsets.

It starts and ends with people, trust, shared values, vision, and empowerment. The lack of agility in many organizations doesn't really impose a new threshold to digital transformation, as a lack of agile decisions affects all kinds of organizational change projects. We know that 70% of change projects fail globally, and we can expect the same results for digital transformation projects, unless people are on board. Your employees need to embrace the digital culture and be educated on it. The percentage of engaged employees in US companies continues to be in the low 30s. To engage your customers, you'll need to first engage your employees. Many organizations are so focused on the technology that they forget people come first. People are at the center of it all, the main ingredient. Without their full understanding of why we are going through a digital transformation, where we are heading, why there are so many changes, they will show resistance to change and the transformation will be effectively doomed. The basis of any successful digital transformation is therefore having people with the right skillset and enabling them to achieve it. Great talent will conduct the digital transformation of business and boost competitiveness in this global and digital marketplace. Today's challenges require diverse teams with different capabilities and the ability master digital collaboration tools.

7 Culture: A company may jump on the "big data" trend or "marketing automation" etc., but fall flat on implementing because they don't support an innovative culture or have the agility to process and react to the data presented, or quite simply they don't listen to those who speak up and try to collaborate. Culture plays a huge part in digital transformations. Culture is the hardest to change and it starts at the top. Culture is dependent upon people and relations. Changing a culture is hard and needs a lot of sincerity and authenticity from leaders and not just artificial changes because you have to. That leads to huge gaps in perceptions between leaders and employees.

"Culture is the glue that either keeps us doing things well or keeps us doing things poorly."—Professor Etha Bernstein, Harvard Business School

Digital Twins: If your organization is planning to leverage the Internet of Things (IoT) you need to become familiar with the concept of the "digital twin." A digital twin is a digital replica of a physical asset, process, or system that can be used for a variety of purposes. It's like a bridge between the physical and digital world. Businesses can achieve better insights on product performance, improve the customer experience by better understanding customer needs, make better operational and strategic decisions and can even help drive the innovation of new business. Digital twins will not just be a "nice-to-have" technology. They will be necessary for innovation transformation, according to research firm International Data Corp. (IDC). "For every physical asset in the world, we have a virtual copy running in the cloud that gets richer with every second of operational data," says Ganesh Bell, chief digital officer and general manager of Software & Analytics at GE Power & Water. Research firm Gartner Inc. stated, 'within three to five years, billions of things will be represented by digital twins'.

The digital world moves fast and into unfamiliar territory, creating a need for you to adapt quickly. Today, you need to be prepared to learn daily, challenge how things were done yesterday, and get ready to apply new approaches today. The best leaders master questions rather than answers. By being a continuous learner, you will stay ahead of the competition. Learning from experiences is a superior skill in the digital world. You must create a culture of innovation where continuous improvement and adaptation to change are constant. Leaders must also be able to balance managing/optimizing your classic business and leading your new digital model. Classic operational silos are your biggest enemy. Driving a digital business is different. Lead by example with your own personal learning and sharing. Sharing information has become a necessity. Part of a successful culture of innovation is an iterative process for testing, failing, learning, reworking, and repeating the process. Foster a culture of risk-taking and experimentation.

After assisting numerous clients around the world, McKinsey found that companies that are successful in transitioning to a new digitally-powered operating model do a couple of things well. "These companies have been able to transform because they have developed next-generation operating models that provide the speed, precision, and flexibility to quickly unlock new sources of value and radically reduce costs. The operating model of the future combines digital technologies and process-improvement capabilities in an integrated, sequenced way to drastically improve customer journeys and internal processes," the authors said. The report also stated that many institutions understand the need to change and have embarked on numerous initiatives, yet few have been able to get beyond isolated success cases or marginal benefits.

Welcome feedback. Often it is noticed that the management level have a different understanding about the cultural aspects and beliefs whereas at the employee level the perception is quite different. Let employees know they will not be penalized for honesty, even if the picture is not pretty. Having open communication channels builds trust. You can then take this feedback into consideration when making strategic decisions. It will lead to creation of a better culture and an improved organisation.

McKinsey's Four Building Blocks to drive enterprise-wide change include:

> **Building Block # 1** is about having **cross-functional teams** that bring together the right combination of skills to build products and serve customers. Operational change requires teamwork and it's important these teams are empowered to experiment and build skills. That means reconfiguring organizational boundaries and revisiting the nature of teams.

Google spent 2 years studying 180 teams to come up with five key characteristics of enhanced teams. Project Aristotle gathered several of Google's best and brightest to help the organization codify the secrets to team effectiveness. Through Google's Re:Work website, a resource that shares Google's research, ideas, and practices on people operations, Julia Rozovsky, Google's People Analytics and

HR Strategy Leader, outlined the five key characteristics of enhanced teams.

- ❖ Dependability—Team members can count on each other to get things done on time.

- ❖ Structure and clarity—High-performing teams have clear goals and roles within the team.

- ❖ Meaning—The work has personal significance to each member.

- ❖ Impact—The group believes their work is meaningful and is personally important to each one of them.

- ❖ Psychological Safety—Team members feel safe to take risks on the team without feeling insecure or embarrassed.

- ➤ **Building Block #2** refers to developing a **modular architecture**, infrastructure, and software delivery process to support a much faster and more flexible deployment of products and services.

According to the authors, "This approach both accelerates development and prioritizes the use of common components, which in turn leads to development efficiency and consistency. Another important reason for building more flexible architecture is that it enables businesses to partner with an external ecosystem of suppliers and partners."

- ➤ **Building Block # 3** is a **management system** that cascades clear strategies and goals through the organization, with tight feedback loops. The authors said leading companies embed performance management into the DNA of an organization from top to bottom, and translate top-line goals and priorities into specific metrics and KPIs for employees at all levels.

- ➤ **Building Block # 4** refers to fostering an **agile, customer-centric culture** demonstrated at all levels and role-modeled from the top. A culture that prioritizes speed and execution over perfection. "Most companies recognize the need for a next-generation operating model to drive their business forward in the digital age. But how well they actually develop it makes all the difference between reinventing the business and just trying to do so."

Digital transformation focuses on agile business decision making, strategic planning as a continuous process, and, of course, people taking center stage. It must be customer centric.

90% OF CEOS LACK THIS BASIC LEADERSHIP SKILL

Leaders must take a strong personal ownership for the development of their digital skills. Don't wait on your company to recommend this for you. The digital transformation put leaders on the spot to develop personal digital skills. Leaders must be digitally literate. Seek to raise your technological acumen. This does not mean that to be a successful CEO you have to become a data scientist. You just need to be digitally literate. This includes data literacy, ML literacy, and math literacy to name a few. It means that in order to be a successful executive, you need to be familiar with the methods of data science and research. As the digital world is more numbers driven, your ability to identify the relevant metrics and be able to think strategically about how to use data to create value for your business is crucial. The complexity of problems has rapidly increased with the digital transformation, while the time available to solve problems has decreased. Aspire to understand the data you collect and the insights you want to extract. The importance for businesses of evaluating and analyzing data streams in today's world cannot be emphasized enough. Algorithms must be designed around specific customer needs.

I recently read an article on Medium by Ryan Holmes: "90% of CEOs Lack This Basic Leadership Skill." What skill is it? Social Media. He pointed out that only one in three Fortune 500 CEOs is on LinkedIn, to begin with. The rest don't even have a profile. Furthermore, 61% of Fortune 500 CEOs have no social media presence whatsoever. They're not posting on LinkedIn, Facebook, Twitter, or other networks. He goes on to say, "Considering that social networks are now closing in on 3 billion users—nearly half the global population!—there's something very wrong with that picture. I'm not saying leaders have to be experts in social media. But if there's a communication channel where your employees, customers, competitors, investors, partners, and stakeholders are all spending their time, shouldn't you at least make an effort to be there, too?"

Pope Francis is the first digital and technology driven Pope in history and has surprised the world today with his own TED talk, where he has challenged tech companies to refocus their priorities and place people first, after products. The Pope has also spoken about technology revolution and transformation and the speed of development of science advances. Another very interesting sign of disruption.

The 2016 presidential election ushered in a new era as much of it was played out in social media. Leaders need to understand the importance of their responsibility as opinion leaders and role models. Leaders should always model Respect, Civility, Integrity and Emotional intelligence on whatever platform they are on. I am saddened at the type of irresponsible behavior displayed by some leaders on social media. When you take on a leadership role you can no longer afford to respond poorly when things get stressful. Always practice social media decorum. The effects of making reckless statements can be long lasting and it gives this upcoming generation a poor example of what true leadership is.

Closing the social media skills gap for leaders is not difficult. Where digital/social media illiteracy is a severe limitation, you can get help from younger digital natives and take advice from social media experts, or if you don't have the time, you can get a social media assistant to open and handle your accounts for you.

Digital transformation is a complex change process touching all facets of an organization, challenging all conventions, business practices, and a key factor to the ongoing success of most companies. Being able to orchestrate, architect, and predict the impact on outcomes that matter to the business is key. It needs patience, time, knowledge, and also perseverance. And sometimes you may even think you are trying to "push a big ball up a hill," and it will bounce back from time to time, but patience is key, tempered with a lot of drive. Great leaders have always been expected to succeed, even in the midst of uncertainty. The present era of digitization is beyond conversion of physical to digital information. It is about the confluence of big-data, AI, IoT, and Cybersecurity. Successful companies will combine IoT with Artificial Intelligence technologies, which enable smart machines to simulate intelligent behavior and will help them to make well-informed decisions. So, businesses must move rapidly to identify how they'll drive value from combining AI and IoT—or face impending disruption. The role that leaders play will continue to change, becoming even more digital-focused and team-centric. Leaders need to stay one step ahead by continually evolving with the trends and ensure that their organizations do not lag behind in the digital transformation. One of the most important issues facing the world in the era of digitization is achieving the right balance of data security and respecting customer privacy. Be trustworthy with data. Cybersecurity threats are emerging rapidly at the same time as the volume of the connected devices and software is increasing. Your data security must be included in this digital transformation. The cyber threat landscape continues to grow and evolve. Cybersecurity Ventures predicts that cybersecurity will become a $1 trillion enterprise between 2017 and 2021. Additionally, too little attention is currently being placed on the importance of getting the integrity of the foundational data and having the right measurements. Our digital legacy will be measured by future generations, to a large extent, based on our ethical stewardship of digital ecosystems and cutting-edge technologies like ML, IoT, and AI.

CHAPTER EIGHT

DEALING WITH UNCERTAINTY

Many companies are currently grappling with the unprecedented speed of technology and the disruptions and challenges it brings. The businesses of today must think far beyond the traditional confines of an enterprise; they need to consider the entire ecosystem to ensure that they are making the right decisions which can help with survival. Companies must learn to unlearn old things and learn new ones to stay current and relevant. If you are in the midst of a team who constantly says, "That›s the way it has always been done here," or "Our business model is bulletproof." Think again! The Companies of the Future are going to become digital and weightless, supplying virtual products and virtual services. The focus shifts from a portfolio of products and services to a portfolio of platforms and solutions.

More and more of the successful companies of the future are going to be creating and supplying us with intelligent solutions that have no physical presence. Future supply chains will possess the efficiencies of customer data mining and knowledge management. AI enabled decision support systems that are personalized will be connecting vendors and suppliers to create a network of commercial efficiency for customers. Continuous digital transformation is needed everywhere in all industries, especially now that the Millennials and Generation Z have grown up in a digital world and are the main consumers to-be.

Conventional wisdom talks about taking customer feedback and building a product based on their needs. Digital wisdom on the other hand creates a product that a customer may not even know they have need of. Always focus on the customer experience and look at what digital means through their eyes. It's the best and fastest way to figure things out. Forward-looking leaders understand the seismic shifts that are taking place and quickly adapt. It's about anticipating future trends and customer needs by being aware, predictive, and flexible to the changing marketplace. Visionary innovation beyond customer expectation is key for survival. It is not enough to ask customers what they need today. You need to spend more time on your own thinking to figure out what they need tomorrow.

"If I had asked people what they wanted, they would have said faster horses."—Henry Ford

Here are 10 incredible products and services that didn't exist 10 years ago.

1 **Android** – Google founder Sergey Brin and engineering director Steve Horowitz debuted Google's Android operating system in November 2007. Today, there are an estimated 2 billion active devices running Android software.

2 **Google Chrome** – Google unveiled its Chrome browser on September 1, 2008. "On the surface, we designed a browser window that is streamlined and simple," Google CEO Sundar Pichai wrote on the company's blog.

3 | **The iPad** – The iPad was announced on January 27, 2010, by Steve Jobs at an Apple press conference. He said, "It's unbelievably great. Way better than a laptop, way better than a smartphone."

4 | **Instagram** – First launched in October 2010 with 25,000 people signing up on the first day. By April 2012, the company was bought by Facebook for $1 billion. Instagram now has approximately 200 million daily active users.

5 | **Pinterest** – Pinterest is a visual bookmarking tool and virtual pin board. It was founded in March 2010. Today, with 175 million monthly active users, the company is valued at $12 billion.

6 | **4G** – 4G networks were an upgrade of the 3G wireless network. They have only been around for about 7 years. Sprint's HTC Evo was the first 4G phone when it came out in March 2010.

7 | **Uber** – Uber is a location-based app that makes hiring an on-demand private driver easy. The company was founded in March 2009. Today, Uber remains the world's most valuable start up at about $70 billion, and its business is still growing.

8 | **WhatsApp** – WhatsApp was incorporated in 2009 by Brian Acton and Jan Koum, both former employees of Yahoo. WhatsApp is a messaging app. Facebook bought the app for $19 billion in 2014.

9 | **Kickstarter** – Kickstarter is a platform for launching and backing independent companies and products. Since its inception, 13 million people have backed projects and $3.2 billion has been raised on the site.

10 | **Spotify** – Launched in October 2008, in Sweden. They launched a public beta in 2007, but it wasn't until the company signed licensing deals with Universal, Sony, and more that Spotify officially launched. Nine years later, Spotify has 140 million active users worldwide.

Just look at today's technology, unimaginable 30 years ago. So there will be many products and services within the next 10 years, ones that we can't begin to imagine, which will revolutionize our world.

Look at these companies:

- ➢ The most popular media owner creates no content (Facebook)
- ➢ The world's largest taxi company owns no taxis (Uber)
- ➢ The world's most valuable retailer has no inventory (Alibaba)
- ➢ The largest accommodation provider owns no real estate (Airbnb)
- ➢ One of the fastest growing banks has no actual money (SocietyOne)
- ➢ The largest phone company owns no telecoms infrastructure (Skype/ WeChat)
- ➢ The largest software vendors don't write the majority of the available apps (Apple/ Google)
- ➢ Amazon just passed Wal-Mart as the nation's biggest retailer, and they own no stores.

What do they have in common? There are a lot of things that they have in common; for example, the most disruptive companies build platforms that solve complex customer problems. Today, business process design is driven by the need for cost reduction and optimization. Tomorrow, it will be driven by the need to create superior user experiences. Some businesses are already bracing themselves, developing new business models, developing applications, building capability, and more importantly developing products and services that will not only offer greater efficiency for them but provide new benefits and experiences for their customers. VNTANA and Satisfi Labs have developed a new platform that will allow companies to develop a hologram concierge to be used in business. The project combines artificial intelligence (AI) with augmented reality (AR) technology to produce a 3D persona that can interact with customers.

If you wait and respond to the changing technology, it won't be very long before you're too late. Companies need to build an innovative culture or die. Amazon, over the years, has increased their releases of new updates or functions, and in 2016, they released over 1,000 new functions or innovations. That is over 3 new functions per day. Bezos has clearly implemented the culture of innovation.

With the explosion of the "Startup" culture that sees some 613 million entrepreneurs worldwide attempting to start 396 million companies, of which approximately 100 million new businesses (or one third) will open each year around the world. If you thought that these disruptive little upstarts aren't going to come to your town or city, think again. They are probably there already—even if you haven't spotted them yet. Once there is some kind of problem that's solved and a disruptive idea has been successfully tested on the market, then it's copied or adapted very quickly into other industries and other markets.

Is your job or business as safe as you thought it was 30 minutes ago? Being able to anticipate the future instead of reacting to what's happening now is going to be key to survival. Your business and your job are on the line because change is happening so fast.

Uber disrupted the taxi industry. Uber's platform started a host of new taxis and a cab sharing economy. In fact, it worked so well that "to Uber" has even become a verb in the dictionary. Uber are now copying their concept and using it to disrupt the logistics industry. Uber are now able to deliver a package in 30 minutes to your front door. That idea has worked well too, so now they are copying that same formula yet again, this time to the fresh goods industry. Learn to copy the best practices/processes of any Industry which may suit your business model. Like resource sharing is the underlying theme of Airbnb. So if it works for you, then copy it. Don't be shy or apologetic.

Just look at the story behind Apple's iTunes. iTunes was disrupted by Spotify. Yet it was iTunes itself that disrupted the music market. But one upstart disrupted another. Spotify came along and disrupted Apple. Spotify took the same digital product and gave customers an unlimited amount of music for a fixed fee each month. It shook the entire industry. That same disruptive model for digitized media was rapidly copied to other industries. With Netflix, you can watch unlimited movies for less than $10 a month. You can read unlimited news, magazines, or book titles for a fixed price per month. Amazon Prime has moved into the space. Eventually, every industry will be disrupted because in some way, every market, every industry, is connected to others.

In 1996, Kodak was a titan of an imaging company with a $28 billion market capitalization and over 140,000 employees. In 2012, they were broke. They still had 17,000 employees, but in the very same year that Kodak filed for Chapter 11 bankruptcy protection, Facebook bought Instagram for $1 billion, and they only had 13 employees. Companies with old technologies and ways of thinking will soon be obsolete. Disruption is ruthless and spares no one. The next generation of technology is already here. It is going fast, very fast. Even Moore's law itself is already outdated. We now have Rose's law. Rose's law is a doubling of Moore's law, so it's quadrupling every 12 to 18 months.

AGILITY AND CONTINUOUS LEARNING IS KEY TO SUCCESS

There is a noticeable gap between the businesses which are thriving and those which are struggling to survive. Far too many of the companies are underestimating the scale of the internal change needed to get this right. Many companies struggle due to the lack of agility and the ability to make the right decisions. Lack of preparedness will likely continue to be the key issue they face. In the past, digital transformation has been perceived as IT-led, and something to compartmentalize in that department. Yet, it will touch all aspects of business. Companies need to completely rethink their operating models to adapt and prepare to disrupt or be disrupted.

Embracing agile principles means new ways to work which require new ways to lead and manage. As with all technology disruptors it is most important to cultivate and proliferate a mindset of learning and development in the organization. Learning organizations quickly obtain new knowledge and adapt to it. They encourage critical-thinking, disruptive thinking, risk-taking, exploration of new ideas, and welcome feedback to foster innovation. Learning organizations learn from mistakes. They address the knowledge gap and train and coach employees.

GE CIO Jim Fowler, at the MIT Sloan CIO Symposium, stated how GE has advanced into a "future ready" company, where "the technology is going to become the process" and where employees will form "mission-based teams" to solve specific business problems and then disband to solve new business problems.

Agility should be the centerpiece of any strategy dealing with AI and digital transformation. Agile organizations focus on organizational flexibility, shorter operating windows, managing partnerships and alliances' and teamwork. The speed and dynamism of decision-making and the ability of the organization to adapt to changing demands and technologies is crucial to success. Agile as a way of working is changing goals, breaking work down into small slices, changing organization structures, removing the functional barriers, collaborating more, visualizing work, reflecting often, organizing the workforce into multidisciplinary teams, and developing cultures of continuous improvement that leverage agile practices.

Amazon's notoriously competitive workplace is guided by a set of rules; one of them is *disagree* and *commit*. Disagree and commit is a management principle which states that individuals are allowed to disagree while a decision is being made, but that once a decision has been made, everybody must commit to it. Amazon added, "Have a Backbone; Disagree and Commit" as its 13th leadership principle.

The technology shifts that the IoT brings will transform the technology industry in unprecedented ways. New digital business models are emerging, and new ecosystems are forming to realign business and customer relationships. The extended distributed IoT platform brings major opportunities to the business landscape when enabling a wide range of new digital services. New business opportunities will be born through cross industry partnerships. Agility is about building partnerships. Amazon, Apple, Facebook, and Microsoft compete intensely publically, but behind the scenes they are cooperating. Everyone uses each other's cloud, Microsoft's software is sought after on the Mac and Windows products are on the Google Play Store. Microsoft recently announced a deal with Amazon to connect Cortana and Alexa, their voice-activated AI assistants. This news also illustrated how these companies are leveraging their respective strengths.

Agility does not depend on accurately predicting future disruptions, but prepares companies to deal with any disruption. Timing and pace of disruptions are always difficult to predict accurately. Agility enables enterprises to keep up with industry trends if not surpassing them. In an uncertain world, if you take too long to bring a product to the market it could become obsolete during the process. Spending too much time analyzing the options, building road maps, and selecting the best technology can delay the business benefits that await. We need to plan for products to be delivered in shorter amounts of time. Take more risks. Encourage trial and error. Test, fail and learn. As Mark Zuckerberg declares on every wall in the Facebook office— "Break things, and move on," and "Done is better than perfect," which was meant to inspire people to innovate quickly and to not ask for permission, therefore removing barriers for fast innovation and ideas. Launch a group of smaller pilot projects, and always be clear on outcomes but don't punish failure as it will stifle creativity and innovation. One of the advantages of digital platforms and technologies is the low cost of experimentation and learning. There is no reason not to get started with pilots and prototypes to learn quickly and adjust as you go. Get the product out, take continuous feedback, and improve it until you arrive at the best product-customer fit. An example is Gmail—5 years in iterative beta, Google got the best product-customer fit. See opportunities where others may not. What's impossible today might well be the new normal tomorrow. The surprises and disruptions around every corner become reminders that the best way forward is to stay in motion. Business leaders need to recognize that technology adoption patterns have changed in the past decade starting with the adoption of smartphones. Our world, as we know it, is changing fast to more of a self-service, on-demand paradigm. Consumerization of technologies is changing how we operate as individuals on a day-to-day basis. More and more people are using smartphone apps for shopping, searching for information, messaging, video calling, and a million other uses that are a far cry from the original use—making phone calls.

To innovate, one needs to let go of the need for certainty and embrace uncertainty with experimentation and rapid prototyping, while keeping an eye on long-term vision.

Carl von Clausewitz identified two responses for managing uncertainty—intellect and courage. In well-led organizations, uncertainty stimulates adaptiveness and creates opportunities.

In today's fast-paced world, we experience uncertainty and change quite a bit, and it is easy to become fearful rather than hopeful. We should get used to this is the new normal. Adapting is key, change happens all the time and everywhere. Certainly is gone. How do you thrive in an uncertain world? By turning an uncertain into certain with help of modern innovation methods. In our fast-paced world, the risks we have to manage evolve quickly. We just need to make sure we manage those risks so that we minimize threats and also be in a position to maximize their potential.

The speed of change is real and is also highlighted by facts like average lifespan of a company in S&P 500. According to a new study of turnover in the S&P 500, conducted by the growth strategy consulting firm Innosight, the lifespans of big companies are getting shorter than ever. In 1965, the average tenure of companies on the S&P 500 was 33 years. By 1990, this reduced to 20 years and is forecast to shrink to 14 years by 2026. Furthermore, about half of the S&P 500 companies is expected to be replaced over the next 10 years. It is a great strategy to fail small and fast. Working with multiple worldviews or hypotheses simultaneously while developing strategy makes survival possible.

"Anyone can hold the helm when the sea is calm."
—Publilius Syrus

Business leaders warned: It's not if, but when you will be hacked

The world is changing fast. We're in a business landscape that is seeing huge rates of technological innovation. Today we have new smart devices and cloud computing—but these often present new opportunities for criminals to find a way to access your data or your systems. The scale of tools available to hackers grows by the day. Massive data breaches are making headlines almost daily.

A survey from the British Chambers of Commerce (BCC) recently revealed that 20% of companies in the UK have been hacked by criminals in the last year alone. This means it's only a matter of time until you might get hacked. And the consequences are serious. Not only does this lead to a PR nightmare, but there is loss of customer data which may end up in the wrong hands. It can result in a declining revenue as potential customers may be afraid to upload personal information or use their payment methods on your website.

Companies need to invest in upgrading their Information Technology department (IT). IT is often an area of underfunding in many companies. Keeping your company's infrastructure secure doesn't have to be an expensive task; apply sensible rules and guidelines and don't go overboard, keep things simple and maintainable. How businesses respond to these challenges and exploit the benefits of smart technologies will be a key contributor to their success. We will need leaders who can manage the present while designing and navigating the new ambiguous and multifaceted atmosphere.

SECTION THREE

THE FUTURE OF LEADERSHIP

CHAPTER NINE

LEADERSHIP AND SELF DECEPTION

In the rush to understand numbers only, we get caught up with analyzing big data and often we fail to look for the meaning behind the numbers. We have put our trust in surveys and soulless statistics which can lead us to deceptions—or at least a greatly diminished understanding of reality. Many people are convinced that new technologies will eradicate all our troubles—which is actually a mere manifestation of wishful thinking. If and when we stop deceiving ourselves with the myriad of magical remedy on sale as "Artificial Intelligence the Great Savior", things may start to improve.

According to T. S. Eliot and Reinhold Niebuhr—human beings cannot bear much reality, hence the need for "necessary illusions." Well, before Eliot and Niebuhr, the German philosopher Hans Vaihinger (1852–1933) had already written about these illusions. In this regard he developed the philosophy of "as if,"—which was published in German as a book in 1911 and translated into English in 1924. In this work, Vaihinger proposes that we should live (as indeed we already do) in a make-believe world. He argued that since reality cannot be truly known, human beings construct systems of thought to satisfy their needs and then assume that actuality agrees with their constructions; i.e., people act "as if" the real were what they assume it to be.

This is one of the many manifestations of human deception. This indifference is similar to the initial reaction of one who is diagnosed as having an incurable disease, and then goes through the five stages described by Elizabeth Kubler-Ross in her book *On Death and Dying:* 1) denial (unconscious or unconscious refusal to accept facts, information, reality); 2) anger (people dealing with emotional upset can be angry with themselves, and/or with others); 3) bargaining (attempting to bargain with God and promises of good behavior); 4) depression (discouragement); 5) acceptance (peace and realism).

The religiosity in human nature often leads us to worship what we have a high regard for. Today, technology is largely admired because of its great efficacy. The limitations of this kind of thinking is becoming increasingly apparent. None of the sciences offer us a way to integrate all the knowledge generated in the various disciplines. This is particularly problematic since action in the world cannot be confined to information drawn from one discipline. For example, the future of "developing countries" cannot be viewed solely from the quantifiable perspective of economics.

The Newtonian revolution represented the first real coherent triumph of what we now call science. Two fundamental things make up the Newtonian world: matter and energy. Matter and energy exist in the emptiness of absolute space and time—the "sterile machine." The three laws of motion were compiled by Isaac Newton in his *Philosophiæ Naturalis Principia Mathematica* (*Mathematical Principles of Natural Philosophy*), first published in 1687. Newton's laws of motion are three physical laws that, together, laid the foundation for classical mechanics. The laws and principles created the foundation for general theories and predictions that could be tested through experiments.

The Newtonian world was therefore deterministic. The assumption was that fundamentally, the universe is governed by simple rules. There is an absolute order to the universe, and anything we consider disorder or complexity was simply a function of our limited knowledge. Simplicity, predictability, and determinism were central to the Newtonian worldview.

According to Gilles Deleuze, a French philosopher, and Félix Guattari, a French psychiatrist, our current reality is dispersed: everything is very molecular. "Molecular" is what pulverizes, fragments, and disorganizes. Any definition of "becoming molecular" is only ever going to be just an approximation, a "region of best fit" on a map of a context/field. "But we don't know yet what the multiple entails when it is no longer attributed, that is, after it has been elevated to the status of the substantive." (*A Thousand Plateaus*, 1980, p. 4)

"We need a kind of thinking that reconnects that which is disjointed and compartmentalized, that respects diversity as it recognizes unity, and that tries to discern interdependencies. We need a radical thinking (which gets to the root of problems), a multidimensional thinking, and an organizational or systemic thinking." —Edgar Morin.

We are just thinking millions of jobs will be displaced by AI so just implement a UBI and everything will be fine. This is what everyone wants to hear. We are not taking into context the emotional states when people lose their jobs. What about social unrest? What about mental issues since most of us connect our self-worth to our jobs? We need to have deeper conversations with individuals from different disciplines and not only those aligned with science and technology.

For Spinoza, Goethe, Hegel, as well as for Marx, man is alive only inasmuch as he is productive, inasmuch as he grasps the world outside of himself in the act of expressing his own specific human powers, and of grasping the world with these powers. However, Karl Marx's rationalism led him to adopt the idea of limitless scientific progress with no side effects. The main bases were positivist science and the belief that this course would be funneled by a principle of certainty. In the current cult of technology, the task would be to implement in our lives the idea of earthly salvation. However, this is limited since this principle is materialistic and temporary.

How do we think about the world, above all, how do we organize information? How do we approach research? How do we live and think in a pluralistic universe, with complexity and ambiguity?

The term organization of knowledge may suggest a particularly technical and endeavor of relevance only to specialists, with completely no bearing for the way humans lead their lives. But the organization of knowledge has far-reaching consequences. Despite the apparent resistance to this process of "thinking about thinking," the question is not just what we know, but how we know, and how we organize our knowledge.

The process needs to be systemic, and more than cross disciplinary, it should be transdisciplinary, in order to, among other things, include the inquirer in the inquiry, the innovator in the innovation (Purser & Montuori, 1999). Real understanding and effective action therefore require an approach that is not dictated by disciplinary boundaries.

As Morin wrote:

The observer should not just practice a method that permits her to shift from one perspective to another... She also needs a method to access a metapoint of view on the diverse points of view, including her own point of view. (Morin, 1981, p. 179). Real change will only be possible if and when there are a sufficient number of people from a diverse background and ways of thinking who are able to contribute. In Newton's world, order reigned, and what we perceived as disorder was simply the result of our human ignorance.

In the words of theoretical physicist Paul Davies (*Cosmic Blueprint*, 1989): For three centuries, science has been dominated by the Newtonian and thermodynamic paradigms, which present the universe as either a sterile machine, or in a state of degeneration and decay. Now there is the paradigm of the creative universe, which recognizes the progressive, innovative character of physical processes. The new paradigm emphasizes the collective, cooperative, and organizational aspects of nature; its perspective is synthetic and holistic rather than analytic and reductionistic.

Paradigms that control science can also develop illusions, and no scientific theory is utterly immune to error. Moreover, scientific knowledge alone cannot treat philosophical or ethical questions.

The illusion of control transmits with it a surplus of certainties, which creates so many problems. Such excess is typical of the belief in a progress whose main features are a hypothetical linearity, as well as the absence of unpleasant side effects. Nevertheless, experience demonstrates that all this is actually fragile and uncertain. That is why it is important to know a minimum about human nature, which can bring us the realism that we so much need. In his book, *The Meaning of Human Existence*, American biologist Edward O. Wilson states that we have four fundamental traits: 1) our instincts are very powerful and often brutal; 2) our intelligence is moderate; 3) our wisdom is dangerously limited; 4) our science is overly confident.

According to Wilson, "people prefer to be with others who like them, speak the same dialect, and hold the same beliefs." An amplification of this evidently leads with frightening ease to racism and prejudice. Self-deception is particularly present when it comes to intelligence. According to the Spanish philosopher Julián Marías, definitions are always universal, whereas human things are individual and sensible. Thus the things you perceive through your intelligence are your things. If you have a mind warped by some kind of ideology, you only will be able to perceive the world that this ideology imposes on you.

We want everything to be smooth, fast, and quantified, but the world is most of the time not so clear, simple, and not as quantifiable as we wish. We do not have the power to entirely reduce the world to our wishes and expectations, but we have been trying to condense and quantify what cannot be abbreviated nor calculated.

Hungarian-born British thinker Arthur Koestler believes the mind of the human species includes a pathological component. Many further attitudes of the philosophy of "as if" could be added. According to Koestler the philosophy of "as if" is helpful because we humans are not rational, contrary to what we usually claim. Koestler claims that the most intuitive diagnosticians—the poets—have always maintained that the human being is evil. But the anthropologists, the psychiatrists, and the scholars have never taken them seriously. On the contrary, they keep blind to all evidence—and this could be a rather ironic demonstration that they also have adopted the philosophy of "as if".

However, with or without scientific theories or explanations, our behavior remains basically unpredictable. Koestler gives as additional examples such as the purges of Stalin and Mao Tse-tung in which millions of people were murdered. The alleged goal was "to cleanse the society to prepare humanity for the golden age of the classless society". It is obvious that saying "everything is going to be all right" is much more comforting than saying "it will not always work." It seems we are afraid to ask the right questions.

All this leads us to the Anthropocene issue. Scientists have been evaluating the need to establish a new geological era named Anthropocene—"the human age." The Anthropocene aims to record humanity's impact on the planet but there is fierce debate behind the scenes. The consequences are well known: *Homo sapiens* have warmed the planet, raised sea levels, eroded the ozone layer, and acidified the oceans. In other words, despite the usual claims to the contrary when it comes to the natural world, "the human age" has been characterized by irresponsibility, violence, and destruction. "We want to help people imagine their role in the world, which is maybe more important than many of them realize," says paleobiologist Scott Wing.

Romain Gary, French/Lithuanian writer and diplomat stated: "The word 'humanity' contains inhumanity; inhumanity is a deeply human characteristic." Xenophanes of Colophon, an ancient Greek philosopher (c. 570–c. 475 BC), had already said: "Even if a human mind could successfully visualize the world as it really is, that mind would have no way of knowing that it had done so." People like to see themselves as "practical" individuals, with their feet firmly planted in reality. But what reality are they talking about? Paul Feyerabend reinforces this perception: "The appearance of absolute truth is nothing more than the result of an absolute conformity."In 1991, the British sociologist Anthony Giddens developed the concept of "ontological security." It refers to our need to give a sense of order to our lives. When we are exposed to things outside ourselves, and how it compares to our idealized version of the world, we feel a sense of ontological insecurity. This basically leads to "wishful thinking." The main objective is to mitigate our existential insecurity. This is what raises and maintains our constant quest for certainties. Thus the search for meaning, the fear of uncertainty, and the discomfort in the face of the world's complexity seem to have the same root.

We must understand that we are in a transition from a mechanistic era to a historical period in which we will increasingly have to deal with the complexity of the world. Therefore the search for certainties cannot be called illegitimate. It manifests itself in many ways, we should not forget that some fundamental questions about the human condition and the meaning of life have been approached through the history of civilization. History is an indispensable to our understanding of the world. Everyone knows that when one wants to explain something difficult to understand, telling a story is a traditionally effective tool. This profound human need to believe has been producing what the American thinker Reinhold Niebuhr calls "necessary illusions."

How to avoid self-deception

There is a consensus that the only legitimate mode of thinking is the one that prevails in our culture, which is mechanistic and tries to oversimplify and compute everything. This is the main result of the proliferation of algorithms. The best way to expand our intelligence is to expand our wisdom. Intelligence enriched by wisdom. Intelligence can be defined as general cognitive problem-solving skills; wisdom can be understood as the use of intelligence so as not to bring harm to other people, ourselves, and the natural world. Intelligence certainly has to do with perceiving the environment and interacting with it. That is what the biology of knowledge calls "structural coupling." All this means is that we have got to read and think a little more. Our intelligence is not the simple accumulation of what we live, read, hear, and repeat. It is what we think and do out of all that. Science and technology are vital, provided they are used by intelligence guided by wisdom. But these combinations are often improperly practiced.

According to the Gregory Bateson well-known observation: "The major problems in the world are the result of the difference between how the nature works and the way people think." The world we are able to perceive is complex, multiple, and diverse but we keep trying to describe it only through our usual mechanistic, shallow, and limited language. Chilean scientists Francisco Varela and Humberto Maturana focus the process of knowledge in the observer as a living being. Hence the need to create discussion networks through which people could exchange explanations about their living experiences.

For all this, we need a complex anthropology. The human being is not only a *Homo sapiens* and *Homo demens*, as stated by Morin. The *sapiens* relate to Nietzsche's Apollonian man, in whom intelligence prevail: he is wise, sensible, and rational. "The Apollonian tendency is associated with the instinct for form, beauty, moderation, and symmetry. It is the basis of all analytic distinctions."(Nietzsche, *The Birth of Tragedy, 1872*). The *demens* is Nietzschean Dionysian man, in whom the passions predominates: he is irrational, unruly, and untimely. The Apollonian and Dionysian man complete each other in the sense that these two terms create our society.

I would like to include a third element. If we want to make complex anthropology even accurate, it is essential to add the *Homo ineptus*. Humans are silly, unaware, and neglectful. This third dimension, like the previous two, is present in varying degrees in all of us. Throughout history, the *ineptus* has accompanied the *sapiens* and the *demens*. The *ineptus* believes that the course of history is predictable and that the objective is always to improve the human condition. Nevertheless, this belief does not prevent him from always acting against his fellow men. The *ineptus* is subtly destructive. The Brazilian writer Paulo Francis once said that human stupidity is the most underestimated force in history, and we cannot doubt it. Just look at the political rulers who have withdrawn from the international conferences in France and Japan aimed at mitigating climate change. This is Homo ineptus. The *Homo ineptus* is our greatest enemy. The survival of our species is increasingly threatened by its presence. Many individuals focus on the obvious damages caused by the demens but don't see how undetectably harmful the ineptus can be. More than ever, we leaders who not only possess knowledge but those who have wisdom and understanding, leaders who look at the big picture and want to solve real world problems. Such leaders don't only concentrate on the here and now but also look at taking care of the future.

It's sad though when man begins to see himself as *Homo deus* (man as God) when he is mortal and imperfect. A sure way to blind him about his limits and make him think he is infallible. During the Industrial Revolution, mechanization of tasks reduced humans to keepers and feeders of machines—the cotton mills, for example. In the natural environment, mechanization of agriculture and forestry meant fields and woodlands could no longer be small and with mixed crops, but needed to be straight, large (machine economics), and growing monoculture food or tree crops (machine inflexibility). That change had a devastating impact on our rural environment and its wildlife. In Industrial Revolution societies, jobs took priority over families, leading to social fragmentation. Expect similar significant changes to whatever area of the environment or human activity AI is applied to. On a spiritual level, the *Fall of Man* (the symbolic Biblical narrative) is still continuing and AI is another example of it. The soul of man is pointing in the wrong direction. Instead of pushing further into the material world, we should be spending our effort and resources discovering our huge inner potential. Then, when we have sorted out our negativity, we might become safe enough to possess nuclear energy, bio-tech, and AI, etc., all of which currently, unfortunately, act to multiply the effect of our destructiveness.

British philosopher John Gray stated, "Nothing is more commonplace than to lament that moral progress has failed to keep pace with scientific knowledge. If only we were more intelligent and more moral, we could use technology only for benign ends. The fault is not in our tools, we say, but in ourselves..." The idea of progress rests on the belief that the growth of knowledge and the advance of the species go together—if not now, then in the long run. The biblical myth of the Fall of Man contains the forbidden truth. "Knowledge does not make us free. It leaves us as we have always been, prey to every kind of folly."

For Edgar Morin, all knowledge, however precise it may seem, includes variable degrees of error, uncertainty, and illusion. We all have, to a greater or lesser degree, a propensity for self-deception, which can manifest itself in the following ways: a) rationalization self-justification; b) selective retention; c) Psychological projection (attaching our own short comings to another person); d) Selective listening and attention.

It's one of the ways by which many leaders allow themselves to be manipulated. They surround themselves with sycophants and loyalists who stroke their ego and tell them what they want to hear—smooth words. There is a classic *Sopranos* episode where Carmela Soprano tells her husband Tony that his crew only laughs at his jokes because he's the boss. Tony then starts to say things that aren't funny at all while his crew laughs and hangs on his every word. The day you became the leader of your organization you did not suddenly become the genesis for all of your organization's best ideas.

THE SEVEN TYPES OF FOLLOWERS

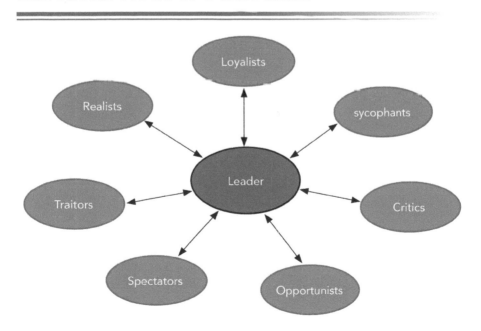

"Strategy, as well as knowledge, continues to be navigating an ocean of uncertainties among archipelagos of certainties. Everything that includes opportunity includes risk, and thinking must recognize the opportunities of risks as the risks of opportunities."—*Edgar Morin*

One might then suppose that emotions may blind us, so to reduce error we should ensure intellectual and emotional development are separable. Spinoza wrote that emotions are indispensable components of rationality. Without the emotions, reason does not produce rationality, but rationalism. Rationality recognizes the importance of emotions, feelings, and subjectivity as part of human nature but this does not mean that it is exclusively determined by them.

According to a new paper by Villanova's Daniel Ziegler (2016), you can understand these classic defense mechanisms even after you strip away their psychoanalytic roots, using Rational Emotive Cognitive Behavior Therapy (RECBT):

This is how RECBT works with each of these defense mechanisms:

1 **Repression** – This is the fundamental defense mechanism in Freudian theory: What you forget can't hurt you.

2 **Projection** – In projection, you take what you think are unacceptable impulses and "project" them to others. They are ideas about ourselves that we can't accept.

3 **Displacement** – Transferring your unacceptable feelings toward someone you're supposed to love or perhaps fear. For example, if you're treated badly by your boss, you may go home and express your anger by yelling at a family member.

4 **Rationalization** – In this defense mechanism, you use an excuse to justify an experience that reflects negatively on you.

5 **Reaction Formation** – The basic idea behind this rather circuitous defense mechanism is that you turn your unacceptable impulses into their opposite.

6 **Denial** – Classic denial means that you escape certain facts or feelings by ignoring or distorting them.

7 **Regression** – The Freudian view of regression is that when you're stressed, you revert to an earlier psychosexual stage when you felt happier and more secure.

8 **Intellectualization** – Like rationalization, in intellectualization you come up with a reason to explain away the negative results of an event or encounter.

9 **Sublimation** – In the Freudian view, sublimation is perhaps the healthiest of all defense mechanisms. You take unacceptable impulses—and turn them into behaviors that will not cause problems, and may even do some good. Sadly most people never get to this stage.

Even scientific thinkers resist attack from adverse theories and arguments. True rationality is by nature open and engaged in dialogue from contradictory points of view. It negotiates with the doubtful. True rationality can be recognized by its capacity to recognize its own deficiencies. As Francois Recanati observed: "Understanding statements, far from being reduced to pure and simple deciphering, is a non-modular process of interpretation that mobilizes general intelligence and draws broadly on knowledge about the world."

Long considering itself proprietor of rationality, Western Europe judged all cultures in terms of technological performance and saw nothing but error, illusion, and backwardness in other cultures.

"Who are we?" is inseparable from, "Where are we?" "Where do we come from?" "Where are we going?" Questioning our human condition begins with questioning our purpose in the world.

Neuroscience has discovered that there is no function in our brain that allows us to differentiate between dream and reality or between the imaginary and the concrete. To deal with error, uncertainty, and illusion, Morin recommends the use of rationality and proposes the controls described below:

1 **Control of the context.** Changes only occur through investments in energy, adequate resources, and logical approaches.

Therefore, the contextual control requires clear answers to the following questions:

- ➢ What is observable, what can be changed?
- ➢ Should the changes be initially micro-structural or macro-structural?
- ➢ The agents of change have political and economic power to do the desired changes
- ➢ If they don't, what changes can be done with the resources and power currently available?

2 **Control of the practice.** It comes from the above described, and also from the perception that the sequence concept of practices to results is not linear but they interact with one another in a circular relation.

3 **Control of the mind.** In our brain there is no structure or function that allows us to clearly distinguish between hallucinations and the perception of the real, dreams and reality, imaginary and concrete.

Control of the mind is exercised through memory, aided by logical operations. The questions to be asked are:

- ➢ Are there reliable chronological records that survive thorough rational analyses based on verifiable measures?
- ➢ Are we prepared to think in terms of the whole without losing sight of the isolated parts?
- ➢ Are we prepared to think in both short-term and long-term, when it is necessary?

The revelation that the world we live in is subject to uncertainty and unpredictability has been revealed in the discoveries of microphysics, thermodynamics, cosmology, and neuroscience. Dealing with uncertainty and unexpectedness requires a strategic attitude, which allows us to modify our actions and also our expectations—over time.

Morin: "One must expect the unexpected. And when the unexpected manifests itself, we must be able to revise our theories and ideas, and not forcibly introduce the new fact into a theory incapable of embracing it." The recent rise of high-profile corporate scandals has raised many questions. One of them is leadership effectiveness. Leadership development has traditionally been quite narrow, with a decided focus on the analytical realm of leadership. In short, what happened with the individuals in leadership positions in these failed organizations? Were they simply devotees of agency theory (cf., Jensen & Meckling, 1976), narrowly focused on doing whatever possible to ensure the best possible quarterly results and related stock performance for their firms? However, the exponential growth of big data, IoT, AI and robotics, coupled with the evolving needs, and expectations of employees, points to the potential need for a more holistic approach to leadership.

Gregersen, Morrison, and Black (1998) published the results of their study on global leadership development. According to responses from Fortune 500 companies, 85% of the companies did not have enough leaders, and 67% had leaders with fewer capabilities than were required to do their jobs.

In response to leadership lapses, they prescribed the ACES model of leadership development. Their model seeks to improve leadership training by expanding it to cover analytical, conceptual, emotional, and spiritual realms of leadership.

The ACES Model of Holistic Leadership:

1 Analytical – Developing leaders who are adept at understanding and managing discrete complexity. Analytically-skilled leaders understand and manage the individual "trees" in the "forest" quite well. Key Skills: Quantitative analysis, Logical reasoning, and Decisiveness.

2 Conceptual – Developing leaders that are adept at both understanding and managing interrelated complexity and fostering creativity. Leaders with strong conceptual skills understand and manage the "forest" within which the individual "trees "are growing. Key Skills: Qualitative analysis, Creativity, and Curiosity.

3 Emotional – Highly attuned emotional leaders are skilled at understanding and managing human emotion as an inevitable phenomenon in a business setting, and they leverage this to influence follower behavior. Key Skills: Persuasive communication, Empathic understanding, and Self-monitoring.

4 Spiritual – Developing enlightened leaders who recognize the value of spirituality. Spiritually enlightened leaders enable their followers to connect both individual tasks and the mission of the larger firm to deeply held moral and ethical values. Key Skills: Self-reflection, Integrity, and Meditative thinking.

The most effective leaders intentionally strive to integrate all four domains into a truly holistic approach.

Economist and journalist Tim Hartford notes that the big data quickly became an obsession among business men, scientists, governments, and the media. In his 2014 Significance Lecture for the Royal Statistical Society, titled "The Big Data Trap," Hartford discussed the pitfalls of putting too much faith in what can be gleaned from the masses of found data that is continually being collected. For most businesses, what really matters are the so-called "found data," that is, the gigantic compilations of searches on the web, purchases, payments with credit cards and mobile phones, and their interpretations and commercial applications.

Given the human tendency to worship numbers many may be led to believe, it is actually possible to totally mathematize and artificialize the natural world. Harford also notes that big data do not solve the problem of insights. It is also a perfect example of what Arthur Koestler once noted about our human species: the contrast between our unmatched technological prowess and our also incomparable incompetence to solve our social problems.

The Need for a New Way of Thinking

The world is full of uncertainty. Change is so rapid, and technology in particular is playing such a dramatic role in this acceleration, that we can't in good faith expect things to stay the same for very long. Unraveling the complexities of global economics and its social impact is an enormous challenge. Disturbingly, in times of transition, complexity and uncertainty, there is a tendency to seek out absolute foundations, certainty, simplicity, and a framework that will make sense of the world and reduce our anxiety.

Additionally, we all have traits that others see, but we are unable to see in ourselves. We call these "blind spots." We all have blind spots. These are things that others know about you, but about which you are completely clueless. In a leadership role, some of these blind spots can be particularly costly not only to you but others as well.

Failing to recognize your cognitive biases is a bias in itself. Notably, Princeton psychologist Emily Pronin has found that, "individuals see the existence and operation of cognitive and motivational biases much more in others than in themselves." In 1955, American psychologists Joseph Luft and Harrington Ingham created the Johari Window to help us better understand how we interact with others. They taught us four areas: open, hidden, unknown, and blind spots.

I once worked with a client who was confident all of his employees knew the top goal and challenged me to prove him wrong. The next day I presented a list of different goals that his employees said were most important. Although the leader saw himself as the goal-oriented, visionary-type, they felt he was good at micromanaging. Bias becomes embedded from the moment we are born and develops throughout our lives by influences we may not even perceive.

Sidney Dekker noted three errors of analysis, anchored to hindsight bias:

1 **Predetermined outcome:** "We think that a sequence of events inevitably led to an outcome. We underestimate the uncertainty people faced at the time, or do not understand how very unlikely the actual outcome would have seemed."

2 **Linear sequencing:** "We see a sequence of events as linear, leading nicely and uninterruptedly to the outcome we now know about. Had we seen the same situation from the inside, we would have recognized the possible confusion of multiple possible pathways..."

3 **Oversimplification:** "We oversimplify causality. When we are able to trace a sequence of events backwards (which is the opposite of how people experienced it at the time) we easily couple "effects" to preceding "causes" (and only those causes)..."

Along with these errors in thinking, there are other important cognitive biases related to decision-making when facing uncertainty.

> Confirmation bias: The tendency to interpret new evidence as confirmation of one's existing beliefs or theories. We place extra value on evidence consistent with a favored belief

- ➤ Anchoring and insufficient adjustment: We tend to base decisions on known "anchors" or familiar positions, with an *adjustment* relative to this starting point.
- ➤ Groupthink: We strive for consensus at the cost of a realistic evaluation of alternative courses of action.
- ➤ Egocentrism: We focus narrowly on our own perspective and discount the viewpoint of others.

We use social heuristics, which look for similarity on how someone dresses and acts according to the way everybody else acts. When we do not act in accordance to the social heuristics then these instincts of disgust come into play, without stopping and reconsidering that our intuitions which are not logical are controlling them. For instance, when seeing a homeless person, our instincts automatically start to insert intuitions about that person; although they may be distinct, we can't see the separation of their interplays.

To prevent the self-deception we must practice:

- ➤ Self-awareness – we must make, reflect, and review our decisions and past actions. We must also be willing to acknowledge our short comings and make the necessary changes. In Satya Nadella's book, *Hit Refresh*, he states, "Since my remarks at Grace Hopper, Microsoft has made the commitment to drive real change—linking executive compensation to diversity progress, investing in diversity programs, and sharing data publicly about pay equity for gender, racial, and ethnic minorities. In some ways, I'm glad I messed up in such a public forum because it helped me confront an unconscious bias I didn't know I had, and it helped me find a new sense of empathy for the great women in my life and at my company."

  In September 2017, Mark Zuckerberg posted an apology to his Facebook page. In the post he states, "For the ways my work was used to divide people rather than bring us together,

233

I ask forgiveness and I will work to do better". We need more leaders who will own their mistakes and take the necessary steps to correct them.

- ➤ Pay close attention all the developments not just the good but the bad as well. Look at the long-term as well as short-term effects.

- ➤ Study the past. To move forward we can only connect the dots from looking at history.

- ➤ Ask the tough questions and face the truth. Our blind spots may result from making false assumptions instead of confronting problems.

- ➤ Surround yourself with individuals from multiple disciplines and seek diverse viewpoints.

- ➤ Pay full attention to critics and criticisms. Don't only welcome feedback from those who agree with you.

- ➤ Request feedback—The 360 degree feedback on a regular basis is always a great check of where you are today and what to work on for the future.

- ➤ Ask for help. Do you see what I see?

"Looking through a Renaissance lens, what to do now becomes startlingly clear. We need to welcome genius. To understand that disruptive change and technological revolutions can spread both immense good and harm. To celebrate diversity and overcome prejudice. To raise public and private patronage. To embrace change, and strengthen public safety nets in ways that embolden us all. To build new crossroads and welcome migrants. To tear up the (mental) maps that unhelpfully divide people. To stoke virtues—especially honesty, audacity and dignity. To champion collective endeavours as well as individual freedoms," says Goldin and Kutarna (2016). Self-deception limits true progress. You must be prepared to face the hard truth. It may mean standing alone and swimming upstream when everyone else is floating downstream but it is the only way to truly succeed in this new technological era.

CHAPTER TEN

EMOTIONAL INTELLIGENCE: THE IGNORED INTELLIGENCE

In an economy where artificial intelligence is everywhere, a leader's ability to relate with employees emotionally—emotional intelligence (EI)—will be the differentiating factor that defines "high intelligence." The primary responsibilities of leadership are setting direction and enrolling people. Emotions are central to both these activities; emotions move people. Ed Hess of the University of Virginia's Darden School of Business writes in HBR, "The new smart will be determined not by what or how you know but by the quality of your thinking, listening, relating, collaborating, and learning." Despite the advent of robots and automation, humans will be required for jobs that require creativity, critical thinking, innovative thinking, and high emotional engagement. More than before, we need leaders to be emotionally sensitive to their employees in this automation era where people are being replaced by machines or unreasonable expectations are placed on them. Employees need a leader who will coach them and support them to be their very best and transition them through change. A leader lacking in EI is not able to effectively gauge the needs, and expectations, of those they lead. Leaders who react from their emotions without filtering them can create mistrust amongst their employees and can seriously put in danger their working relationships. Reacting with erratic emotions can be detrimental to engagement and overall culture. Good leaders must be self-aware and understand how their communication (verbal and nonverbal) can affect the team.

The primary responsibility of leadership is setting a vision and enrolling people. Emotions is central to this; emotions influence people.

Emotional intelligence as a component of interpersonal skill, aids in managing personal feelings along with the moods and emotions of others (George, 2000). Emotional intelligence is different from personality in that it brings together a varied group of abilities which explain how people recognize and manage emotions (Jordan, Ashkanasy, & Hartel, 2002). Therefore, EI influences relationship development. Too often, leaders attempt to eliminate emotion in their decision-making processes. However emotion plays a part in every decision, whether we realize it or not. A leader has a difficult but important job: leading a team of unique individuals to follow the vision and mission and to motivate them to work collaboratively toward a common goal. Not all leaders can do this effectively. Why do some leaders succeed while others fail?

Successful leaders get to where they are by achieving results through others. They connect with the people they want to influence. They understand their own emotions and also have the ability to understand other's feelings and to adapt themselves to the people around them. The greater the ability to understand themselves, their people, and to receive feedback, the more likely they are to choose an approach that will create the best result for their organization. Although there are exceptions, most great leaders succeed because they have a high degree of EI. The "human" touch makes managers better leaders. Until a few years ago, Intelligence Quotient (IQ) was considered to be the major indicator of success. Companies were looking for leaders with a high level of hard skills even though they lacked soft skills. Today, however, it's quite the opposite. EI taps into a fundamental element of human behavior that is distinct from your intellect. There is no known connection between IQ and EI.

EI refers to the collection of abilities used to identify, understand, control, and assess the emotions of oneself and others. It is more complex and powerful than just being "nice." The term was first defined in 1990 by two behavioral researchers named Peter Salavoy and John Mayer, and it was more broadly popularized by Rutgers psychologist Daniel Goleman in his 1996 book, where he discussed the importance of EI to business leadership. In one of HBR's most enduring articles, "What Makes a Leader," he states unequivocally:

"The most effective leaders are all alike in one crucial way: they all have a high degree of what has come to be known as EI. It's not that IQ and technical skills are irrelevant. They do matter, but...they are the entry-level requirements for executive positions. My research, along with other recent studies, clearly shows that EI is the sine qua non of leadership. Without it, a person can have the best training in the world, an incisive, analytical mind, and an endless supply of smart ideas, but he still won't make a great leader".

The ability to be intuitively in tune with your emotions, as well as having sound situational awareness can be a great tool for leading a team. The act of knowing, understanding, and responding to emotions, and overcoming stress in EI is the key to professional success. Working collectively with others means interacting with a variety of personalities and whether this involves managing direct reports or a project, other people will have a huge impact on the results you achieve.

Understanding the emotional aspect of human interactions can help reduce conflicts and can help build more cohesive teams. Numerous studies have shown a positive relationship between emotionally intelligent leadership and employee engagement and performance. The Levo Institute polled Millennials on the key elements of career development, and 80% of the respondents indicated EI as important, while 87% termed their leaders' EI to their motivation at work.

Former Bank of America executive Dee Hock captured the importance of a leader's EI in the following observation: "The first and paramount responsibility of anyone who purports to manage is to manage the self: one's own integrity, character, ethics, knowledge, wisdom, temperament, words and acts...it is a complex, unending, incredibly difficult, oft-shunned task...however, without management of self, people are not fit for authority no matter how much [of it] they acquire..."

According to Talent Smart, EI accounts for 58% of a person's job performance. Talent Smart president Travis Bradberry points out, "Your emotional intelligence is the foundation for a host of critical skills—it impacts most everything you do and say each day." A survey by CareerBuilder found that 71% of 2,662 US hiring managers interviewed chose emotionally intelligent candidates over those with higher IQ when hiring.

EI can't be mustered up by machines. Yet a majority of managers undermine the importance of people skills to their success. Empathy and vulnerability are purely human, and the real key to moving forward in any endeavor.

Daniel Goleman and Dr. Richard Boyatzis created a framework of behavioral qualities that demonstrate EI. It is composed of four domains:

- ❖ Self-Awareness
- ❖ Self-Management
- ❖ Social Awareness
- ❖ Relationship Management

Personal competence comprises your self-awareness and self-management skills. Personal competence is your ability to be aware of your emotions and manage your behavioral tendencies.

- ❖ Self-Awareness is described as: "The ability to recognize and understand personal moods and emotions and drives, as well as their effect on others."

- ❖ Self-Management is your ability to use awareness of your emotions to positively direct your behavior.

SELF-AWARENESS

Why is this so important? Self-awareness is the keystone of EI. It's about establishing a more accurate internal barometer—one that is aligned and tuneful with the world around you.

Here's the problem: A middle manager for a large manufacturing chain thinks of himself as a "results oriented" kind of guy. If asked about his leadership style, he'll tell you that he is assertive and clear in making sure his employees know what needs to be done. If his team doesn't meet performance targets, he knows it is because his staff didn't do their work properly, not because of his leadership. Ask that manager's staff about what he's like and you'll hear a very different story. What the manager considers "assertive," his staff will tell you is he gets angry easily, and is manipulative. And those performance problems? They will say that everyone is so tired of his threats that they don't care whether they make their numbers. Clearly, this manager isn't aware of the negative impact he has on his staff or of how his emotions affect his leadership. What he lacks is Emotional Self-Awareness.

Self-Awareness begins by Self-Assessment: This can be defined as having the ability to recognize one's own emotions, values and drivers, strengths, weaknesses, and understanding and also knowing how your emotions can affect others around. It's being aware of your own reactions to people, things, situations, and events. The first step in improving your EI is to recognize your emotions, understand the root cause of your feelings, and how you react to them. It's also understanding the consequences of your reactions. Keep in mind that your emotional state is a dynamic condition, and it can vary considerably from moment to moment throughout the day. Your reactions to things may not always be immediately clear or obvious; it is important for you to understand why you have a given emotional reaction to something. Especially when you are feeling a strong wave of emotions, pay particular attention to being "in the moment" and attentive to the "here and now," and ask yourself why you are feeling the way you are.

As a goal, the development of self-awareness is to gain an understanding about the nature and "internal source" of your gut reactions, as well as how to manage and harness these reactions to maximize positive outcomes. It entails being completely honest with yourself; it also requires that you be totally objective as you assess and evaluate yourself. Once you identify this, you can start working on improving your self-regulations. Without reflection we cannot truly understand who we are, or why we make certain decisions. Self-awareness helps you to identify the traits that serve you well and the ones that work against you. Those that have a strong understanding of who they are and what their values are can improve themselves on a regular basis. Laura Wilcox, former director of management programs at Harvard Extension School explains: "The core of high EI is self-awareness: if you don't understand your own motivations and behaviors, it's nearly impossible to develop an understanding of others."

Self-awareness also means understanding the consequences of your actions. How will your conduct be received or interpreted by others, and how might they react? Do not make the common mistake of assuming that other people think the same way you do, or hold the same moral or ethical values, or even share your sense of humor. Self-awareness also means understanding the limitations of your own observations, with the caveat that your observations may be misleading or your assumptions incorrect. Consider that your physical state can impact your emotions as well as your ability to reason, make decisions, and to execute other cognitive thought processes. Keep in mind that your instinctive reaction is to avoid confronting these uncomfortable situations; simply by being aware of this fact can help you overcome your internal resistance and achieve breakthroughs. Self-reflection can come in a number of forms. Listening to music, prayer, spending time with God, even a thoughtful walk or jog can provide you with the opportunity to know yourself better.

Emotional Self-Awareness isn't something that you achieve in one leap. It's small steps every day. It's a conscious choice to be continuously self-aware.

How to Develop Self-Awareness

- ➤ Develop a daily self-reflection practice. Make time for adequate introspection

- ➤ Don't make sudden decisions. Pause and listen to yourself and pause and listen to others.

- ➤ Name and understand personal emotions rather than transferring them to others.

- ➤ Recognize and consider what is at the root of a feeling or emotion before reacting to an employee or making a hasty decision.

- ➤ Maintain a journal of emotions to recognize your feelings' patterns through the course of time and use the insights to effectively mould your reactions.

- ➤ Ask peers for feedback. Get feedback about your leadership style from those you work with, listen to what people say, and implement these changes into your life. Do you engage with your direct reports to get 360-degree professional feedback? Do you set monthly, quarterly, or annual goals for improvement and personal development? This can help reveal some blind spots you may have.

➤ Be open to uncomfortable feelings or feedback without reacting in adverse ways.

➤ Filter your thoughts before you put them to action.

If you can't control your motions, team members might feel their leader is not stable enough to maintain control over his or her emotions, much less the situation at hand, and they lose faith in their leader, thereby deteriorating his or her effectiveness. It can be challenging to critique yourself, which is where collaborative feedback comes in. Emotionally intelligent leaders constantly seek feedback to analyze and strategize how to constantly improve themselves. As with all attributes of EI, the greater your ability to become proficient at building your self-awareness skills, the greater your ability to get what you want out of life.

"Success is nothing more than a few simple disciplines, practiced every day."—Jim Rohn

Korn Ferry Hay Group research found that among leaders with multiple strengths in Emotional Self-Awareness, 92% had teams with high energy and high performance. In sharp contrast, leaders low in Emotional Self-Awareness created negative climates 78% of the time. Great leaders create a positive emotional climate that encourages motivation and commitment.

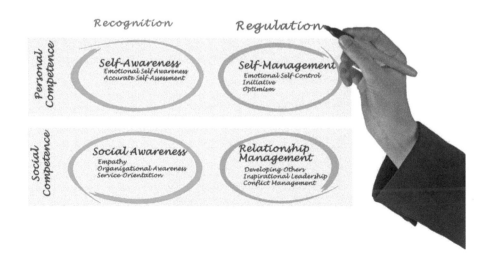

SELF-MANAGEMENT

Effective self-management requires competency in self-awareness as its foundation. The second pillar of EI is self-regulation—also known as self-discipline. It's essential, but not enough in itself just to understand self-awareness. It's just the first step. The next step is translating this understanding into a practice of self-regulation. Feelings vary in intensity; higher levels of emotional intensity tend to thwart rational thought and therefore tend to dictate your actions. In cases of extreme stress, your emotions can take over, which is sometimes referred to as an "emotional hijacking." While it may be very difficult to use your rational brain under such circumstances, you can definitely learn to moderate, control, and override your emotions in almost all aspects of daily life. While there is a "cause and effect" relationship between you and your environment, do not simply accept that your emotional reactions are automatic and beyond your control—they are not. You can rise above any reflexive urges within you, and manage your reactions so that you respond in a positive, cooperative, and constructive manner.

Self-regulation: Also known as discipline. Are you in control of yourself or do you frequently make emotional outburst or impulsive decisions or harbor preconceived notions about others? This involves controlling our negative emotions in order to keep the team moving in a positive direction. Leaders can't afford to lose their temper with so many eyes on them. Leaders with high EI are able to regulate themselves and stay in control. You can modify your behavior for the better if you can identify your own bad habits and catch yourself when you're doing them. Instead of reacting to their emotions, they are able to engage their thinking capacity to come up with better decisions. For example, resist the temptation to interrupt someone simply because you don't agree, or don't like, whatever they are saying. Patience is a virtue in the art of self-management. Leaders who are 'hasty' often speak before they think which results in having to retract a statement or make a public apology.

Self-regulation applies to more than our external behavior. Self-regulation also applies to our internal, emotional behavior. Steven Stosny, Ph.D., explains in his *Psychology Today* article "Self-Regulation," that behaviorally, self-regulation is the ability to act in your long-term best interest, consistent with your deepest values. Violation of one's deepest values causes guilt, shame, and anxiety, which undermine wellbeing.

Let's illustrate this point: "I need to avoid yelling at my staff because it demoralizes them. I'm not going to allow myself to act like that. I have the unique ability to make a huge impact on my staff, and I'm excited to make that impact as positive and valuable as possible."

Self-regulation is about acting with consideration for the impact it will have on others, and also about your commitment to personal accountability. When you stay calm and positive you can think and communicate more clearly. The clarity of emotions can make you nonjudgmental in your approach.

To be more self-regulated:

- ➤ Act in accordance with your deepest values.
- ➤ Have a clear knowledge of what aspects trigger you off then have a plan of steps to take to prevent you flying off the handle.
- ➤ Take ownership: Own your mistakes, decisions, and their consequences.
- ➤ Do necessary tasks you hate daily to strengthen your willpower.
- ➤ Have a friend or business partner to hold you accountable for your goals.
- ➤ Strengthen self-regulatory "muscles" by visualizing success.

It's also important to try to take control over the stream-of-consciousness, or "internal conversations" that are continually going on inside of your head. Everyone has literally tens of thousands of thoughts running through their heads each day. These different thoughts can have an impact on our moods and emotions; while they can be, and often are, positive thoughts, we sometimes have the tendency to fill our heads with negative thoughts and ideas. Try to redirect negative thoughts and put things in a more rational and logical perspective. For example, instead of saying to yourself: "This employee is pushing my buttons," tell yourself: "I will look at this situation from her point of view." Negative generalizations are particularly harmful; they can blind us to the truth and create a distorted image of situations. Not everything goes according to plan. So, you should also accept that situations may come your way that you did not expect—and perhaps don't like.

Emotional Self-Control: Australian researchers found that leaders who manage emotions well had better business outcomes. With practice, you can learn to become more patient and stay in control by giving yourself the time to mentally assimilate things before taking action. Depending on the situation, the time needed may be only a few seconds, or it could be as long as a few weeks or even months. Whatever the circumstances, try to avoid rushed closure, and keep your mind open, even if it feels uncomfortable.

Social competence is made up of your social awareness and relationship management skills; social competence is your ability to understand other people's behavior, attitudes, and motives in order to respond effectively and improve your relationships.

- ❖ Social Awareness is your ability to determine the emotions of other people and understand what is going on.
- ❖ Relationship Management is being aware of your emotions and the emotions of others and using this mindfulness to manage interactions successfully.

SOCIAL AWARENESS

This skill makes leaders unlikely to jump to conclusions or judgment. They are more likely to get to the root of the issue and the cause of strong emotional reactions of others. We all have our own unique perspective and position on things in life; sometimes our thoughts align with others and at other times we might see things quite differently. Social awareness is not about how we regard different facts or situations, but rather manifesting an awareness of the emotions that others may have about those facts or situations. For example, you may be very enthusiastic about a change initiative being launched at work, but your employees may be filled with anxiety and trepidation about it. From your perspective, the new initiative might be a great opportunity for advancement, but not everyone may feel the same way.

In other words, an essential social awareness capability is exemplary listening skills. This means not only catching every word someone is telling you, but also the tone, pace, volume, etc., of their message. In today's society, this is actually most important when you are speaking to someone over the telephone. Do not, under any circumstances, multitask while speaking on the telephone. Do not read email, surf the web, read a newspaper, or even look at a magazine cover. You will be distracted, you will miss something (or everything), and the chances are good that the person you are speaking with will know that you are not paying attention. Similarly, when dealing with someone face-to-face, make sure to make eye contact; do not, for example, look at your laptop or stare out the window when speaking or listening. By avoiding these mishaps, you will not only facilitate your own communication cues, but also help get your message across. Also recognize that you may sometimes misread someone; do not automatically assume that you have correctly interpreted all signals from others.

Much of what comprises effective social awareness skills is empathy. But why empathy so important?

To be understood is a need of most...that defines the strength of connection. Leaders and manager who practice empathy in the workplace are better equipped to understand (and meet) their employees' needs. Empathy is the ability for someone to understand and share the feelings of another person. It's a key component of successful human relationships, and the foundation of EI. Sympathy is rarely an ideal response to an employee or customer's problem. Instead, show empathy. Empathy allows you to be professional and caring at the same time.

Are you able to easily put yourself in someone else's situation to give constructive feedback, or listen to others' issues? Empathy is the ability to put yourself in someone else's shoes and understand how they may feel when addressing challenges and problems with them. When one has empathy, the capacity to feel compassion is open. Empathy is defined as the ability to understand and share the feeling of another, even in instances when you believe the other person may be wrong or you disagree with the other person's action, attitude or behavior. You pick up cues to what's being felt and thought. You read between the lines to what is not being said. With empathy, you sense unspoken emotions.

As a leader, you need to have the skill to see everything from different perspectives and being skilled at empathy allows you do so. Neuroscientists have identified the different sections of the brain involved with two distinctive types of empathy: emotional empathy and cognitive empathy. With emotional empathy, we identify the feelings of a person through verbal and nonverbal cues, and experience what they are feeling. With cognitive empathy, we can understand the perspective of another person and the forces that informed their outlook cognitive element is a lot easier to engage with than the emotional, and potentially it is this differential that is at play in management where empathy is discussed, however not actualized, in the relational context. It's a natural way to create genuine, authentic connections...thus trust and loyalty.

Does having empathy contribute to a leader's performance?

That's a question researchers at the Center for Creative Leadership set out to answer when they looked at a sample of over 6,700 leaders from 38 countries. Here's what they found: "Our results reveal that empathy is positively related to job performance. Managers who show more empathy toward direct reports are viewed as better performers in their job by their bosses. The findings were consistent across the sample: empathic emotion as rated from the leader's subordinates positively predicts job performance ratings from the leader's boss."

Leaders possessing high EI don't solely focus on the bottom line. Their style is about growing an organization and the people who are responsible for the bottom line. They are considerate to everyone. They have respect for others. Empathy means not just listening to team members, but also making them feel heard and understood. Leaders should constantly seek to understand the perspective of their team members to effectively communicate changes and feedback—both good and bad. Putting your employees first can lead to happy employees. And, happy employees have been shown to be more creative, more productive, and more likely to be retained. A 2015 study by the Center for Creative Leadership found that higher empathy ratings from a leader's subordinates regularly predicted higher performance reviews from the leader's own boss.

Fundamentally, leadership involves relationships. For effective relationship building, leaders must understand the perspectives of the people with whom they are working. Without empathy, it's difficult or impossible to reflect on the impacts your actions might have on others. An empathetic leader knows when they need to stop talking and listen. Empathy also helps a leader to understand the unique circumstances others are facing, and how those circumstances impact their work.

You can demonstrate empathy by **social awareness:**

➤ Show people that you genuinely care for them and their well-being

➤ Practice active listening—listen intuitively to understand the other person's point of view. Try to comprehend not only the content of what others are saying, but also pick up the feelings behind the words that are being spoken.

➤ Acknowledge others' feelings and opinions and respond to them.

➤ Share your own emotions with team members to help them feel understood.

➤ Advocate for your team to make sure members feel supported and heard.

➤ Take an active interest in their concerns.

➤ Make a habit of trying to see things from your employee's perspective.

The most effective leaders are able to put themselves in others' shoes and to understand how and why employees are reacting to organizational events. At the same time, their empathy does not prevent them from making tough decisions.

Moreover, empathy cannot be used as a lip service tool. It has to be really felt and the outcome has to be a response in a meaningful way. Showing empathy to your employees isn't a weakness, but a strength. When you practice empathy, you can listen deeply. Show that "you really care,"—when you, as a leader, really care about the person, you start to show your personal interest in them to lead them well to achieve their best. So, as a leader, we need to care about people and not pretend to. Congruence and sincerity in our engagement with others is essential.

RELATIONSHIP MANAGEMENT

This is the fourth pillar of EI. In many respects, relationship management draws from all of the other EI skills discussed above, and is a product of how effectively you use them. It is really a combination of "emotional" and "behavioral" components; in this regard, it is more complex than the other EI strategies. It is a person's ability to manage and maintain healthy relationships.

Relationship management involves many things, including sensing and monitoring your emotions and the emotions of those around you, making choices in the context of these emotions, and acting accordingly. It also involves a certain degree of planning and follow-up (such as buying a birthday card and mailing it to your friend so it arrives on time). Whatever the situation, your goal should be to create trustworthy and honest relationships with an appropriate level (and type) of emotional content.

Relationship Management is a measure of your ability to use your awareness of your own emotions as well as the emotions of others, to manage interactions successfully. Note that "interactions" can mean anything from a brief encounter with your local banker, to your interactions over many years with your boss, spouse, family, etc.

If you want to run a successful business, you have to proactively work to maintain positive relationships and establish trust with both employees and peers.

Managing and maintaining relationships is rarely easy; it takes a lot of work, including time, effort (both physical and mental), and a willingness to grow and learn. Relationships are a two-way street—you must do your part to make it work. On the other hand, there may be times when you find (or feel) that you are doing most of the work to maintain a relationship. While relationship management should never gravitate to a system of "keeping score" of your efforts, it is important to talk about a serious imbalance of effort in any relationship with the other person.

Striking the right balance is important in all aspects of relationship management, particularly in professional relationships; for example, it is generally appropriate to express some interest in the personal lives of your colleagues, and also to share some things about yourself, but be careful not to let it get too personal. So, it might be fine to talk about the big fish you caught over the weekend, but it would be inappropriate to share the details of the big argument you had with your spouse about your fishing trip.

You can help build relationships by being curious and inquisitive about others, as well as open about yourself (but not too revealing); try to connect in an engaging but not overbearing fashion. While you might prefer talking about yourself (most of us do), try instead to open the door to allow other people to talk about themselves; ask them questions and demonstrate that you are interested in their story. Also, I strongly advise against taking the view that some people are "beneath" us, and do not warrant our energy and effort. So, don't "save the effort" only for those relationships that you feel are most important. Instead, try to bring out in yourself that inner person who is engaging and interested in everyone, and make it part of your natural way of being.

Relationship management skills help you deal with challenging situations, and develop mutually beneficial interpersonal relationships. This is the key to navigating awkward situations, resolving conflicts, and strengthening communication. Effective leaders are not only aware of what is going on with their people in one-to-one conversations, they are able to pick up the mood and feelings of their work environment. Tuned in emotionally, they are aware of the many factors that can influence the feelings of their employees. They work to develop an organizational environment where giving effective praise is a natural and frequent interaction. As a leader, part of your quest to develop EI should include helping others on your team to do the same. Leaders who react from their emotions without filtering them can severely damage relationships. Careful relationship management cultivates emotionally engaged employees.

Another relationship management issue that we all contend with from time to time, especially in business settings, is the concept of buy-in, or teambuilding—whatever you want to call it. There will be times when you want to rally people around your mission, or simply agree with your way of doing things. For example, when launching a new project, people are more likely to support it if they have been given the opportunity to contribute to planning it ahead of time. Make sure you give them this opportunity. In this regard, you need to be open and accessible, which also helps build trust and understanding. Similarly, when you make a decision that affects others, a little "transparency" can go a long way. Explain the basis for your decision, such as what the issues or problems are, and why you made the choices you did. When your decisions impact others, you owe it to them to explain it. People are more likely to support a decision if they know how or why the decision was made.

Making employees feel understood and accepted is a powerful bonding tool. An informed discussion about not taking things personally is a great preamble to offering constructive criticism for a relationship-based problem that needs resolution. The reflexive response is almost always defensive; it is an expected response to fend off an unpleasant realization and the even more painful sensation that the criticism is likely to be true. But as a manager, your overarching goal should be to make your staff members as successful as possible. If you are to help them fill a gap in their "relationship skill set," you are advised to step lightly (at least at first), and offer constructive mentoring and your heartfelt support to help them mature into a better professional.

Additionally, do you moderate interpersonal conflict discreetly and effectively? Conflict is bound to happen, even among the closest of colleagues. Emotionally intelligent leaders should provide team members with opportunities to address issues and air challenges before they can negatively affect team spirit and to prevent future problems before they arise. Leaders can facilitate discussions without taking sides or downplaying anyone's opinions for those affected to come up with solutions that make everyone involved feel respected.

Indeed, even a few words can make a big difference in relationship management. This is one of the most underutilized tools in the relationship management toolbox. We have all been trained to some degree in basic social niceties, such as saying "please" and "thank you." With very little additional effort, you can offer simple words that mean a great deal to others, and that can go a long way towards building excellent relationships. Be generous with simple praise and compliments; be conscientiously thoughtful of others and look for opportunities to say simple things—even a well-placed "thank you" can be very well received by the other person. In your personal relationships, always try to thank others for simple things, like doing the dishes, taking out the garbage, or running a simple errand.

I called an employee to a meeting. The look on her face was, "Did I do something wrong?" When she sat down, I told her, "Thank you for the great job you are doing." Her response was, "But I didn't do anything out of the ordinary." She then gave the biggest smile. We shouldn't only thank employees when they achieve goals or accomplish targets. How about just thanking them for being part of the team? I started doing this for all my employees and it really strengthened our relationship. To be effective it must be genuine and spontaneous. We are so quick to call employees to a meeting when they do something wrong. How about quickly calling them to your office to thank them when they do something right or just for their role on the team. It's good to thank your team collectively and in group settings but this adds a personal touch. A simple "Thank You" goes a long way. It is always nice when your boss calls you to their office and tells you how happy they are with your work.

In business, a little praise can make a huge difference. It can be highly motivating and yet costs you nothing to say something like: "Dave, your memo on the new software system rollout was very good. I was impressed by how clearly and succinctly you spelled out the details of our planned implementation. I'm sure it will be well received by everyone involved. Keep up the good work!" Dave's confidence and job satisfaction will both improve, and he will also delight in sharing the story with his family at the end of the day.

So, how exactly does one build and maintain positive workplace relationships?

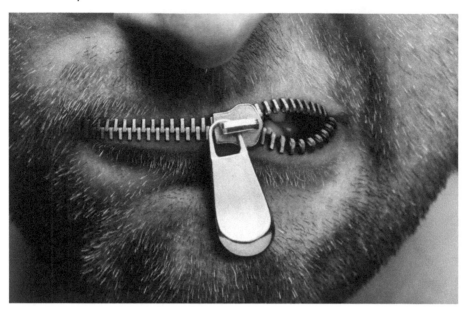

Practice Relationship Management by: Be a good listener and observer—take note of people's body language to know how someone truly feels.

- ➢ Set aside time to grow relationships.
- ➢ Validate your coworkers' experience and point of view.
- ➢ Assign tasks that play to your employees' strengths.
- ➢ Communicate openly and effectively with employees at all levels.
- ➢ Appreciate your team's contribution. Even though some people deny it, everyone craves recognition and validation. It makes that person feel accepted and valued.
- ➢ Never insult anyone.
- ➢ Never, ever use sarcasm.
- ➢ Avoid jokes that disparage a person or a group.

Clarity of communication is most important when taking feedback and criticism from others; taking feedback well can be a "true test" of your EI, as it is often difficult if not painful to have negative things about you revealed. Both social and self-awareness skills are very important as you gauge and assess your reaction to criticism, so be sure to activate your EI skills and listen carefully to the advice being offered. Be grateful, express gratitude for the feedback, and acknowledge the message in a clearly positive manner. Similarly, when you give feedback and criticism, make your comments direct and constructive; what you say should be "actionable" in the sense that the other person can take action to make improvements. Avoid offering criticism without also providing useful suggestions, and be diplomatic—choose your words carefully!

Additionally, if you must "argue," think in terms of "debate" where you try to convince the other side of the validity of your viewpoint based on facts and merits. And remember to respect the feelings of the other person at all times. You don't have to agree with a person's feelings or emotions, but don't try to trivialize or dismiss their feelings either. Avoid telling others how they should or should not feel—their feelings are theirs, not yours, and it is not up to you to tell others what their emotions should be. I believe that respect is inherently a reflection of yourself; by showing disrespect for others, you reveal an element of disdain or disrespect for yourself. This concept is actually at the heart of all relationships, whether casual or intimate, personal or professional; you cultivate in others what you carry inside of yourself. If you do "lose your temper" and let your emotions get the best of you, try to be the first person to admit it.

Whether you are "right" or "wrong" about the issue is scarcely the point. Indeed, in my experience, one of the strongest urges in all of humanity is the desire to be right.

Emotionally-intelligent leaders exemplify traits such as self-awareness, authenticity, and empathy. They read their colleagues and clients. They are able to analyze and interpret data and synthesize and effectively communicate. Some of the biggest corporations in the world now include EI in their training and development programs. According to a study done of leaders from prominent Fortune 500 companies, EI was found to be an incredibly valuable asset for leadership. Shell,

Boeing, BMW, and FedEx have used EI in management training. Sanofi-Aventis, the 4th largest pharmaceutical company in the world, implemented an EI training program in Australia and estimated an almost $6 return for every $1 they invested in the training.

What happens when leaders aren't emotionally intelligent?

➢ Leadership who are low in EI tend to act out because they're not able to manage their own emotions. They may be prone to behaviors such as yelling and blaming. This can create a stressful environment for employees who are always walking on eggshells trying to prevent the next outburst.

➢ Not being emotionally intelligent can inhibit collaboration from subordinates. The team will hesitate to contribute ideas, for fear of how the leader will respond. They will not feel comfortable to approach you to discuss solutions or provide feedback.

➢ Not being emotionally intelligent can also mean an inability to address situations that could be fraught with emotion. Once you are leading others there will be conflict. A leader who isn't clued into others' emotions may have a difficult time recognizing or dealing effectively with conflict.

What happens when leaders are emotionally intelligent?

➢ Leaders who are emotionally intelligent foster safe environments, where employees feel comfortable to take the initiative, take calculated risks, and to share their ideas. They don't dwell on mistakes or failures but see them as learning opportunities.

➢ When a leader is emotionally intelligent, they can leverage emotions for the good of the organization. Leaders often have to implement change, and if they are aware of how others will react to changes then they can anticipate this and plan the most appropriate ways to carry out the change.

➢ Emotionally intelligent leaders don't take things personally and are able to forge ahead with plans without worrying about the impact on their egos. They don't hold grudges and are not easily offended. They frequently and openly recognize the contributions of others.

An example:

You notice that David made a mistake on his report and it's the second time it has happened. It's obvious that you're annoyed, but you should wait a moment until you calm down. Don't tell him off in front of everyone, rather ask him for a quick chat and instead of saying "you made a mistake in your report, again!" say: "David, I've noticed that there are some errors in the report again and I'd like to know if there is anything I can help you with to avoid this problem in the future." You tell him that you've noticed a mistake, but instead of punishing him, you offer him help. If David has a problem or needs help, he won't be afraid to open up and say that out loud once you offer him your support. But if he was just too lazy to double-check the report, your offer will most likely make him feel bad about it.

Leaders with high EI can deliver feedback in team members' preferred method of communication, tailor communication according to different personalities, and adapt their leadership style to what's most effective for motivating and helping the larger group.

Although some people tend to have more EI than others, it is definitely a trait that can be developed. The more we can relate to others, the better we will become at understanding what motivates or upsets them. EI allows for more effective business interactions. If you're a manager and you lack EI, you won't be able to motivate your team, and you won't get along with others. It will also negatively affect communication, morale, and team spirit among your employees.

Understanding and practicing EI can help you to build better relationships with employees and clients. The benefits of actively engaging in a better understanding of EI can lead to more adaptable teams, effective personnel management, and a decrease in interpersonal conflict.

8 QUALITIES THAT DEMONSTRATE EMOTIONAL INTELLIGENCE IN LEADERSHIP

EI is the foundation for a host of critical skills—it impacts most of everything you do and say each day.

1 Intuition

Do you try to identify and solve problems before they arise? Intuitive leaders make decisions based on wisdom. Logic is important, but can't be the only determining factor for making a decision. Effective leaders balance feeling and logic in making decisions. Effective leaders are in touch with their instincts about the right thing to do in the absence of supporting data. A leader who trusts their gut takes calculated risks. They are able to make decisions even without all the information and they inspires others to trust their judgment. Great leadership is about having the confidence to make decisions and not second guess them. Those who inspire others to follow into the unknown, do so possessing self-confidence. They are great judges of character without being judgmental. Such leaders cultivate strengths in their team members and help them get to the point where they're confident and capable to lead others. This includes recommending training for team members or suggesting they apply for internal vacancies you think they are suitable for. They empower their team. Encourage team members to support and rely on each other, work collaboratively, and share knowledge and skills for better team outcomes. The goal of leadership is to make more leaders and not more followers.

In a study conducted by IBM, 200 CEO's stated: "Today's business environment is volatile, uncertain, and increasingly complex. Because of this, the ability to create something that's both novel and appropriate is top of mind."

2 Adaptability

Are you flexible to changes on your team and within your organization? Are you resilient when confronted with difficulty? Adaptability is a key trait of emotionally intelligent leaders. Whether you're dealing with an interpersonal conflict between team members or poor performance, leaders need to be able to quickly respond to new and changing information. They also need to be able to respond to change with humility and compassion. An emotionally intelligent leader has the ability to cope up with uncertainty and imperfection. They can handle all kinds of situations whether it's about managing an undisciplined subordinate or a high demanding job. They do this by appealing to reason and acknowledging others' feelings, thus enabling people to feel that the decisions make sense. Leaders should encourage teams to present constructive feedback in team meetings and also address the human side, the emotions of others when implementing change. Emotionally intelligent leaders show flexibility and adapt constantly. They are always on the watch to recognize change and act anticipating.

3 Motivation

Do you truly love what you do? Are your goals in line with your current aspirations? Are you able to calm yourself down when you're upset or cheer yourself up when you're down? Are you able to motivate others? This brings us to internal motivation as Daniel Goleman describes it, "a passion for work that goes beyond money and status." Effective leaders are passionate about what they do, and they show it. The positive emotion of the leader elevates the team's emotional state, and inspires members to perform with more enthusiasm. They harness that motivation toward increasing performance and overall results. They are not weighed down by negative emotions as anger, hate, or jealously. Just like adaptability, optimism is critical for leaders to motivate and uplift a team to give their best. Good leaders are highly optimistic and believe in the inevitability of success. Emotionally intelligent leaders are more motivated to face situations with confidence. They encourage others to believe that the most challenging goals can be met even with the most daunting obstacles. Now, optimism doesn't mean you're insistently positive, no matter what. It means you can see the bigger picture of a difficult situation, envision the results you want, and work towards that in spite of the many obstacles. Leaders should encourage team members to look at all sides of a problem, come up with creative solutions to challenges, and let them they can reach the goals by working as a team. Leaders who are successful are those who have an optimistic attitude, right kind of flexibility in thoughts, and a positive attitude.

Goleman, Boyatzis, and McKee (2002) have argued that EI is a critical component of leadership effectiveness, particularly as leaders deal with teams. Emotionally intelligent leaders serve as a benefit to teams in two ways. Leaders motivate team members to work together toward team goals. They challenge the members of the team to work toward increasing team effectiveness and performance, facilitate team member interaction dynamics, build interpersonal trust, and inspire team members to implement the articulated vision.

Barbara Fredrickson, a researcher at the University of North Carolina, sums it up this way: "People who experience and express positive emotions more frequently are more resilient, more resourceful, more socially connected, and more likely to function at optimal levels."

4 Authenticity

Do teammates confide in you? Do employees feel comfortable bringing concerns to you when they arise? Leadership is about creating an environment of mutual trust where team members feel supported and comfortable. Research suggests that 8 out of

10 people don't trust leaders. Emotionally intelligent leaders are authentic. Leaders who show their emotions and vulnerability are also better at connecting with many employees on an emotional level. Such leaders don't put on a façade. They don't have one set of guidelines for when people are watching them, and another for when they're alone. Their words match their actions. They genuinely care about people and the people they lead can feel their sincerity. If you pretend to care about other people, they won't respond much to your interest. If you actually care, they will open up to you. If you are faking it, the people around you see right through that.

5 Effective Communication Skills

Leaders possessing high EI are good communicators. Leadership has been described as a process of social influence in which a person can enlist the aid and support of others in the accomplishment of a common goal. Therefore, two way communication is key to leadership success. Once a person is able to manage the thought process, being articulate comes naturally. Clarity in stating a thought or directive gives employees the ability to understand what is expected of them. They also know that communication keeps people motivated and connected. Great leaders are able to communicate their vision in such a way that it motivates their team. They are great communicators: quick to listen and slow to speak. They practice intuitive listening. This is crucial to gaining a complete understanding of situations. Without this full understanding, one can easily waste everyone's time by solving the wrong problem or merely addressing a symptom, not the root cause. The skill of intuitive listening is the heartbeat of all communication. Great leaders function at this level. They listen beyond what is being said; the hidden meaning.

Studies show that effective communication is 7% the words we say and 93% tone and body language. EI also means having awareness about one's verbal as well as nonverbal communication skills, something which is actually critical for a business leader. Misunderstandings and lack of communication are usually the basis of problems between most people. Failing to communicate effectively in a workplace leads to frustration, wasted time, confusion among employees, and in some cases business failure or loss. Good communication results in alignment and a shared sense of purpose.

The Center for Creative Leadership suggests practicing active listening in order to strengthen your empathic ability. Here are a few guidelines for practicing active listening:

- ❖ Make listening your entire focus, instead of only waiting for your turn to speak.
- ❖ Ask questions to help you understand the other person's perspective.
- ❖ Don't judge what the person is saying.
- ❖ Summarize what you think they've shared with you.

6 Sense of Humor

Humor is a great way to win over and influence a team. It minimizes status distinctions between leaders and followers, and encourages interaction. If a leader is serious all the time, then it creates a very austere environment. Some leaders are afraid to relax, because they want to be taken seriously. It's usually a sign of insecurity. An emotionally intelligent leader presents balance. Leaders who use humor allow people to feel comfortable around them. It is humanizing and puts others at ease. Leaders who use humor tend to be much more approachable than the person who never laughs. The more approachable you are, especially as a leader, the more comfortable people will feel around you. Humor acts as a catalyst to influence and inspire others. It helps foster an upbeat atmosphere that encourages interaction, engagement, brainstorming, and creative thinking. All of which leads to greater productivity.

7 Professional Development

Do you encourage team members to learn and cultivate new skills? Do you help team members identify strengths and target areas of improvement? Do you deliver constructive and feedback? Leaders are continuous learners and encourage their team to do the same.

Managers with low EI may be hesitant to train people well since this could mean losing them as a team member or far worse, them taking their position. Emotionally intelligent leaders put the interest of their team first. They can prioritize the development of others over their own desire to have the best team possible. Such leaders help employees identify talents, improve on strengths and weaknesses, and support employee developmental efforts. Managers need to communicate expectations clearly, to give employees the tools they need to do a good job, to set reasonable deadlines, and to offer help if needed. When giving instructions, ask if they understand your instructions—don't assume—as you may not be the great communicator you think you are. If your employees are making mistakes, or not performing up to par, consider that maybe it's because you may be partly at fault.

Here's a scenario: An employee makes a huge mistake for the third time. I have to fire her. This is only my first week in the company so I am not looking forward to dealing with this. I call her to a meeting. I can see she is very nervous. Her palms are sweating and the paper she has in her hand is wet as she asks me, "Are you going to fire me?" What I learned that day meant a huge shake up in the organization:

1) This was not the job she applied for.

2) Her training schedule was curtailed to expedite the transition process because they were short staffed.

3) She was uncomfortable approaching her supervisor for help because she always seemed so busy and acted like she was disturbing her.

If you want people to do a good job. Train them well. Make sure they are in a function where they can use their significant skills and support them. Many organizations are too quick to fire employees when they are the ones at fault.

Anyone can be a boss, but a good one will use leadership skills to inspire, coach, and mentor employees to deliver results. If you want to win the support and commitment of your team and improve engagement you will have to use influence and inspiration rather than solely relying on designated power. Listen, encourage, recognize, and show that you value their contributions and you genuinely care about them. EI is a critical skill for leaders who want to inspire and motivate a team. Set a good example, praise in public, criticize in private, respect your employees' capabilities, give credit where credit is due, and learn to delegate. If the leader is unable to empathize with their employees, they will surely find it difficult to obtain respect or loyalty.

Research confirms women have higher EI than men

Although, our current era has the highest-to-date level of acceptance of women leaders in society, there is still an obvious gender gap. Statistics in the S&P 500 companies show that women comprise 44% of the total workforce on average, yet only 25% of the senior leader roles. The number of women leaders drops significantly in technology, science, and industrial service industries. We need more women in senior leadership roles.

A study conducted by Zenger Folkman on 16,000 industrial leaders revealed that women have higher EI. Results showed a higher average of effectiveness (54.5%) as compared to their male counterparts (51.8%). A similar study conducted by the Hay Group division of Korn Ferry revealed that women scored higher in almost all related competencies. Businesses that recognize this strength can find better leaders in their female executives. However, this does not imply a monopoly but teaches us to embrace diversity.

Emotional intelligence in AI

Regardless of its ability to compute technical information, AI lacks the emotional capability. As we all tread towards a future interlaced with AI, there is an increased demand for a more human touch in AI. Artificial emotional intelligence or Emotion AI is a branch of artificial intelligence that aims to bring EI to AI systems. Our interactions with technology are becoming more conversational and more relational. Subsequently the devices we use are increasingly expected to interact with their users the way people interact with one another. According to ZDNet, emotional capabilities are vital to helping AI process emotional input from humans, such as understanding when people are angry versus when they are sad. Emotions are already provided as training data sets in Deep Learning algorithms from Tsinghua University and the social network Weibo. Advanced AI systems are expected to work hand in hand with humans: engaging students and personalizing their learning experience, assisting doctors and nurses in delivering care to patients, and improving productivity in a work environment. These systems need to have EI; they must be able to read the emotions of their users and adapt their operations accordingly.

ZDNet also noted that by 2020, the average consumer may be having more daily online conversations with AI solutions than with human representatives. Moreover, companies are investing into software programs that can identify "emotions." SASI (Semi-supervised Algorithm for Sarcasm Identification) for example succeeded to recognize sarcasm in Amazon reviews correctly up to 80%. Apple has recently acquired Emotient that detects emotions from facial recognition. Similarly, companies such as Google, Microsoft, and Amazon are hiring comedians and scriptwriters to make their AIs more human-like.

Affectiva is at the forefront of emotion AI technology. Affectiva not only captures emotions of the users but also relates them to their cultural contexts. CEO of MIT, scientist Rana el Kaliouby says, "AI promises to bring automation, accessibility and improvement to quality of life. Emotion AI will make the experience more personal, authentic and persuasive." While Siri can tell a joke or two, humans crave more, so we will have to train our devices to provide for our emotional needs. In order to create a great user experience, AI designers or scientists are developing meaningful frameworks with which to design AI personalities. Chatbot builders are also hiring writers to write lines of dialogue and scripts to inject personality into their bots. Cortana, Microsoft's chatbot, employs an editorial team of 22 people.

According to most observers, we're a few decades away from AI making significant inroads into becoming more emotionally attuned to the ways of humanity. As Microsoft's disastrous experiment last year with its AI chatbot "Tay" proved, being human is not an easy thing. Emotion AI is projected to grow to a multibillion dollar industry in the next 5 years.

However, the way we currently understand and model emotions still needs a lot of work. Approaches to modelling emotions as in Game Theory does not translate across cultures. The deepest roots of emotion and intuition remain elusive to researchers. They cannot be measured, individually or in aggregate, with any high-degree of accuracy. The range of human intellect and EI—much of which researchers still do not understand—cannot yet be captured with a high degree of accuracy as data points for AI and ML training sets. At some point—in the future—there may be viable applications which are derived from data which are compiled and assimilated from computer vision queues, wireless monitoring of physical movement (heartbeat, breathing, etc.), and neurological monitoring.

The anticipated future demand for robots as service robots for everyday life has increased the need for "natural" human-robot interaction. One of the important topics of natural interaction is the detection of emotions which enables the robot to react appropriately to the emotional state of the human. A machine can detect the outward manifestation of an emotional state, however, the correlation between a recognized outward manifestation and the actual state differ. Yes, a machine can pick up heart rate variability, micro expressions, facial blood flow, pupil dilation, tremors, etc. but what is happening inside, to trigger the emotion, requires context, mostly unrelated context. How can a machine equate a pleasant smell with a negative emotion? Illogical yet a real condition for many humans.

You Can Increase Your Emotional Intelligence

According to Talent Smart, EI can be developed. It just takes practice of the right behaviors. EI requires effective communication between the rational and emotional centers of the brain. Plasticity is the term neurologists use to describe to the extraordinary ability of the brain to modify its own structure and function following changes within the body or in the external environment. As you practice new EI skills, the billions of microscopic neurons lining the path between the rational and emotional centers of your brain branch off small "branches" to reach out to the other cells. As you train your brain by repeatedly practicing new emotionally intelligent behaviors, your brain builds the pathways needed to make them into habits. Before long, you begin responding to situations with EI without even thinking about it. And just as your brain reinforces the use of new behaviors, the connections supporting old, negative behaviors will die off as you learn to limit your use of them.

The most effective leaders we have known possess great reserves of empathy, awareness of their own feelings, and awareness of their impact on others, interpersonal astuteness. More importantly, they apply these capabilities judiciously as best benefits the employee and company. In today's world of AI, big business, multiple locations, and global operations, employees can feel alienated from management and disconnected from the company at a personal level. The most effective leaders find ways to make themselves personally visible and approachable. They create personal connections with their people. Make the time to engage employees individually and in groups, listen to their ideas, suggestions and concerns, and respond in ways that make people feel heard and respected. It builds trust and will improve your leadership effectiveness.

In today's AI era, employees are fearful about their future and whether AI will take away their jobs. Emotionally intelligent leaders are able to ease their fears by acknowledging their emotions and communicating openly and honestly. If change is coming then give employees bite size pieces of information so they can digest it and prepare themselves for it. Don't just come one day and upload everything on them. If the company is downsizing then be humane and help prepare them for the transition. You can't expect employees to give their best when they feel fearful or those who remain feel guilty. Even if it's a decision you can't control then still be humane about it. Some employees may have been with the organization for a long time and their income and livelihood depends on their jobs. Treat them with respect and give them your kind consideration.

CHAPTER ELEVEN

GO DIGITAL: STAY HUMAN

In his book, *The Fuzzy and the Techie,* Scott Hartley says that at Stanford University, USA, the term "fuzzies" refers to students who prefer the social sciences and the humanities—the liberal arts. While the term "techies" is customarily used to describe the students who choose to study the STEM disciplines (science, technology engineering, mathematics,), which are linked to the "hard sciences." This was popularized by Charles Percy Snow, who created the term "two cultures" to symbolize the separation of the scientific (techie)

and literary (fuzzy) cultures. Therefore we can say the culture of the humanities is more associated to natural intelligence and the culture "hard sciences" can be likened to AI. "Soft" and "hard" skills (the fuzzy vs. techie).

The separation of the cultures has generated two one-dimensional areas of knowledge and outlooks. On the fuzzy side, it has resulted in a theoretical, romantic, and expansive worldview. While, on the techie side, this has produced illusion of control, power lust, and narcissism. Today, the predominant assumption seems to be that techie people are well prepared to see in the world a sharpness that fuzzies do not have.

As the famous quote says, "A person without data is just another person with an opinion." This statement has been often credited to W. Edwards Deming, but actually it is said to be of uncertain authorship. It's a good example of how techies view fuzzies. For analytical and quantitative-minded people, the expression "data" means numerical and thus supposedly "objective" and "concrete" information. Mechanically minded people have built an entirely artificial model which has led them to perceive everything in a linear and sometimes distorted way. It is evident that complexity requires us to think of the world in new ways, which are alternative to planning and forecasting. The problem is that we are only prepared to think in one unique way, because our culture has been conditioned (mainly by the Socratic method) to see planning and forecasting as practically the only reliable and legitimate practices. Spanish philosopher Ortega y Gasset in his book, *The Revolt of the Masses* first published in 1930, give some insights on this. They are as follows: a) progressive specialization has led to increasingly narrowed worldviews as a result, the experts know a great deal about only a few things; b) even so, most people admire them, treat them as oracular sages and they become convinced of their wisdom; as a result, the public tends to consult them about everything—and they gladly give their opinion about what they know and don't know about.

Their one-sided and limited knowledge makes them offer biased and narrow opinions. The consequences are misleading, if not disastrous, especially when it comes to broad issues such as climate change and discrimination. Mechanically minded people are usually good to make dichotomous decisions but complex, non-dichotomous decisions include a greater degree of ambiguity and require reflection. Scott Hartley adds: "We can't eliminate bias from society, but we can pair fuzzies and techies to train our algorithms to better sift for, and mitigate, our shared human foibles". The fuzzies bring context to code, and ethics to algorithms. They bring the soft skills that are so vital to spurring growth.

Ortega cites a famous example: the great differential of Albert Einstein's physics in relation to that of Isaac Newton is due to the fact that Newton was not very versed in philosophy. Unlike Einstein who, among many others, knew the thoughts of Kant and Ernst Mach, who helped to open his mind. Some of the biggest challenges imposed by technological advances are philosophical in nature, meaning good technologists must absolutely never leave the humanities aside.

In short, we do not have emotional and social skills at the same level as we have scientific and technological abilities. Sadly, we value our techie side much more than our fuzzy side. The techie side is directed at the superficiality of human behavior and not at the depths of human nature. This phenomenon is chiefly due to our formal education, which favors quantification and analysis and undervalues intuition and synthesis. This fact limits our ability to deal with phenomena such as subjectivity and the inherent unpredictability of human nature. Such predisposition has led us to accept a simplistic and shallow outlook that may be opportune for business but not for the lives of people. Yet many feel compelled to embrace it, because they believe that it is a survival imperative—which may however result in the opposite. The liberal arts are not only important in complementing the STEM disciplines. Arts and mindful thinking is a very important part of developing and implementing anything. They are important to combine our human and mechanical dimensions. This can prevent us from being robotized.

In Blaise Pascal's book *Pensées,* he identified two antagonistic ways of thinking: the *esprit de géométrie* (the mathematical mind) and the *esprit de finesse* (the intuitive mind). The mathematical mind is associated with the explanatory/demonstrative knowledge. It works with principles that are clear but distant from the common uses and practices. The intuitive mind is associated with the instinctive/intuitive knowledge. It seeks to understand and validate what he called "the reasons of the heart." The intuitive mind (*esprit de finesse*) understands things synthetically, at once, and not through the analytical method, which it is a characteristic of the *esprit de géométrie* (the mathematical mind).

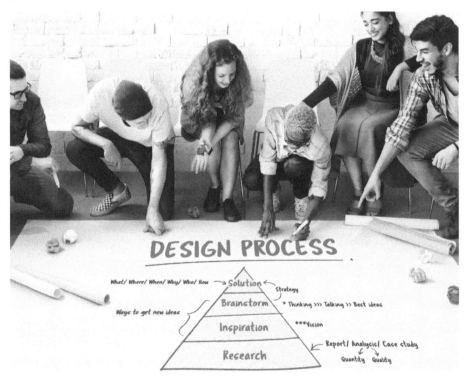

Our current education system has turned many schools, colleges, and even universities into mere commercial enterprises. Education is being increasingly seen as a business, not as a human development endeavor. Instead of pushing everyone to major in a STEM field, we need to recognize that the liberal arts provide a crucial human perspective in a world increasingly governed by machine algorithms. Our fixation with data often masks stunning deficiencies, and the risks for humankind are enormous. Blind devotion to number crunching endangers our education system, businesses, and our governments.

Too many businesses have lost touch with the humanity of their customers, while marginalizing workers with people skills. Obviously, the value of STEM education is a strong as ever and, as technology continues to drive innovation in new industries, it will be increasingly critical. However, we must also remember that a liberal arts background enriches organizations at all levels. Critical thinking, art, political science, and every other course of study in the liberal arts exists not to teach an "unmarketable skill" but to teach us how to ask questions, express ourselves, draw connections between disparate elements, and keep the human element at the center of our choices. Those skills are arguably more important than ever as we see the increase in technologies that have the power to impact billions of people.

In Pascal's own words, "all mathematicians would therefore be intuitive if they had good sight, because they do not draw false conclusions from principles that they know. And intuitive minds would be mathematical if they could adapt their sight to the unfamiliar principles of mathematics". He is obviously talking about the need of complementarity between these two types of mind. Both fuzzies and techies are needed to tackle future challenges in health care, politics, design, and innovation. The future will require teams of people with multiple disciplines and experiences. While "software may eat the world," everyone will need to dine at the software table. The combination of skillsets creates brilliant ideas that will improve human life. The complementarity of the two sides may not completely solve the problem, but it can mitigate it, and this will also mitigate the irresponsible optimism of the techie side, as well as the pensive immobility of the fuzzy side.

Technological advances can be hollow without advancing our ability to ask better questions about who we are and what we live for. As we collect more and more data, we must inquire as to its source and application. As algorithms come to command our world, we must remember that, even veiled in mathematics, they are not objective and the biases within the data sets must be accounted for in the analysis of them. Most engineers have skills to build things, but what will they build? Machines are built to serve humans, and human needs, and humankind has problems of its own which technology can help to solve or abate. People need to collaborate across disciplines to address complicated and human-centric design problems.

At the present time, however, the growing predominance of the mechanist mind (that is, the mathematical mind) over the intuitive mind is evident. This means that the mathematical approach to complexity tends to increasingly rule over the complexity of nature and biology. In other words, we human beings, more and more dehumanize ourselves, whether or not we are aware of it. Yet most of mechanistic ideas are easy to sell to public opinion, because most people share or worship the mechanist mind.

American Philosopher, Hubert Dreyfus, was critical of the grandiose promises of artificial intelligence. He argued that artificial intelligence rested on several flawed assumptions, principal among them is the idea that the mind is analogous to computer software and the brain to computer hardware. His critique was based on the insights of modern philosophers such as Merleau-Ponty and Heidegger, and was directed at the first wave of AI research which tried to reduce intelligence to symbol manipulation. In a 2005 interview with blog Full-Tilt Boogie he stated, "They came to my course and said, more or less: We don't need Plato and Kant and Descartes anymore. That was all just talk. We're empirical. We're going to actually do it." When Dreyfus' ideas were first introduced in the mid-1960s, the AI community's response was derisive and hostile. However, by the early 1990s several of Dreyfus' radical opinions had become mainstream. His work eventually became an inspiration to researchers in the development of AI. Historian and AI researcher Daniel Crevier writes: "time has proven the accuracy and perceptiveness of some of Dreyfus's comments."

We need new paradigm shifts in how we think about technology— and its role in education. There is a disparity between the exponential advancement in technological capabilities and the linear growth in human capabilities to comprehend these advances. All this narrows and obscures our mental horizon, and this is the price we will have to pay for such a heavy conditioning. Underlying all these phenomena is the predominance of quantity over quality and of the mechanical over the human.

We must never lose sight of the fact that humans are the essential link in Artificial Intelligence. Deep Learning—AI also requires deep-thinking humans. The advances in machines require greater engagement of our humanity. Several thinkers, like the Brazilian philosopher Mario Ferreira dos Santos, have long highlighted that our dehumanization has increased at least since the Renaissance, and has continued with the gradual replacement of the feudal economy by the industrial, commercial, and financial economics. Since then, the statistics and monetary values have gradually become the main indicators of political and military power. Basically, as Santos says, human history has always been a struggle between reason and intuition, science and religion, estimation and measurement. We must recognize the limits of technology and reinforcing the importance of critical humanistic thinking. Technology requires input and expertise from every corner of society. Our technology ought to augment rather than replace, and ought to provide us with great hope rather than great fear. Humans are not secondary in the new age of automation and technology. They are primary—they come first.

Spanish philosopher Julián Marías points out that from the human perspective, the world is both sensible and intelligible. In other words, what we feel (see, hear, taste, palpate, smell) is connected to what we perceive. This is the great absolutist dream of the behavioral worldview: despise the subjective side of people; evaluate them only for what they do and ignore what they feel and think. And, by doing this, all too often we run the risk to see as big hits what actually are big mistakes. From the 17th century onwards, the *mathesis universalis* has spread throughout all the Western culture. According to Descartes and Leibniz the "right" way to use reason would be the mathematical *approach,* which should be extended to all areas of human knowledge. All aspects of the world should be reduced to equations, numbers, and other mathematical formalisms.

In his book *Essais*, the French philosopher Albert Camus wrote a sentence that became famous: "If the world were clear, art would not exist" (*si le monde etait claire, ne serait pas l'art*). The obvious inference is that we need the arts to better understand the world—here included, by extension, the so-called human sciences.

Our perception/expression crisis has been enhancing the well-known detachment between the two main ways of thinking in our culture. The first one—which is the dominant mode—produces mechanistic intelligence. The second one—which is connected with the so-called humanities—produces non-mechanical intelligence. We obviously need these two kinds of intelligence and knowledge, as they moderate the excesses and correct the shortcomings of each other. We need to be practical and utilitarian, but we also need to develop our human capabilities. This is what I call a pragmatic way of life.

The old and seemingly immovable effort to measure what cannot be measured was one of the causes of the gap between the scientific and humanistic cultures. Many current thinkers say that we should apply our intelligence, looking for ways of at least narrowing this gap. Judging from the perspective of today's societies, this seems most likely beyond our capabilities, however intelligent we think we are.

Given the dominance of the analytical and quantitative mentality in our culture, the development of AI has been examined almost exclusively from that angle. Enter, the Dunning-Kruger effect. A cognitive bias wherein persons of low ability suffer from illusory superiority, mistakenly assessing their cognitive ability as greater than it is. This bias result of these explorations makes them inadequate for the understanding of the comprehensiveness of reality. An examination of the subjective (and therefore human) aspects of the big data issue can complement these results, pointing out its limitations and improving their understanding and efficiency. "Hard" sciences are not able to provide all the clarity we need and the arts and the human sciences do not have this capacity either. The fact is technology thrives when the STEM fields and the humanities allow their unique capabilities to fuel the common goal of forward progress. But I found myself imagining all the engineers and programmers in positions of power that won't let this evolution happen. How do we create a better, more successful model incorporating both STEM-types and artistic types is the challenge because the people in power will invariably be the STEM people? Conventional wisdom states the future belongs to those with STEM degrees and the rest of us will fall down the economic ladder. But the fact is we need a healthy balance of technology and human management in our lives and in our society.

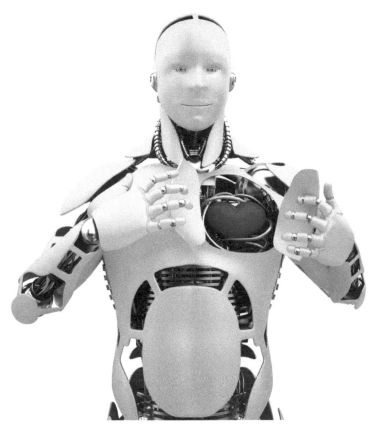

STAY HUMAN

Edgar Morin's seven complex lessons in education

1 Detect error and illusion – The purpose of education is to transmit knowledge, and yet education is blind to the realities of human knowledge, its systems, infirmities, difficulties, and its propensity to error and illusion.

2 | **Grasp principles of pertinent knowledge** – The predominance of fragmented learning divided up into disciplines often makes us unable to connect parts and wholes; it should be replaced by learning that can grasp subjects within their context, their complex, their totality.

3 | **Teach the human condition** – Humans are physical, biological, psychological, cultural, social, and historical beings. This complex unity of human nature has been so thoroughly disintegrated by education divided into disciplines that we can no longer learn what human being means. The human condition should be an essential subject of all education.

4 | **Work for an earth identity.** The future of the human genre is now situated on a planetary scale. Knowledge of current planetary developments that will undoubtedly accelerate in the 21st century, and recognition of our earth citizenship will be indispensable for all of us.

5 | **Confront uncertainties.** We have acquired many certainties through science, but 20th century science has also revealed many areas of uncertainty. We should teach strategic principles for dealing with chance, the unexpected and uncertain, and ways to modify these strategies in response to continuing acquisition of new information.

6 | **Understand each other.** Mutual understanding among human beings, whether near or far, is henceforth a vital necessity to carry human relations past the barbarian stage of misunderstanding. Therefore, misunderstanding must be studied in its sources, modalities, and effects. This is all the more necessary in that it bears on the causes instead of the symptoms of racism, xenophobia, and discrimination. And improved understanding would form a solid base for the education—for peace—to which we are attached by foundation and vocation.

7 | **Take responsibility for ethics for the human genre.** Education should lead to "anthropo-ethics" through recognition of the ternary quality of the human condition. In this sense, individual/species ethics requires control of society by the individual and control of

the individual by society; in other words, democracy. And individual species ethics calls for world citizenship in the 21st century. Ethics cannot be taught by moral lessons. It must take shape in people's minds through awareness that a human being is at one and at the same time an individual, a member of a society, and a member of a species.

Sadly, science and technology have no moral or social consciousness drivers. There is an adage that says: "To someone holding a hammer, everything looks like a nail." AI experts and companies are trying to persuade everyone that our human limitations will be absolved by this technological evolution. Treating everything as a nail is focusing on developments for the sake of it rather than focusing on using AI to solve problems. Today we need technology that works with us, that amplifies our voices and improves the human condition. Technology is about making the lives of humans better. One missing aspect is the total lack of moral objectivity behind much of tech today. The often-used question philosophers have asked for centuries; it's not that we could, but should we? We need to understand that most of the tech elites aren't philosophers, intellectuals, and thinkers of the sort, they're businessmen. They run massive corporations and their focus is on the bottom-line.

John McCarthy's initial definition for AI: "Artificial Intelligence [AI] is a science, it is the study of problem solving and goal achieving processes in complex situations." McCarthy further states, "It [AI] is a basic science, like mathematics or physics, and has problems distinct from applications and distinct from the study of how human and animal brains work." Notice the phrase: "distinct from applications and distinct from the study of how human and animal brains work". The reason why we need philosophy is to help us ask the right kind of questions, and create the right kind of definitions for words and concepts that may be used along the way. In addition, we need to produce rational arguments in order to explain what we are proposing, and have some understanding of scholarly work on such notions as "truth" and "belief" as it relates to these artificial beings.

We are approaching a new world order, which will function vastly different from what we know today and it will be unwise to try and govern it with the same mindset that worked for us over the last few centuries. Just like in the times of John Locke (English philosopher and leader of the Enlightenment age), we will have to go back to the backbone of society and determine what our social contract should look like under the new realities of the Fourth Industrial Revolution. "Social Responsibility Contract" will be arrived at after the emergence of a new level of our collective consciousness. The current paradigm, including its methods, assumptions, and biases need to be "swept away." To be clear, we now must take up the issue of "Industry 4.0" and its impact, and allow ourselves to gain insight into the structure of our society and its issues; all of this is necessary and preliminary work leading to a global alignment of our collective consciousness; at that point, the momentum will cause the "Social Responsibility Contract" to be enacted.

I do hope that humanity may rise to engage and collaborate in the formulation of new global perspectives and standards, and objectively cross-examine the seeming ideological bias of Industry 4.0 deployment and its potential for cultural and social discrimination and erosion. Indeed the drivers and any side-effects and trade-offs must be scoped and thoroughly analyzed, as well as potential alternatives. And what about accountability? For some strange reason, I am drawn to remember the initial debate of censorship on the internet in its 1983 public rollout and the prehistoric AI of filtering/blocking software which was massively controversial and captured some of the same issues? That wasn't all that long ago (how quickly technology has evolved) and at the time, it was considered that circumvention technology would be developed. It seems the opposing sides to that debate have now reversed and I wonder how circumvention technology may still be relevant in humankind's evolution if higher levels of consciousness are triggered following an Industry 4.0 implementation.

Our issues today are structural; we need to embrace a new transcendent level of awareness of our society and perspectives;

and not just blindly roll-out the red carpet for Industry 4.0. It's the "transcending" that is unfortunately taking too long to occur. As some of you may know, there are forces out there working very hard to maintain (low) levels of consciousness, awareness, and even disunity. On the other hand, there are others suggesting that we should technologically update (disrupt) every activity possible and do so without considering the longer term ramifications such changes will have on the very fabric of society.

The biggest challenges that humanity is however facing when it comes to the renegotiation of the social contract, is the risk that the small percentage of people who are really in control of the world's strides may not be willing to let the rest of humanity in on the negotiation and design of this new world. This situation could be aggravated once we reach the singularity, as it would by then be impossible for human beings to resort to the basic principles of the social contract by attempting to overthrow the order of the day. The message is thus a very somber, but urgent one; the time for humanity to respond to the new challenges of Industry 4.0 and any chance of renegotiating our social contract is quickly running out.

A handful of companies have been gobbling up AI-startups in the last 5 years. An even smaller handful touch nearly all data being passed around the internet. Whole cultures and groups are going unrepresented in our AI revolution. As the Western world continues to play a leading role in building the framework for AI, its culture and ideals get entrenched deeper. Most AI platforms are being trained on a bed of English language semantics, for instance. Today, it is being built to be compatible with a very small-subsection of the world. The danger is that the rest of the world will have to adapt to this narrow definition. And when that happens, will the thousands of other cultures and social norms begin to fade away? Will AI become a subtle sociocultural colonization?

Most humans are neither rational nor objective, they're subjective. Sometimes, scientists inadvertently create biased (sexist, racist, etc.) tools, so when scientific tools are applied to human phenomena there is subjectivity of the scientist at work. Humans are not equivalent to apples, ball bearings, leaves of a tree, Euler's bridge, rice on chess boards, and other examples of mathematical and physics theorems. Can we trust that AI will work with objectivity all the time? Will, a healthcare-AI developed by hospital corporations and insurance firms act in the patient's best interest, or will it prioritize a certain financial return?

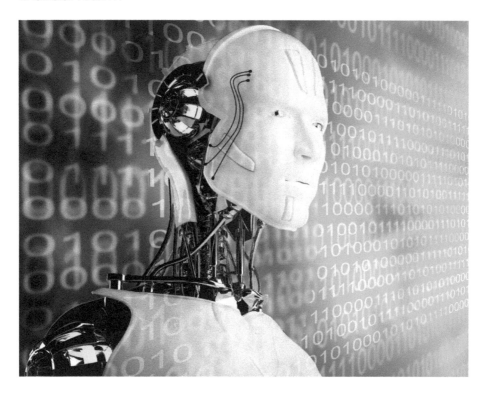

We stand at the brink of an evolutionary explosion unlike anything in the last millennium. The famous "Magna Carta" which means "The Great Charter," was a defining moment in humanity's advancement toward an unbiased relationship between power and those subject to it. In 1215, King John agreed to the terms of the Magna Carta, following the uprising of a group of rebel barons in England. It set the stage eventually for the Enlightenment, the Renaissance, and democracy.

Today we need a Magna Carta for the new AI economy. Who will be in the development? Who will be out? What about women and ethnic minorities who already face discrimination? Who will be the King Johns of today? This revolution needs framing. Therefore, collaborative design is critical for AI. Intelligent technology needs deliberate design in order to reflect and serve human needs and values. AI systems are at risk of producing unreliable insights even if algorithms were perfectly implemented. A Princeton University study demonstrated that Mechanical Learning (ML) systems inherit human biases found in English language texts. Failing to carefully review and de-bias such models has real-world consequences. With AI becoming integral in every area of our lives, how do we design systems that don't backfire?

Biases in AI have been widely documented over the last few years. The first international beauty contest judged by machines—"Beauty AI"—was supposed to use objective factors to determine beauty. The judges, consisting of a five-robot panel picked winners from the photos submitted by volunteers using algorithms to analyze specific traits that they perceived were relevant to outer beauty. The results: only white women were identified as beautiful. This happened because it was working off the data it was fed. Bottom line, if we don't have diversity in the AI world, more of this is going to happen. AI will pass on the biases of its creators. We need women of diverse backgrounds to be part of this AI revolution if we want there to be a comprehensive perspective in the new world of AI. Just look at the racial and gender bias reports that have riddled Silicon Valley.

Diversity in technology has never been so important. Will AI favor survival of the fittest, the most liked, or the most productive? The field of advanced computer engineering is not known for its diversity, but never have diverse perspective and representative data been more important than in the field of AI technology. Homogenous development teams lie at the root of many of the challenges already manifesting in AI today. Cognitive diversity is the key. This is why cross-industry collaboration will be essential to developing technology that works for everyone.

In life, passion fuels purpose. The very act of conception and the continuance of the human race is deep-rooted in passion. It is passion that inspires so much of the creativity we see here. Passion is like fuel in a car. It gives the needed push. However, purpose should always precede passion. Passion without purpose is like a journey with a dead end. The dichotomy is that the people with a sense of purpose forget about profitability and hence sustainability of their endeavors. While, the people who are after profit forget the purpose behind their endeavors. Also these two fail to come to terms with each other. Great leaders are those with a combination of both these qualities. We need that combination of passion built on a solid foundation of purpose, to help create sustainability.

In a world of programs making programs, and machines making machines, you have been reduced to a number, judged by an algorithm. We must remember the strength of people is our humanity. We cannot reduce people to just algorithms.

AI is as good as its data. Unfortunately the paradigm of modeling human experience and human nature has only been able to describe the parts of the existence which describes humans as mechanical machines—matter. The other part of life—feelings, emotions, interactions, has no science. This is why science has not been able to fully understand the human mind. As it turns out, the next frontier of progress is going inside, understanding our own intelligence, and what makes the human alive, driven, and passionate.

The ethical advocacy role is something I've been considering a lot recently. We definitely all have a role to play in proactively standing up for social values in the face of new technology so that it works "for us" and "with us," rather than against us.

In trying to humanize machines, we are forgetting what it is to be truly human. The greatest strength that a human being has, is the power of connection. Relationship building is the key to all human activity. We are social beings, but we sometimes overlook this in this AI age. Being human is about showing compassion, generosity, kindness, respect, and most importantly having love for one other. When we look around the world, the effects of hate are destructive. Unless we daily cultivate the precious fruit of love in our hearts, we are in danger of becoming unsympathetic, selfish, and cold. Leaders who stand on the foundation of love don't just focus on the balance sheets when making decisions but also the humane side, and this is what is prominently missing in our corporate self-seeking world today. It's about connecting goals with how they'll positively impact the lives of others. There is nothing that can replace the "human touch" and this is something we all yearn for. Look around. Most of our problems are caused by the lack of empathetic affectionate human interaction. We need to go back to basics of what it means to be human to figure out how to truly thrive in the future we are creating.

CONCLUSION

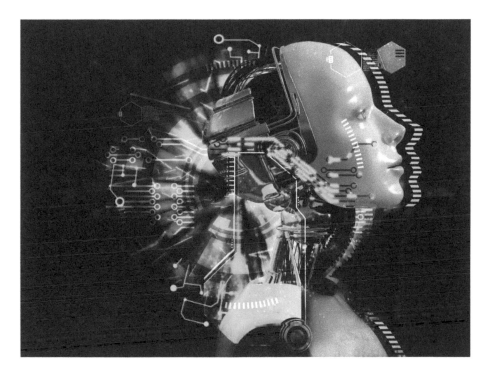

AI promises to be the biggest technological shift in our lifetime. For the foreseeable future, AI is there augmenting our capabilities, allowing us to do more, with better accuracy, in less time. However, every industry will have to fundamentally reassess how it operates in order to incorporate AI and coexist with machines that will become invaluable partners in solving real problems. Technology is changing and the ramifications of this evolution will be felt in every aspect of life. How we interact is going to change in ways many people just can't imagine right now. One thing is certainly clear: Breakthrough technologies will continue to transform experiences for businesses and consumers alike. Leaders must be willing to embrace their civic duty—the actions of an individual must benefit the society as a whole. The new leaders of tomorrow must be ready to face a complex set of unknowns never faced before.

REFERENCES

||||||||||||||||||||||||||||||||||||||||||||||||||||||||||||||||||||||||||||||||||||||||||||||||||||||||

Alvesson, M. Leadership as social integrative action:A study of a computer consultancy company. Organization Studies, 1992, 13, 185-209

Artificial Intelligence Innovation Report - Deloitte -https://www2. deloitte.com/.../Deloitte/at/.../artificial-intelligence-innovation-report.pdf

Goleman D, R. Boyatzis & A. McKee A: Primal Leadership: Unleashing the Power of Emotional Intelligence, Harvard Business School Publishing, 2013

Gregersen, H., Morrison, A., & Black, S. (1998) . Developing leaders for the global frontier Sloan Management Review, 40, 21–32.

F. Torney, B.G. Trewyn, V.S.Y. Lin, K. Wang Nat. Nanotechnology 2 (2007), pp. 295-300

MORIN, Edgar (2000). "Afronter les incertitudes". In Les sept savolrs nécessaires à l'éducation du future. Paris: Seuil, p. 87-102

Neubert, M. J., Wu, C., & Roberts, J. a. (2013). The Influence of Ethical Leadership and Regulatory Focus on Employee Outcomes. (D. G. Arnold, Ed.)Business Ethics Quarterly, 23(2), 269–296. doi:10.5840/beq201323217

Ortega Y Gasset, José (1994). The revolt of the masses. New York: W. W. Norton.

Sinsheimer, Robert L. (1969) The Prospect of Designed Genetic Change. Engineering and Science, 32 (7). pp. 8-13.

http://www-03.ibm.com/ibm/history/ibm100/us/en/icons/watson/

https://www.agclassroom.org/gan/timeline/farmers_land.htm

https://www.bls.gov/

https://www.bloomberg.com/view/articles/2017-07-19/china-s-cashless-revolution

https://www.dupress.deloitte.com/dup-us-en/focus/human-capital-trends/2017/developing-digital-leaders.html

https://www.economist.com/news/leaders/21728617-life-age-facial-recognition-what-machines-can-tell-your-face

https://en.wikipedia.org/wiki/Hubert_Dreyfus%27s_views_on_artificial_intelligence

https://www.enterprise.blob.core.windows.net/whitepapers/futureproof_tomorrows_jobs.pdf

https://www.forrester.com/Robots+AI+Will+Replace+7+Of+US+Jobs+By+2025/-/E-PRE9246

https://www.forrester.com/report/The+Future+Of+Jobs+2027+Working+Side+By+Side+With+Robots/-/E-RES119861

https://futurism.com/goldman-sachs-report-chinas-ai-sector-is-catching-up-to-the-u-s/

https://futurism.com/images/the-history-of-chatbots-infographic/

https:// futurism.com/ thousands-to-receive-basic-income-in-finland/

https://www.innosight.com/insight/corporate-longevity-turbulence-ahead-for-large-organizations/

http://www.infogalactic.com/info/Deep_learning#Deep_neural_networks

http://www.law.du.edu/documents/privacy-foundation/history-of-artificial-intelligence.pdf

http://www.mckinsey.com/global-themes/digital-disruption/whats-now-and-next-in-analytics-ai-and-automation

https://www.mckinsey.com/business-functions/digital-mckinsey/our-insights/how-to-start-building-your-next-generation-operating-model

https://www.microsoft.com/en-gb/athome/close-ups/futureproof/

http://www.oxfordmartin.ox.ac.uk/publications/view/1314

http://www.pwc.com.au/people-business/assets/workforce-of-the-future.pdf

https://www.pwc.com/gx/en/issues/data-and-analytics/publications/artificial-intelligence-study.html

http://www.sloanreview.mit.edu/projects/reshaping-business-with-artificial-intelligence/

https://www.statista.com/chart/9443/ai-acquisitions/

http://www.talentsmart.com/about/emotional-intelligence.php

https://www.theatlantic.com/magazine/archive/2013/11/the-man-who-would-teach-machines-to-think/309529/

https://www.weforum.org/press/2016/01/five-million-jobs-by-2020-the-real-challenge-of-the-fourth-industrial-revolution/

https://www.weforum.org/agenda/2017/01/four-principles-for-leadership-in-an-uncertain-world/

Ziegler, D. J. (2016). Defense mechanisms in rational emotive cognitive behavior therapy personality theory. Journal of Rational-Emotive and Cognitive-Behavior Therapy, 34(2), 135-148. doi:10.1007/s10942-016-0234-2

EPILOGUE

We have come to the end of this book. Thank you for staying with it. I hope you have known at all times that the author has your best interests in mind. **The Future of Leadership: Rise of Automation, Robotics and Artificial Intelligence** offers the most comprehensive view of what is taking place in the world of AI and emerging technologies. It combines wisdom from the ages with the author's insights; thus, giving a winning formula for success.

I wish you the very best in life!

Sincerely,

Brigette

NOTES

9 789769 609211